THE NATURE OF FLORIDA

By the Same Authors:

The Sierra Club Guide to the Natural Areas of Florida
The Sierra Club Guide to the Natural Areas of New England
The Sierra Club Guide to the Natural Areas of Idaho, Montana, and Wyoming
The Sierra Club Guide to the Natural Areas of Arizona, New Mexico, and Nevada
The Sierra Club Guide to the Natural Areas of Colorado and Utah
The Sierra Club Guide to the Natural Areas of Oregon and Washington
The Sierra Club Guide to the Natural Areas of California
The Random House Guide to the Natural Areas of the Eastern United States
Our Polluted World
Zoos
The World's a Zoo
Veterinarians and What They Do
Foresters and What They Do
Exploring the Forest
Exploring the Seacoast
Exploring the River
17 Million Jobs
American Ferryboats
The Story of Standards
Our Wonderful Eyes
Human Relations in Small Industry

THE NATURE OF FLORIDA

John Perry
and
Jane Greverus Perry

THE UNIVERSITY OF GEORGIA PRESS

Athens and London

Published in 1998 by the University of Georgia Press

Athens, Georgia 30602

The paper in this book meets the guidelines for

permanence and durability of the Committee on

Production Guidelines for Book Longevity of the

Council on Library Resources.

Printed in Canada

02   01   00   99   98   P   5   4   3   2   1

Library of Congress Cataloging in Publication Data

Perry, John, 1914–

The nature of Florida / John Perry and Jane Greverus Perry.

p.   cm.

Originally published: Gainesville, Fla. : Sandhill Crane Press,
1994.

Includes bibliographical references (p.   ) and index.

ISBN 0-8203-2008-0 (pbk.   : alk. paper)

1. Natural history—Florida. I. Perry, Jane Greverus.

II. Title.

[QH105.F6P47   1998]

508.759—dc21   97-36054

British Library Cataloging in Publication Data available

Originally published in 1994 by The Sandhill Crane Press.

TO THE RANGERS,
FORESTERS, NATURALISTS,
WILDLIFE BIOLOGISTS,
AND OTHER MEN AND WOMEN
WHO CARE FOR OUR FORESTS,
PARKS, AND PRESERVES.

Many places are mentioned in the text. The reader may wish to know where they are and how to find them. We suggest obtaining the *Florida Atlas & Gazetteer*, described in Appendix A.

CONTENTS

INTRODUCTION
John Perry

The Florida landscape has been changing at a dizzying pace. On the one hand, wetlands have been drained, natural forests replaced with plantations, and high-rise condominiums now crowd coastlines. On the other, the state of Florida is buying back more land for preservation than any other state or the federal government. Each state park has been required to prepare a management plan to restore conditions prevailing when Europeans first arrived. Natural areas within state forests are being preserved and restored.

My wife, Jane, and I were not strangers to this state when we moved here in 1978. We had explored inland waterways by canoe and pontoon boat; we had hiked and backpacked on sections of the Florida Trail; we had visited many parks and refuges. We wanted to write a natural history of Florida for the pleasure of learning more about it and as a tribute to our adopted state. Here it is.

Jane and I had worked together even before we were married on New Year's Day in 1943. She had come to Washington D.C. as a congressman's secretary, then served as economist with several federal agencies and four presidential commissions. I had been an industrial management consultant, then an assistant director of Smithsonian's National Zoo, spending much of my time on international wildlife conservation. Much of our work together was after hours, weekends, and vacations, writing books, photographing and producing educational slide films on natural history and ecology. We hiked, backpacked, camped, canoed, and cruised in all fifty states, always with notebooks and cameras, gathering material for present and future projects.

When asked what each of us contributed to a book, we had difficulty answering. We were inseparable. In photography, we each carried two cameras. Our library research was so well practiced we could extract what we needed from a four-drawer filing cabinet in less than an hour. I did more of the final drafting; Jane was the better copyeditor. In the canoe I paddled at the stern; she was outstanding at the bow.

Jane was backpacking until age seventy-three, when the doctor made her stop. We canoe-camped for several years later. When she had to use a cane, she put a tennis ball on the end for beach walking. When she needed a walker, we found one she could use on rough ground, sometimes for five or six miles in a day. After she recovered from a nearly fatal illness, the walker was replaced by an electric scooter. We mounted it on the back of the motor home and continued traveling.

This book was in the hands of the publisher when we made our last expedition together, to the Everglades. Two days after we returned, the scooter was replaced by a wheelchair, but Jane never quit. She never lost her optimism, her sense of humor, or her love of friends. In her final week, when she was clearly terminal, she insisted on going to Audubon and Sierra meetings.

Jane died on April 16th, 1997, at the age of eighty-seven. I cannot dedicate this book to her, for it is hers as much as mine. It may not be our last book. We had planned another, gathered a rich store of material, sketched chapters. If I find a publisher, it will be coauthored.

Chapter 1

A Most Unusual State

E ven now, after years of living in Florida, we are often reminded of our first visit forty years ago. When we left Maryland the trees were bare, grass brown, snowdrifts melting. We made a late camp in South Carolina and entered Florida next day.

First impressions were sensual: brilliant but soft light, shades of blue and green, warm breeze carrying the odor of salt marshes. We crossed dunes and saw strings of pelicans skimming wave tops. That night we camped under palm trees.

Other recollections of that first visit are kaleidoscopic: orange groves, bromeliads, sawgrass, wood storks, sandhill cranes, flocks of coots, scurrying fiddler crabs, coquinas vanishing into wet sand. Walking a Gulf beach one night, we saw a giant manta ray leap high, silhouetted against the low-hanging moon.

This was not the Florida John's parents knew in the 1920s. Until the Coral Gables real estate boom crashed, they went south each winter, stayed at fashionable hotels, played golf, and returned with suntans, kumquats, and baby alligators.

For most visitors and residents today, Florida is an artifact. Florida is Disney World and Busch Gardens. Florida is a housing development built on fill, a dredged channel to the Gulf. Florida is an irrigated golf

White Pelican

course, rows of motels, causeways to barrier islands, highrise condominiums, acres of mobile homes, shopping malls, dinner theaters, shuffleboard courts, bingo parlors. Most visitors and residents don't enjoy or understand the natural Florida because they don't know it's here.

Yet not far from malls and theme parks are quiet places of extraordinary beauty, unique in the United States. Here are great watery wildernesses, wide prairies, pine forests, rivers flowing silently through cypress swamps, thousands of lakes and islands. Even at the height of the tourist season, you can walk or canoe all day in solitude or explore little-used back roads.

One Sunday we turned northeast from the crowded waterfront of Sarasota. Soon we launched our canoe on the Little Manatee River, a slow-moving, tannin-stained stream meandering between sandy bluffs with subtropical vegetation overhead. For hours we drifted quietly, encountering many birds and turtles, a few alligators and raccoons, no other canoeists.

On another morning, across the state, we discovered the Volusia County Scenic Highway. It leaves the busy coast road a few miles south of Flagler Beach. We found it by chance and thought it delightful: quiet, narrow, winding through an old-Florida landscape of creeks, marshes, and hammocks. Live oak canopies close over the road. On either side grows dense subtropical vegetation.

It was only the beginning of that day's discoveries. We noted for future use an inviting canoe landing on a tidal creek. Next to an open gate was a small sign half hidden by brush: "Bulow Creek State Park." We parked and hiked down a dirt track through a young forest of slash pine, oak, and magnolia, and soon saw the blaze of the Florida Trail. The track ended at Bulow Creek.

Later, on Old Dixie Highway, we came to the main park entrance. Just inside is a grove of huge ancient live oaks. The largest--the Fairchild Oak--is said to be 2,000 years old. Here, too, we were the only visitors.

Such quiet places can be found throughout Florida, many areas accessible only by canoe or other shallow-draft boat. More than a thousand miles of trails have been developed by the Florida Trail Association. Many miles of back roads aren't shown on ordinary road maps.

Ask new residents why they came here and they may say, "We were tired of shoveling snow." But Florida's appeal is more complex and subtle, an ambience felt even inside the Magic Kingdom. "Sun" is the word most used in naming condominiums, insurance offices, and pawnshops, but close behind are "Palm" and "Cypress." Visitors may not take note

Mammoth

of arching mangrove roots, festoons of Spanish moss, bromeliads on electric lines, and egrets fishing in lakes and canals, but they sense this is a special place.

Florida is young. In the time of dinosaurs, Florida had not yet risen from the sea. Even after it became part of the continent, much of the peninsula was inundated several times in geological history. At times Florida was home to primitive rhinoceroses, camels, saber-toothed tigers, three-toed horses, mammoths, mastodons, and other prehistoric creatures.

Tigers and mammoths are long gone, but Florida's fauna and flora are unique among the states. Southern Florida shares many species with the Caribbean. Occasionally a new species arrives by wind or wave and finds the habitat congenial. In recent times, by deliberate act or accident, humans have introduced dozens of species that survive and reproduce in this subtropical setting. You might see a monk parakeet or jaguarundi from the south, a coyote or jackrabbit from the north.

Paradoxically, the environment hospitable to such strangers is exceptionally fragile, easily disrupted. Because the terrain is so flat, a ditch changes the ecology of the area it drains. A road blocks the surface flow of water. When beachgoers trample a path over dunes, the exposed sand is windblown. Boat propellers kill sea grasses that nurture fishes.

This environment, which has attracted so many human visitors and residents, is under great stress. It is doubtful that many more people can be accommodated. For example, water is now rationed in much of central Florida. On both coasts, as more and more fresh water is pumped from wells, salt water is seeping in.

After that first visit, we returned to Florida often. Then came an opportunity to write a series of guidebooks to the natural areas of the United States. For the first time we could choose to live almost anywhere.

We chose central Florida, shunning busy coastal resorts and retirement communities. Our desks look out on one of many lakes. On the far shore bald eagles have built a nest where they raise two chicks each year. Ospreys soar overhead as we breakfast on an open deck. Regular lake residents include green-backed, great blue, and tricolored herons; great and snowy egrets, common moorhens, wood and mallard ducks, red-winged blackbirds, kingfishers, anhingas, and more. Two white ibises were poking their long bills into our lawn this morning. Our feeder is patronized by doves, sparrows, cardinals, blue jays, and squirrels. Grackles perch on the railing, loudly demanding food. When they have chicks, purple gallinules come to the kitchen door and take bits of bread back to their nests.

Sparrows nest in several compartments of the purple martin house. When we clean the house in January, we find the sparrows' rooms packed tight with twigs, leaves, and grass; the martins' rooms have only a half-inch of sand. Back goes the house to the top of the mast, and in February the first purple martins appear. A month later, it's a cheerfully noisy swinging party. Martins seem indiscriminate in mating. By the end of June, parents and young have departed.

Swifts dash overhead. Mockingbirds are abundant. We see flickers, downy and red-bellied woodpeckers, occasionally a pileated attacking a telephone pole. We hear killdeers before we see them.

The lake attracts seasonal and occasional visitors. Last year a limpkin called lonesomely at night; a few nights later, his call was answered.

Each spring a few dozen ring-billed gulls spend a busy week or two with us. Forster's terns stay longer. Twice we have had white pelicans. Wood storks once looked us over and found us wanting, and once, to our astonishment, a pair of black skimmers made a two-day visit. Red-tailed hawks have a favorite tree.

Not being expert birders, we miss a lot. Our friend Chuck Geanangel, one of the best in Florida, stands on our balcony and sees far more than we do. "Cedar waxwings!" he declares, pointing. Hears more, too: "Summer tanager!"

Otters are permanent lake residents not often seen. Alligators come and go. The neighbors' grandchildren catch many bass.

Marsh rabbits favor the shoreline vegetation. Once four baby rabbits, flushed from cover by a lawn mower, dashed frantically into a neighbor's pool. We rescued them.

Before our pre-breakfast swim, we rescue whatever has fallen into our pool. Always spiders and beetles. Occasionally a ring-necked snake. Anoles, shy under other circumstances, welcome a saving hand and cling to its warmth.

Toads took up residence in the pool's overflow pipe. We gave them a front porch, a floating board from which they jump up to the walk for their night's hunting. One sits in the outlet each morning, throat pulsing, watching us and our Labrador swim.

The pool is surrounded by flower beds. Shopping for plants, we saw a green tree frog on a leaf. We bought plant and tree frog together. When the plant was set inside the enclosure, the tree frog disappeared. A night later we heard it calling. The next night an answering call came from across the pool.

Green and brown anoles and at least two other lizard species inhabit pool enclosure and garden, capturing insects, doing pushups, inflating colorful throat fans. They mate while clinging to the screening, show frustration when male and female are on opposite sides. As the browns increase, the green anoles are seen less often .

Huntsman spiders are welcome house guests. They hide in draperies, spin no webs, and destroy cockroaches. Along our balcony, in the garden, and in the grass, webs of other spiders sparkle in morning dew. Colorful, crablike spiny orb weavers hang their webs from the screen roof. Once, as we rescued a female spider from the pool, her egg sac broke and dozens of tiny spiders swarmed over the water; we netted most of them. Often we find a spider submerged in a drain basket; returned to dry land, it scampers away. We did not identify a tiny spider seen only once; approached by a fingertip, the spider put its two-inch web into rapid vibration.

Around our lake, each year is different. Last year was the year of the spider. Their webs, jeweled by strings of dewdrops, decorated balcony railings, flower beds, and tufts of grass. This is the year of the dragonfly, and fewer spiders are seen.

A neighbor gave us stalks of milkweed, leaves spotted with eggs. We put the stalks in a vase on our breakfast table. Two eggs became voracious caterpillars requiring a fresh leaf supply daily. One morning a cat-

Zebra Longwing

erpillar glued its tail to a twig. It hung there for a few days, then began twitching, shedding all caterpillar garb and equipment, leaving a glistening emerald-green chrysalis. The chrysalis twitched and contracted, becoming acorn-shaped with a ring of gold dots.

In a few more days the shell became transparent, revealing the colors of a monarch butterfly. The chrysalis split. The monarch spread and dried its wings. We placed the twig outdoors, and the new butterfly soon flew away.

We now grow milkweed to attract monarchs. We dug a passion flower plant from a field. It attracts zebra longwing and Gulf fritillary butterflies.

Florida was once famous--or notorious--for its snakes. On our home grounds we occasionally see garter snakes, corn snakes, ringnecks, and black racers. The cottonmouths ("water moccasins") reported on our waterfront proved to be harmless water snakes.

Our book is not an advertisement for Florida real estate. In writing about the glories of Florida, we must also take note of drastic changes in the original landscape. Gone are Florida's original upland forests, half of its natural wetlands, much of its coastal mangroves and sea grasses. Native wildlife has suffered catastrophic declines. Despite abundant rainfall, water shortages have become chronic. Vast moonscapes are the aftermath of phosphate mining. The Everglades National Park has been frightfully, perhaps fatally, damaged. Municipal and industrial wastes are dumped on land, into lakes, streams, and harbors, and pumped underground through injection wells.

Two aspects of this devastation are striking. First, it has happened with terrifying speed. Second, it was often innocent, even well intentioned. To be sure, greed played a large part; fortunes have been and are being made at the expense of Florida's future. But great changes in the environment were made in the name of progress.

These are crucial times for Florida. Until recently developers, farmers, miners, and commercial fishermen had their own way. The "good ol' boys" controlled the legislature and county commissions. Enforcement of state environmental laws was lax to nonexistent.

One good ol' boy, a county commissioner, said, "Times are changing, John. Used to be all it took to get elected was a pickup truck with a gun rack."

Now State and local governments are confronting the consequences of unchecked and unregulated growth. Construction and maintenance of bridges, schools, prisons, libraries, parks, sewage plants, and solid waste disposal systems have fallen far behind needs. The accumulated backlog seems unmanageable. Still the land speculators and developers cry, "More progress!"

Aldo Leopold wrote, "Land-despoliation has evicted nations, and can, on occasion, do it again." To understand the present one must know the past; the nature of Florida arises from its history. We have tried to summarize the events of several billion years.

Our purpose is not to denounce the rape of this gentle and lovely subtropical land, although we must tell what happened. Rather, it is a loving appreciation of endearing young charms that have not fleeted away. Florida is young, in its vegetation, its wildlife, and its people. Although fragile, its natural systems have the resilience of youth.

More than enough of natural Florida remains for a lifetime of enjoyment. Public recognition is growing that artifact Florida cannot survive without natural Florida. If we first enjoy, then understand, and thus come to cherish what remains, it can be saved. Some of the lost will be regained.

Chapter 2

A Many-Splendored State

Traffic moves quickly on Florida highways. The road ahead demands attention. To pause for a glimpse of egrets or water lilies would be incautious. The passing landscape is a blur of billboards, pastures, and citrus groves. Florida has no snowy peaks or colorful badlands, no great waterfalls or cataracts. Except for its ocean beaches, natural Florida is seldom dramatic on a grand scale.

"Why are we doing this?" Jane asked one day as we drove south on US 27. "What's the hurry?" In blanking out billboards, we were blanking out the scenery beyond them; we had seen nothing for miles. Now we turned onto a side road where we could roll as slowly as we wished, or stop when Jane spotted sandhill cranes. We parked beside a marsh and strolled along a farm road, looking at birds and wildflowers. Fresh deer tracks were printed in a patch of mud.

On another day, driving on a barrier island, we saw a path leading west toward the Indian River. No sign prohibited entry, so we parked and explored. The path, we discovered, is on a dike forming a 3-mile U, enclosing what had been a shallow impoundment, now dense with mangroves. Dozens of golden-silk spiders had spun large webs from tree branches. Below were smaller webs of colorful, crablike spiny orb weavers. We saw many zebra longwing butterflies.[1]

---

[1] We will identify places on public land. This site is privately owned and could be closed at any time. A similar public site, Jack Island, is not far away.

Fox

Pelicans splashed down just offshore. An osprey cried overhead. The only person we met, a fisherman, told us he'd seen a young raccoon and a young fox playing together.

Such natural riches must be enjoyed at close range, at walking pace, with frequent pauses. An owl might be in the next tree. Look for a five-lined skink on the rotting stump.

Living in Florida, we can afford the luxury of wandering and discovery. If an afternoon is unrewarding, we can try again. If visitors know what Florida offers and where to find it, they need not risk their limited days .

Florida has a splendid array of public parks, forests, wildlife areas, and beaches; thousands of miles of hiking, canoe, and equestrian trails; thousands of lakes, rivers, and streams for boating, fishing, and swimming. Birders can add many species to their life lists. Amateur botanists will find trees, shrubs, and wildflowers not seen elsewhere in the United States. Offshore lie countless islands and coral reefs.

Florida still has many quiet places where one can say: "This is how it looked when the first Europeans arrived."

The State

Florida is about as large as Alabama, Illinois, or Wisconsin. From its western border to Key West by road is 860 miles, a longer drive than crossing Texas on I-10. The peninsula projects southward 500 miles between the Gulf of Mexico and the Atlantic Ocean. Because of their influence, the southern peninsula's climate is subtropical, although Florida is entirely within the temperate zone; Key West is just north of the tropic of Cancer.

Florida's coastline--the perimeter--is longer than that of any state but Alaska: 1,350 miles. Because the coast is heavily indented with sounds, bays, inlets, and tidewaters, the actual shoreline is more than six times as long.

The state's land area is 54,153 square miles. Florida has 7,800 lakes (30,000 counting ponds) covering about 4,500 square miles, more in wet seasons, less in dry. Most lakes are smaller in dry periods, and some ponds vanish altogether. In wet weather, the floodplains of streams and rivers often look like lakes.

The original wetlands covered half the state. Almost all southern Florida was wet. A central theme of Florida's history is a succession of ambitious drainage schemes.

Only Louisiana and Rhode Island are flatter than Florida, whose highest point is 345 feet above mean sea level. A T-shirt boasts, "I climbed Mount Dora!" (Mount Dora is a pleasant small city, its highest point slightly above 200 feet.) At Torreya State Park, a bluff 150 feet above the Apalachicola River overlooks a sweeping forest landscape. Such vistas are rare.

Flatness suggests monotony, but natural Florida is far from monotonous. In the Rocky Mountains, a plant association such as that dominated by lodgepole pine may extend through more than 2,000 feet of elevation. In Florida, differences of a few inches often produce different and colorful plant communities.

Florida has great variety. The several parts of the state differ from one another.

The Panhandle

The Panhandle is a region of deep pine forests, clean rivers with broad floodplains, swamps, shallow bays, sand beaches, and barrier islands.

Some call it "the other Florida." For most people, "Florida" is the peninsula. In libraries we found ten times more information about the peninsula than about the Panhandle. Although it has 20 percent of the state's land area, the Panhandle has only 8 percent of the population.

Summer, not winter, is the Panhandle's high season. Many tourist businesses close after Labor Day. "It gets cold here in winter," we were told.

Cold? January daily averages are only 10° F lower in the Panhandle than in the southern peninsula. We think it odd the visitor seasons are reversed, but we take advantage of it and tour the Panhandle after Labor Day. In September the weather is usually delightful, the Gulf warm enough for swimming, most parks and beaches deserted on weekdays.

The Panhandle's northern landscape is like that of southeastern Alabama: rolling and hilly. From the Alabama border the land slopes gently to the Gulf of Mexico, drained by four of Florida's largest rivers. It has extensive pine and mixed hardwood forests and an amazing number of wildflower species, including hundreds common to the southern Appalachians.

The Panhandle attracted early settlers because of its safe harbors, navigable rivers, easy access to immense timber resources, and fertile soils. An 1825 census found about 5,800 Europeans in the Panhandle, only 320 in southern Florida.

Longleaf pine logs were the principal export, but live oaks were the first tree species to cause concern. Live oak was the most durable wood for ship hulls and thus in great demand. Live oaks are salt tolerant and grow well in coastal fringes, where they were easily harvested. Alarmed by the dwindling supply for its naval vessels, the U. S. government purchased live oak forest land in 1828. In 1829, President John Quincy

Adams authorized it as a reservation, the first such natural area set-aside in the young nation's history. The Naval Live Oak Reservation is now part of the Gulf Islands National Seashore.

Forestry is still the chief land use in the Panhandle. Some of the largest private landholdings in Florida are those of timber companies along the Gulf. The big trees are gone, however. The companies grow and harvest pulpwood.

Most of the Panhandle's Gulf coast is fringed by barrier islands, beaches, and extensive tidal marshes. On some sections of the coast, the Gulf is too shallow for swimming. The principal beach resorts are between Pensacola and Apalachicola. For quiet beach hiking, our favorite area is the 18-mile-long St. Joseph Peninsula.

The largest public lands are the Blackwater River State Forest on the Alabama border, the Apalachicola National Forest southwest of Tallahassee, and the Eglin Air Force Base, east of Pensacola. The Blackwater has the nation's largest longleaf pine forest, restored after logging and burning, and several of Florida's cleanest streams, popular with canoeists. We canoed Clearwater Creek recently. Much of the Air Force Base is maintained in natural condition and is open to public recreation. Other sites with notable natural features include:

> Gulf Islands National Seashore
> Falling Waters State Recreation Area
> Torreya State Park
> St. Marks National Wildlife Refuge
> St. Joseph Peninsula State Park
> St. George Island State Park
> Apalachicola Bluffs and Ravines Preserves

In this book we mention the larger publicly owned sites. Some have visitor centers, campgrounds, and other facilities, but each has extensive areas where development is prohibited. Some include primitive or wilderness areas accessible only on foot or by canoe.

The Panhandle has many smaller State and county parks, Wildlife Management Areas, isolated beaches, canoe trails, and hiking trails. Coastal waters offer opportunities for cruising and saltwater fishing. Several barrier islands are outstanding birding areas; bird-watchers come from afar during spring migrations.

North Florida

Our "North Florida" extends from the Georgia boundary to Ocala and Daytona Beach. Three Interstate highways, I-10 from the west, I-75 from the northwest, and I-95 from the north, funnel traffic through the region. Road maps show it's heavily settled, but note the contrast between the two coasts. On the Atlantic are cities and popular resorts: on the Gulf, a few small fishing outposts and modest towns.

Inland from the Gulf, highway maps show what look like large roadless areas. In fact there are local roads, private and public, some unpaved, some poorly maintained. Here and elsewhere in Florida, the *Florida Atlas & Gazetteer* is indispensable.[2]

Much of the land bordering the Gulf is owned by timber companies. Some companies permit hunting, by arrangement with the Florida Game and Fresh Water Fish Commission. A few permit day use by the general public. Company roads are maintained as timber operations require. On a recent visit we drove on rutted tracks that had been muddy and impassable the day before. After a downpour, some fords can't be crossed .

The Gulf coast is a vast region of marshes and tidal flats bordering 60 million acres of shallows. Life is prolific here. Submerged sea grass meadows and emergent vegetation provide nurseries for fishes, crabs, shrimps, and many other marine creatures, a bountiful feast for wading birds, ospreys, alligators, muskrats, and other predators. We saw a gigantic midden of oyster shells, 15 feet high, covering 25 acres, left by early Indians.

The wetlands have few visitors except fishermen and hunters. They can be explored by small boat or by hiking or wading along the fringes. To understand and enjoy this unusual and fascinating region, stop at the visitor center of the St. Marks National Wildlife Refuge, south of Tallahassee. Its dioramas, exhibits, literature, and nature trail describe the flora and fauna of the region. The road past the center ends at an old lighthouse.

In the north central area, just south of the Georgia boundary, is an extension of Georgia's vast Okefenokee Swamp. The Nature Conservancy and the U.S. Forest Service recently acquired Pinhook Swamp, linking the Okefenokee with Florida's Osceola National Forest. Along the paved roads inside the Forest one sees mostly pine plantations, but there is greater diversity in the interior. The Forest has extensive hardwood swamps, one large lake, and many small ponds. Four creeks in the Forest drain to the Suwannee River, two to St. Marys River. Five are classified as Outstanding Florida Waters and thus given special protection. Except for hunters, the Osceola attracts relatively few visitors.

The much larger Ocala National Forest east of Ocala attracts many

[2] Described in Appendix A.

more visitors. It straddles the sand ridge that forms the spine of the
Florida peninsula. On either side of the central highlands are several
hundred lakes surrounded by grassy prairies and forests of longleaf and
slash pines.

The principal visitor attractions are four great springs: Alexander,
Juniper, Silver Glen, and Salt. Creeks drain to the Oklawaha and St.
Johns rivers and to lakes within and beyond the boundary. Baldcypress,
palms, and red maples grow along the waterways, often in dense stands.

We usually avoid these four springs because of crowds. You have
your choice of uncrowded campgrounds, developed or primitive, or one
can camp in wilderness solitude. Backpackers can enjoy trailside camping.

North Florida has two of the state's principal rivers. The Suwannee
flows south from Georgia's Okefenokee Swamp to the Gulf. It's
canoeable for its entire 235 miles, 177 of them in Florida. Much of the
land it passes through is publicly owned and natural, including the Lower
Suwannee River National Wildlife Refuge.

The St. Johns is one of the nation's longest north-flowing rivers. It
enters the Atlantic Ocean at Jacksonville. From Sanford to Jacksonville,
the St. Johns is used by commercial vessels and motorboats, but canoeing is pleasant. Blue Spring State Park on the St. Johns is a winter haven
for manatees; we occasionally meet one in the river. One of our favorite
canoe runs is the Wekiva River, which enters the St. Johns a short distance south of Blue Spring. Hontoon Island State Park is reached by a
small passenger ferry from Hontoon Landing. A short distance downstream from the Landing, boats can enter a maze of creeks within the
cypress swamps of the Lake Woodruff National Wildlife Refuge.

Three interesting sites are near Gainesville. At Devil's Millhopper
State Geological Site, steps descend into an old sinkhole. The undeveloped San Felasco Hammock State Preserve has exceptional botanical
and geological features. Paynes Prairie State Preserve is an 18,000-acre
complex of wetlands and uplands, with much wildlife and an excellent
visitor center.

The Atlantic coast is heavily developed, but you can find quiet places.
The ocean beach is an ever-renewed natural area, swept clean by tides
and storms. Sand dunes, their fragile vegetation easily damaged, are protected by restricting parking and dune crossing to designated places. Few
people wander far from these designated crossings.

Inland from the dunes are tidal lagoons, rivers, and creeks, bordered
by salt marshes. Little Talbot Island State Park, near Jacksonville, is a
complex of islands, beaches, and salt marshes cut by a maze of creeks.
Faver-Dykes, Tomoka, and Bulow Creek State Parks are on tidal waters

near the coast; all three are on fine canoe trails.

These are some of our favorite natural areas; north Florida has many more.

Central Florida

This region extends from coast to coast, and south from Ocala to just north of Lake Okeechobee. The strip along I-4 from the Orlando area to Tampa-St. Petersburg is becoming a metropolis. Development has been intensive on both coasts. Flying over the Gulf coast you can see acres of subdivisions built on artificial flats a few feet above high tide, awaiting the next hurricane.

Four large theme parks are in the region: Disney World, Sea World, Busch Gardens, and Cypress Gardens. The ever-expanding Disney complex has had radiating effects, including dozens of high-rise motels and conference centers.

Central Florida has about 300 golf courses, countless mobile home parks, and proliferating shopping malls. It has more orange groves and grazing land than other parts of Florida. One-third of the world's phosphate rock comes from west central Florida, gouged out of the earth by giant draglines in cuts more than 50 feet deep, 150 feet wide, often a mile long.

Despite all this, central Florida has many delightful natural areas. We know--this is where we live.

On the Atlantic, just north of Cape Canaveral, is the 140,000-acre Merritt Island National Wildlife Refuge, where one can walk for miles on dikes beside fresh- and saltwater impoundments. The birding is outstanding. We often see otters. The Refuge has a fine visitor center, affectionately dedicated to two rangers who died fighting a fire..

Adjoining is the Canaveral National Seashore. It has 24 miles of protected ocean beach and dunes. The central half is a wilderness accessible only on foot.

South from the Cape, the coast highway runs just back of the dunes on barrier islands. Some waterfront sections are heavily developed, but we can usually find an uncrowded beach. Jack Island, north of the Fort Pierce Inlet, is one of several attractive natural areas on the inland side.

On the Gulf side of central Florida, the Cedar Key National Wildlife Refuge is a cluster of islands accessible only by boat, with some restrictions of access. Cedar Key itself was once a busy fishing port, terminus of an early railway from Fernandina, and source of redcedar used in millions of pencils. Now, the fishery and redcedar depleted, it's a pleasant informal resort reached by a causeway through wetlands.

To the south is the Chassahowitzka National Wildlife Refuge, 30,000 acres of marsh and water, an excellent natural area but accessible only by shallow-draft boat.

Still farther south are surprising natural sites in and near the large cities. The Upper Tampa Bay County Park is an attractive remnant of the ecosystem that once surrounded the bay; it has trails, boardwalks, canoe launching, and one of the state's best visitor centers. At Tampa's edge is a 16,000-acre wilderness with several county parks on its perimeter. Popular Fort DeSoto County Park, on the extreme south tip of St. Petersburg, is a cluster of islands linked by causeway, famous among birders for its seasonal assemblies of weary bird migrants.

The interior of central Florida has more lakes than any other part of the state, although unrestricted lakeshore development has been permitted on many. A notable exception is 3,900-acre Lake Arbuckle, completely surrounded by federal and state land.

The St. Johns River emerges from a 90,000-acre complex of marshes and lakes purchased by the St. Johns River Water Management District. Hunters and fishermen know this area, but hikers, birders, and canoeists have yet to discover it.

The Kissimmee River used to meander slowly from near Orlando through a chain of lakes to Lake Okeechobee. Its floodplain, 2 to 3 miles wide, is almost flat. Between 1961 and 1971, to stop natural flooding, the river was replaced by a 52-mile-long canal with locks. The ensuing environmental disaster finally persuaded government officials that the river must be restored. Work has now begun. The first restored section offers fine canoeing and informal island camping. A section of the Florida Trail follows the river.

On the west side of the central ridge, the 500,000-acre Green Swamp is headwaters for five major rivers. Some of it is publicly owned, the rest threatened by development.

An excellent way to enjoy a cross section of the peninsula is a leisurely drive on SR 70 from Sarasota to Fort Pierce. It's less than 150 miles, but allow a long day for the journey. Consult your map and guidebooks; there are many worthwhile side trips. On the central sand ridge, look for Florida scrub.

Central Florida has other natural areas:

The Withlacoochee River State Forest comprises four tracts of 10,000 to 49,000 acres, each quite different ecologically.

Highlands Hammock State Park, the State's first, has trails, boardwalks, and much wildlife. We take visitors here to see what central Florida was like before Europeans came.

Avon Park Air Force Range, 106,000 acres. Most of its extensive

natural areas are open to public use.
Myakka River State Park includes a wilderness area.
Tiger Creek is a preserve of The Nature Conservancy.
Central Florida has many canoe runs into or through otherwise inaccessible wonderlands.

South Florida

Until the late 19th century, most of south Florida was wetland, accessible only by sea. One early visitor described it as "nine-tenths water, one-tenth swamp." After Flagler's railroad opened the east coast, land speculators swarmed. Almost overnight Palm Beach, Lake Worth, Fort Lauderdale, and Miami became world-famous resorts.

The Gulf coast developed more slowly. The interior remained wild until the Tamiami Trail crossed the everglades in the 1920s.

(We use "everglades" for the entire ecosystem, "Everglades" for the National Park that occupies its south portion.)

Recently we listened as staff and governors of the South Florida Water Management District discussed "buildout"--the hypothetical ultimate development of the Atlantic coastal land--and what the demand for water would be then. "Buildup" might be a better term, as high-rises rise higher and higher.

Some fragments of Atlantic beach and dune have been preserved. Palm Beach County has been buying undeveloped beaches. The Hobe Sound National Wildlife Refuge is on a barrier beach, and several miles of foot-access beach adjoin on the north. The Nature Conservancy is preserving and restoring the Blowing Rocks Preserve. John D. MacArthur Beach State Park has remarkable natural habitats plus an outstanding nature center and corps of volunteer guides.

Just inland are several fine natural sites, including Jonathan Dickinson State Park, which has rolling white sand dunes, flat pinelands, and a river through subtropical jungle.

The Gulf coast of south Florida is less intensively developed. Charlotte, Lee, and Collier counties have only one-seventh the population of Palm Beach, Broward, and Dade. Not that it has escaped developers. Condominiums stand on the sandy shores, vulnerable to hurricanes. Housing developments sprawl.

Of the many islands along the western Gulf Coast, those accessible by bridge or causeway have been heavily developed. Some important natural areas have been preserved, notably the J. N. "Ding" Darling National Wildlife Refuge on Sanibel Island. South of Naples, the Marco Island development is the only break in a wide strip of coastal mangroves with countless channels. Local residents intend to keep it that way. Within this strip is Collier-Seminole State Park, at the edge of the Big Cypress. It includes a fine tropical hammock, wilderness canoe trail, and hiking trail.

Inland, northeast of Naples, is the Corkscrew Swamp Sanctuary of the National Audubon Society. It has a long boardwalk through one of the last virgin stands of baldcypress.

The wet interior of south Florida has been drastically altered, but not by urbanization. Looking down from a plane flying west out of Miami's airport, you can see the developed area stop abruptly, as if blocked by an invisible wall. The "wall" is a stabilized line of battle. Beyond lies what remains of the upper everglades, originally a miles-wide expanse of sawgrass through which a thin sheet of water moved slowly toward Florida Bay.

The everglades ecosystem begins at Lake Okeechobee, often called "the liquid heart of Florida." Before people tried to improve on nature, the lake, overflowing in rainy seasons, was the source of water for the everglades.

Today one can drive around Lake Okeechobee without seeing it. A high surrounding dike was built after hurricanes in 1926 and 1928 drove water over the banks, killing over two thousand people. To the south and southeast is the Everglades Agricultural Area, 700,000 acres, larger than Rhode Island, drained for farming and a major claimant for irrigation water. Runoff of nutrients and pesticides from farms pollutes the water entering the National Park.

"Drain the everglades!" The cry began as soon as the first European wet his feet. It was taken up by presidents and legislators, entrepreneurs and confidence men, engineers and speculators, farmers and fools. Some of the bizarre story is told in a later chapter.

From Lake Okeechobee to Everglades National Park, the natural everglades have been ditched, diked, drained, flooded, and managed for conflicting and irreconcilable purposes. Sheet flow is blocked by roads. Everywhere are canals, ditches, dikes, water gates, and other control structures.

To know where to go and understand what you see requires an introduction. The Arthur R. Marshall Loxahatchee National Wildlife Refuge is 221 square miles of flat wetlands surrounded by a pentagon of levees and canals. Once part of the natural everglades, this is now one of three huge water storage areas built by the U. S. Army Corps of Engineers. The Refuge has a fine visitor center, schedule of events, exhibits, dioramas, slide show, nature trails, and canoe trail.

The most famous natural area of south Florida is Everglades National Park. Everything is here: visitor centers, nature trails, wayside exhibits, cruises, campgrounds, ranger programs. Disruption of its water supply has gravely damaged this National Park, largest in the East. Much has been lost, but even today visitors are not disappointed.

And they come, hundreds of thousands of them, a third from foreign lands. Most are content to wander about the Royal Palm Visitor Center, Anhinga Trail, Gumbo Limbo Trail, other waysides, and Flamingo, perhaps take a cruise up to Whitewater Bay. Others leave the crowds behind. More than nine-tenths of the Park is wilderness, and almost half is a lacework of rivers, bays, and tidal creeks, many navigable by motor craft, many more by canoes. The 99-mile Wilderness Waterway is a test of canoeists' endurance.

On the south, the boundaries of Everglades National Park include Florida Bay, with over a hundred islands; on the west, the Ten Thousand Islands. Wilderness camping is permitted on several islands.

The Big Cypress Swamp in Florida's southwest encompasses 1.5 millions acres of freshwater swamps, marshes, wet and dry prairies, forested islands, hammocks, and estuarine mangrove forests. Congress has authorized purchase of almost half of the area, and more than one-third has been acquired. Parts of the Big Cypress can be explored on foot or by canoe. There is a visitor center on US 41.

Adjoining the Big Cypress is the Fakahatchee Strand State Preserve, a wetland with the last known resident population of Florida panther. The strand has a rich flora, including virgin baldcypress, fine examples of strangler fig, royal palms, ferns, and rare orchids. Portions of it can be seen from a long boardwalk, more by canoe and ranger-led wades.

Islands and Keys

Just south of Miami, Virginia Key and Key Biscayne are the first of the islets enclosing Biscayne Bay and its coral reefs, the principal feature of Biscayne National Park. At Key Largo the Overseas Highway begins, a 113-mile chain of 42 bridges and causeways linking islands, the route to Key West. The chain encloses Florida Bay, where over a hundred keys are within the boundary of Everglades National Park. A Park Ranger station is on Key Largo. On and north of the chain, between Marathon and Key West, numerous keys are within the Florida Keys National Wildlife Refuges. The Refuges also include the Marquesas and other islands west of Key West. Still farther west is the Fort Jefferson National Park in the Dry Tortugas, reached by boat or plane.

Coral reefs within the Florida Keys National Marine Sanctuary extend for 200 miles from Biscayne National Park on the east side of the chain, through John Pennekamp Coral Reef State Park, and around to the Dry Tortugas.

The Keys have no fresh water; it must be piped in. Development should have been limited long since, but it continues. The few State Parks on the highway are often crowded. A rare fragment of what was once here is the Lignumvitae Key State Botanical Area, a pristine tropical hammock off Indian Key channel. Access is by tour boat.

And Much More

Florida's natural areas can't be seen on a single visit or in a single year. After forty years, we are still discovering new places. Someone who tries to see too much sees too little.

So take it easy. Don't hop to a different campground or motel every night. That wastes the best parts of each day: early and late. Choose a base and make daily expeditions. Wherever your base is, or wherever you live, there are attractive natural areas nearby.

Chapter 3

How It All Began

Florida's geology seems uncomplicated until you pick up a white rock. The rock is likely to contain fossils of seashells. A hand lens or microscope would disclose smaller creatures.

Canoeing the Peace River near Arcadia, we rounded a bend and saw two scuba divers. *Diving*, in 4 feet of water? One surfaced, waved, and slipped off his mask. They were paleontologists, he explained, collecting fossils by fanning bottom sediments with their hands. He showed us the morning's finds: mako shark teeth, stingray vertebrae, bones of horse and mammoth.

How could fossils of land and sea animals be found together? we asked. They had been washed from different strata in upstream banks, he explained. Their ages were millions of years apart. When the marine fossils were laid down, Florida was beneath the sea. Much later, horses and mammoths roamed on dry land.

The First Few Billion Years

Florida--if its origins can be so called--has been submerged for most of the time since life began 3.8 billion years ago. From the simplest of beginnings, plants and animals evolved in the sea. Most extracted calcium carbonate from the water to form their shells and other hard parts. As they died, their remains showered down on the sea floor, accumulating.

Some 550 million years ago the plate of the Earth's crust that underlies Florida was joined to Africa, part of a continent geologists call Gondwanaland. About 300,000,000 years ago the plates separated. Florida's drifted westward, eventually meeting the North American plate. By now the plate carried a deep bed of limestone.

Tectonic plates move slowly but with great force. When they collide or one slides beneath another, buckling forms mountains and islands. Volcanoes erupt. Then the elevated terrain slowly erodes. Thus the young Appalachian Mountains eroded, and rivers transported sediments to still-submerged Florida. Now layers of accumulating limestone were mixed with clay, sand, and other minerals, including the phosphate rock now mined in central Florida.

Florida was still submerged when terrestrial life burgeoned elsewhere in North America. It was submerged throughout the age of dinosaurs, the limestone bed still accumulating, in places as much as 2 miles deep.

Florida began to emerge from the sea about 30 million years ago, first as a series of islands. Rising further, it gradually became a peninsula twice as broad as the one we know today. This is the Floridan Plateau, tilting gently downward from east to west. The plateau's western half, today under water again, extends about a hundred miles offshore, making the eastern Gulf of Mexico a shallow sea. The eastern edge of the plateau is only a few miles off Palm Beach and Miami. To the south it turns westward, just outside the Florida Keys. At the plateau's edges, the sea bottom drops sharply several thousand feet.

The fossil record in some other parts of the world goes back almost to life's beginnings. Geologists and paleontologists have their easiest tasks where the record of ancient rocks is exposed. In the walls of the Grand Canyon of the Colorado, for example, they can read two billion years of history; we saw marine fossils there in rocks not far below the rim. Marine fossils occur high in the Tetons and other western mountains.

Florida has no high mountains or deep canyons to expose its past. To look back, scientists must drill. Deep drilling is costly, laborious, and slow. The pipe string must be hauled up frequently to remove cores and add new pipe sections. By analyzing core segments, geologists can tell when they were laid down and the conditions then prevailing.

"To get to the age of dinosaurs you'd have to drill down 9,000 feet," said Gary Hacking, director of the Phosphate Museum at Mulberry. "No dinosaurs, though. Florida was under water then. Trilobites? Probably two to three times as deep."

Trilobites, swimming arthropods, were primitive marine inverte-brates abundant throughout the seas. Later, primitive fishes appeared, diversified, and flourished. Other life-forms evolved, including sand dollars, sponges, corals, sea urchins, sharks, whales, sea cows, and sea turtles. All left their remains on the sea floor.

Cores from deep drilling often contain shattered fragments of the larger marine organisms; rarely, intact specimens. Florida's oldest verte-brate fossil was recovered in 1955 in the course of oil drilling near Lake Okeechobee. A core sample included a partial skeleton of a sea turtle from 9,210 feet. Its age was estimated to be about 140 million years. Few holes have been drilled so deep.

Florida's accessible fossils are exceptionally abundant, but few are older than 50 million years. Those of land plants and animals are much more recent.

The world's early plants made the transition from sea to land by way of the intertidal zone, where they adapted to periodic exposure to air. Mosses and liverworts, able to absorb and store water, were among the first to become established on dry land. By 400 million years ago, species of trees, herbs, and ferns had spread from marshes to uplands. In parts of North America land plants grew prodigiously, some of their remains eventually becoming coal. Insects swarmed, among them drag-onflies with 30-inch wingspreads.

Amphibious creatures appeared about 300 million years ago. Later some adapted to full-time life on land. Fossils found elsewhere in North America record their evolution, including the ascendance of dinosaurs of many sizes and shapes. The age of dinosaurs ended abruptly, cata-strophically. They and countless other species became extinct. Some scientists attribute the cause to meteor impacts, others to gigantic volca-nic eruptions. Either would have darkened the sky, depriving plants of sunlight and chilling the climate.

As Florida missed the age of dinosaurs and its abrupt end, it also missed first stages of the great evolution and proliferation of birds and mammals that followed. Mammals had existed before, but they were small and not abundant. When the effects of the great catastrophe abated and plant communities flourished again, bird and mammal species had the earth pretty much to themselves. The North American fossil record shows accelerated evolution and diversification. By the time Florida emerged from the sea, many species of plants and animals were available to populate the new land.

The Great Menagerie

Visitors to the Florida Museum of Natural History at Gainesville or the Mulberry Phosphate Museum are usually surprised to learn what extraordinary creatures once lived here. Some, such as primitive rhinoceroses, tigers, horses, camels, giant tortoises, bats, and crocodiles, resembled their modern counterparts sufficiently to be given their common names. Mammoths and mastodons had elephant-like trunks. Others, unlike anything seen today, have such names as *Megalonyx* and *Ambelodon*.

At the Museum of Natural History at Gainesville, scientists have constructed reproductions of several ancient creatures. A fearsome giant sloth towers over the viewer. You could walk into the open jaw of a great white shark. A prehistoric deer was a delicate creature about 18 inches tall.

Did they all inhabit Florida at the same time, a bizarre menagerie of large and small, predator and prey, strange and familiar? Were ancestors of modern species among them? These questions are addressed by paleontologists, such as the two we met scuba diving in the Peace River.

A fossil is a record left by plant or animal: a mineralized bone, tooth, shell, or tree trunk; the impression of a leaf, a cast, a worm boring, a footprint. Fossils are exceptionally abundant and accessible in Florida. Elsewhere we have seen technicians laboriously chipping bones from solid rock. In Florida you might find a mammoth tooth just lying on a sandbar. With a single bite, a phosphate mine dragline may bring up enough fossils to fill a small museum. Wherever running water erodes soil, fossils are likely to be exposed. Collections of fossils have been found in ancient sinkholes.

Often fossils have been transported by streams, scattered, and mixed with fossils from other creatures and time periods. Paleontologists are fortunate when they find a group of fossils where the animals died. Some of the richest finds have been in shell pits where fossils of many species accumulated. In one such pit diggers uncovered a giant tortoise, 6 feet long, 4 feet high.

Paleontologists deduce. A tooth may tell if its owner had been a grazer or a predator. A thigh bone suggests the size of the whole animal. The age of a fossil can be determined. Using many such clues, a heap of bones may be sorted and arranged into a skeleton. A body may be visualized around the skeleton.

When we took a handful of fossil fragments to the Mulberry Museum, Director Hacking identified each one without hesitating: shark vertebra, horse tooth, stingray scale, parrot fish mouth-plate, crocodile tooth, mastodon bone.

Plants must have been the first colonists of emerging Florida, a food supply for animals, but relatively few fossils of leaves or grasses have been found. Florida's peat beds often contain identifiable bits of wood. Palynologists--scientists who study plant pollen and spores--painstakingly extract fossilized pollen and spores from the peat, examine them by microscope, identify their plant species, and thus define early plant associations.

When Florida emerged from the sea, North America had a great variety of plants and animals ready to disperse into the new land. Land animals established in Florida's first 5 million years included numerous species of reptiles and amphibians, rodents, primitive horses and peccaries; species resembling bears, canines, and felines; and mammals unlike any seen today.

Their evolution continued here over many generations. Fossils found in later sites include not one but two kinds of rhinoceroses; several camelids, peccaries, catlike carnivores, and canids; many species of rodents. Bird fossils are scarce--their remains don't mineralize well--but it is certain that they were numerous and diverse.

Even after Florida emerged from the sea, the boundary between land and water was far from stable. At various times the sea again inundated most of the peninsula. At others most of the Floridan Plateau was above water, extending far out from the present Gulf shoreline. During the last ice age, about 20,000 years ago, the ocean was about 430 feet lower than it is today. As the sea fell and rose, broad savannahs appeared, flourished, and were again submerged. The climate varied. Wetlands dried and became wet again. Warm and cold periods alternated. In some habitats, pines replaced deciduous trees. Each alteration of habitats affected their inhabitants. Some species did not survive the changes.

Florida was never glaciated, but the advancing and retreating ice sheets to the north were responsible for marked changes in Florida's climate and shoreline. Changing conditions in the north caused the southward migration of many species that eventually came to Florida.

A Land Called Beringia

How did such creatures as rhinoceroses, saber-toothed tigers, and mammoths come to Florida? The Florida Natural History Museum at Gainesville displays a replica of a short-legged rhinoceros that lived in Nebraska 20 million years ago. It is one link in a chain of evidence tracing the route rhinos and other creatures followed from Asia to Florida. A small, three-toed, horselike creature was among the early colonists. Other horse species may have arrived later, but several evolved in Florida, and horses became abundant. At least two resembled modern horses. Then, strangely, all horses became extinct in North America. Ancestors of the modern horse appear to have returned to Asia.

In grammar school we heard about the "land bridge" between Alaska and Siberia. A wonderful mental image persisted: people and beasts marching like a circus parade across a narrow strip of temporary land, escaping from inhospitable Siberia to our better world.

In fact, the "bridge" linking Asia and North America was a broad expanse of continental shelf exposed as the sea lowered. Colonized by plants and then--as this food supply was established--by animals, it became a productive habitat. Together with some adjoining lands, it is now called Beringia.

Changes in the ranges of wild animals are common, almost continuous. Climate change, overpopulation, diminished food supply, increased competition by other species--these and other reasons cause movement. For some Asiatic species, Beringia became an inviting habitat. Herbivores followed their food supply, carnivores their prey. Beringia was not a bridge to cross but a hospitable place to live and reproduce for many generations. It lasted for about 50,000 years, until the sea returned about 15,000 years ago.

You may ask: "If Beringia was there because the sea level was low because the water was frozen in glaciers, how did animals live? Wasn't it bitter cold and covered with snow?"

Largely because of ocean currents, most of Beringia was free of ice, and its south coast was relatively warm. The same currents warmed the west coast of what is now Alaska and Canada, providing a favorable habitat, much of it grassland. Its inhabitants included mammoth, woolly rhinoceros, reindeer, ibex, antelope, bear, wapiti, wolf, cheetah, horse, lion, camel, and bison. Their descendants spread gradually southward, some eventually to Florida, some by a more western route to Central and South America.

Plants also spread from continent to continent. Many modern plant species have relatives in both hemispheres. The Florida torreya is a tree that occurs only along the Apalachicola River, notably in Torreya State Park. It has close relatives in California, China, Korea, and Japan. The Florida species is near extinction now.

People also inhabited Beringia and gradually drifted to the east and south. Their cave and rock drawings portray many large prehistoric animals.

Continuing changes of habitats shaped terrestrial wildlife populations throughout the hemisphere. New species entered Florida from time to time, and in Florida their evolution continued. Among them were kinds of cats, deer, pig, and camel. The first elephant-like mammals, forerunners of the mammoth and mastodon, appeared about 15 million years ago.

As new species arrived and evolved, many older species became extinct. For some, the reason was loss of habitat. Fossils of land animals have been found far out in the Gulf, evidence that it was once dry. When the sea rose and the savannahs were inundated by the Gulf of Mexico, savannah dwellers had no place to go. In dry cycles, creatures of the wetlands lost their habitats. Displacement, predation, and competition caused some extinctions.

The role of bacteria, viruses, and parasites in population dynamics is often overlooked. We treasure a book autographed to us by its author, Richard Fiennes, when he was Pathologist to the Zoological Society of London (*Man, Nature, and Disease*. New York: Signet Library, 1964). One sentence is especially relevant here:

> When animals are denied free range and aggregated in small areas, their natural parasites and disease-causing organisms multiply in a geometrical progression, until they develop an ascendancy and cause ill health and death.

No, these creatures did not all live here at the same time. Over the span of 30 million years, many species appeared, flourished, and evolved; some became extinct. At the Florida Museum of Natural History at Gainesville, we saw a statement that, on the average, an animal species lasts for about a million years. Many, such as the horse, lasted far longer in Florida.

The onset of the ice age began a great change in the cast of characters in the Western Hemisphere. Many disappeared forever. New ones appeared. It was not the first glacial period in earth history. Climatologists describe a 100,000-year cycle. In the cold phase, summers aren't warm enough to melt winter ice and snow; huge quantities of water are locked in glaciers and ice caps; the sea level is therefore lowered; the weather is dry.

Lowered sea levels created a wide plain around the Gulf of Mexico and through Central America. This became the route of a great influx to Florida of new species from South America, species such as sloths, armadillos, and capybaras, some far larger than those we know. The route was also followed by animals migrating from the western plains of North America, among them a long-horned bison, a pronghorn, and a jackrabbit.

One might expect that, as the time approached the present, surviving animal species would tend to resemble today's fauna more and more closely. Many familiar-looking species arrived or evolved, among them bears, otters, porcupines, and muskrats. However, the years also saw the advent of strange new animals. Smaller cats evolved into the fearsome saber-toothed tiger. A lion was half again as large as today's African lion. Some among the canids resembled modern dogs and coyotes, but one was a huge wolf.

By comparison with horses and rhinoceroses, mammoths and mastodons had a short run. Earlier elephant-like mammals had been less imposing. The mammoth stood up to 13 feet tall, with a long trunk and great curving tusks. The mastodon was also large, with an elephant-like trunk and tusks, its skull flatter than the mammoth's. Both were widely distributed in North America and many fossils have been found. Both were abundant in Florida and present when the first humans arrived.

At about that time another large-scale extinction of species occurred. Horse, mastodon, mammoth--these and many other mammals vanished not just from Florida but from all North America. Gone from Florida were several species of small mammals that still survive elsewhere in North America.

Man the hunter can't be blamed for earlier extinctions; he wasn't present. He did hunt the mammoth and mastodon. Spear points have been found with some of their remains. Whether he pursued them and other large species to extinction through all North America is debatable. Some believe the scattered human population was too small to have had such devastating impact.

Now the stage is being cleared. Species that would look strange to us are disappearing. Bison, deer, wolf, cougar, fox, squirrel, rabbit, a multitude of birds, snakes, lizards, amphibians, turtles, butterflies, spiders, and grasshoppers--most of the modern players are in place.

Pines, oaks, palms, and other trees, as well as shrubs, grasses, and herbs--most have been present for quite a while. Sea creatures have, in general, had a steadier continuity over tens of millions of years than those of the land. Fossils of the sand dollar, horseshoe crab, and chambered nautilus look like those living now.

The end of the ice age did not mark the beginning of a steady-state ecology in Florida. Changes continue. Indeed, humans are accelerating changes. Draining wetlands seems to be altering the weather. Some scientists expect the sea to rise 2 to 5 feet in the next century. The greenhouse effect may cause the sea to rise more rapidly. Panthers, manatees, and wood storks are among the species being pushed toward extinction by what we have done.

Chapter 4
The Wet Frontier

We spent a day with the late Sam Keen and wish we had recorded all he told us. He had come with his parents to roadless central Florida before 1910. They raised cattle and drove them to the Gulf coast for shipment to Cuba.

They weren't the first ranchers. At Lake Kissimmee State Park, not far from the old Keen spread, present-day visitors enjoy a "living history" reproduction of a cow camp, complete with scrawny cattle and whip-cracking "cow hunters" who look blank when asked about anything more recent than 1876.

Showing us around the land he was managing for a hunting club, Sam talked about the way it had been. Several times he stopped at Indian mounds. The Indians who made them had been gone for two centuries before Sam's family arrived, but he spoke as if they were part of his own past. He was determined to protect their mounds from desecration.

The first humans entered Florida at least 10,000 years ago; some anthropologists believe it was much earlier. They came from many generations of hunters who had pursued prey in Beringia and across the Great Plains. Other humans rounded the Gulf to Middle America, where their descendants developed the incredible Mayan civilization. Without metal or wheel, they erected tens of thousands of pyramidal stone structures, some over 200 feet high. They devised an accurate calendar and a system of mathematics. Their intricately carved glyphs record their history.

Florida's Indians were never as numerous nor as creative. For centuries they were hunters. Settlements appeared in river valleys about 5000 B.C. Pottery making began about 2000 B.C. Before the first Europeans arrived in Florida, an estimated 25,000 Indians lived here: the Timucuans, Calusas, Ais, Apalachees, and Tequestas. Their ceremonial centers had temple mounds, but none as massive as the Mayans', and they had carved no intricate glyphs. They had established a multi-tribal society with the social, economic, and political systems needed to manage large communities. They became capable potters long before northern tribes did. They traded with tribes as far away as the Great Lakes.

Their impact on the Florida landscape was light and transitory. They hunted for food but gradually turned to subsistence agriculture, fishing, and gathering shellfish, roots, and nuts.

Their ages-long journey from Asia ended tragically. The Indians had no defense against European diseases or cruelty. Many died in combat or were executed. Some were enslaved and transported. Some were banished to what later became Oklahoma. The rest scattered. By the mid-eighteenth century, Florida's Indian civilization was obliterated. Decades later, Indians of other tribes drifted in from Alabama and Georgia and became known as Seminoles.

In 1513 Ponce de Leon sighted land near St. Augustine. On Easter Sunday, he came ashore, named the land Pascua Florida, and claimed it for the king of Spain. On his second voyage, he landed near Charlotte Harbor, was gravely wounded in an Indian attack, and died still believing Florida was an island.

Other Spanish explorers traced the coastline as far north as Nova Scotia, and the Spanish claim to "Florida" encompassed it all. De Soto sought gold throughout the Southeast and found none. For good reasons, the Indians became increasingly hostile.

The Europeans Settle

St. Augustine's title as oldest city in the United States is based on the Spanish fortification begun in 1565. Spain made several attempts to establish settlers on the Gulf coast, but each failed. France also coveted whatever could be extracted from the New World, and battles between Spanish and French forces were bloody. Neither power was interested in agricultural development, although a few individuals established plantations, some in futile efforts to grow olives and dates. Cattle ranches were more successful. Still, the impact of the warring powers on the nature of Florida was modest.

The British pushed their claims and aggressions southward, establishing the colony of Georgia in 1733. From time to time, the British and French assaulted each other's outposts. In 1763, Spain ceded Florida to England.

The British had a different kind of exploitation in mind: providing England with timber, indigo, rice, and sugar. They also grew produce for local consumption. Their more systematic agriculture required surveys, plantations, settlers, and slaves. The deliberate alteration of Florida ecosystems had begun.

The Treaty of Paris ended the American Revolution and returned Florida to Spain. Many British plantations were abandoned, but Spain had neither the power nor the will to install an effective government and economic system of its own. The following years were turbulent with raids and expeditions, rustling and slave stealing, piracy and betrayals. Those acclaimed as heroes one day might be jailed as villains the next. A few Englishmen returned and were given Spanish land grants.

Florida Joins the Union

Meanwhile Florida's commerce was undergoing significant change. Most cargoes departing Florida were now consigned to U.S. ports. Return voyages often carried U.S. settlers who believed the United States would soon annex Florida.

That Florida should become part of the United States may have seemed manifest destiny to some, but the sequence of events would have bemused the Marx Brothers. American presidents and Congresses, often at cross-purposes, variously encouraged, endorsed, denied, ignored, supported, and disowned attacks across the border. When Congress declared war on England in 1812, it refused to support the U.S. irregulars then occupying portions of Spanish Florida. British forces moved in, assuring the Spaniards they meant them no harm. Confusion and skirmishing continued after the war, but now American incursions into Florida had some official backing. Andrew Jackson came to "restore order." Spain, then a friendly nation, didn't object. Both governments were startled when Jackson flamboyantly claimed Florida for the United States. Florida was finally ceded to the United States in 1821.

Decades of turbulence had discouraged settlement, agriculture, and commerce. Land titles were a bilingual mess. With the expulsion of the last native Indians, Florida's population had decreased. Except in the vicinity of settlements, the landscape of Florida was still pristine.

Now, however, agriculture began in earnest. Cotton, rice, and indigo were significant export crops. Leaders talked about development: stage routes, railroads, land sales. Steamboats began plying the Apalachicola River in 1827, and Apalachicola for a time was the principal port.

Land to Be "Conquered"

Leaders were advocating statehood, and after much debate and maneuvering Florida became a State in 1845. With statehood came a grant of 500,000 acres to the new State government, to be used for economic development. Five years later the Congress passed a "swamp and overflowed lands" act, deeding to the State lands considered unfit for cultivation and directing the State to reclaim them. That could amount to 22 million acres! No legislation has had greater effect on the nature of Florida.

Most of the early travelers who sang Florida's praises had seen only its northern tier. Here was a favorable climate, ample rainfall, well-drained forested uplands, pure rivers and streams, huge, gushing springs, and safe harbors. Those attuned to nature were awed by the endless forests, incredible numbers and variety of birds and wildflowers, waters teeming with fish; deer, black bear, bobcat, and other mammals abundant.

Southern Florida was strange and terrifying. Sailors feared the coast. To reach Gulf ports, they had to sail around the peninsula's tip. Storms drove ships aground or onto reefs. Many who swam ashore had fatal encounters with Indians or died of exposure and starvation. Survivors told lurid stories of encounters with alligators and rattlesnakes. Key West's chief industry was salvaging wrecks.

Inland, according to the few who penetrated, was an almost impassable watery wilderness. When Florida became part of the United States, only about 320 Europeans lived in its south, most of them at Key West.

Proposals for a cross-Florida canal linking the St. Johns and Suwannee rivers were much discussed in the 1820s. Proponents, including Daniel Webster, argued that it would save 800 to 1,000 miles of dangerous sailing. Had it been built, efforts to develop the southern peninsula might have been delayed for decades. One Congressman declaimed he "should not think it much of a loss to the United States were the whole Peninsula of Florida sunk into the Gulf of Mexico."

Instead, the long history of Florida land speculation began. In granting the State ownership of "swamp and overflowed lands" to encourage land drainage, the Congress had no guidance from maps or surveys, only a scattering of field reports. "Swamp and overflowed lands" were never clearly defined, and dry uplands were often included in claims and grants.

We call them "wetlands" now, and what constitutes a wetland is still a bitterly contested issue. Oddly, the traditional opponents have swapped sides. When Florida was young, land speculators and developers wanted the broadest possible definition of "swamp and overflowed" land, for this was land they could buy cheaply. Today wetlands enjoy some legal protection, so landowners and developers now argue for the narrowest possible definition.

Many wetlands are not always wet. That was the significance of the word "overflowed" in the 1850 legislation. Florida has pronounced wet and dry seasons. Land that is dry for part of the year may be inundated in wet seasons. Many plant species have evolved that require this alternation of wet and dry, called "hydroperiods."

The spine of the peninsula is a line of low sand hills extending from the Georgia border to Highlands County. Most land on either side of these hills, and all of it farther south, is low, relatively flat, and in its natural condition often wet. Central Florida has several thousand lakes, as well as swamps, wet prairies, bogs, coastal marshes, and broad river floodplains.

The Kissimmee River floodplain, flat and seasonally inundated, included more than 1.25 million acres of land that seemed unfit for agriculture or other uses. It blocked cross-Florida travel. Even its outer margins were unsafe for development; land that was usually dry might be inundated by floods once in a decade.

The St. Johns River also blocked east-west travel. It flows north more than four hundred miles from vast marshes near Sebastian through cypress swamps to the ocean at Jacksonville. We often cruise the St. Johns and its network of creeks north of Sanford. A few roads built on embankments now reach or cross the river. Draining and filling have provided some land for riverside developments. Once beyond these, we see what early explorers saw: seemingly endless cypress swamps, lakes, and marshes cut by a maze of wandering creeks.

On one glorious sunlit day, our rented craft was a pontoon boat, a floating platform with comfortable seating, a table, canopy, and quiet motor. River traffic was light.

We turned into a wandering creek that would take us to Lake Woodruff in the heart of a National Wildlife Refuge. Without map or chart, one might soon be lost. The openings to Hog Lake and Twin Lakes look like rivers. Waterways such as Zeigler Dead River and Scoggin Creek are deceptive dead-ends. Other passages have such final destinations as Stagger Mud Lake and Tick Island Mud Lake.

We saw no place where one could go ashore. There is no shore, only forests of cypress, red maple, cabbage palm, water ash, sweet bay, black gum, and swamp laurel oak, standing in water. On foot one could struggle through this region only by clambering over tangled roots and fallen trees, wading, and swimming.

Jane saw a dog! A handsome collie was lying on the branches of a downed tree, just above the water. He tried to stand but was too weak from hunger to climb aboard, so Jane lifted him to the deck. The collie was painfully thin. We offered sandwiches; despite his hunger, he took them gently, while our Labrador watched enviously.

How had he come there, far from dry land, across miles of flooded swamp and creeks? We traced his owner, who could tell us only that the collie had vanished from his yard two weeks before.

There were wetlands along both coasts as well as in the interior. Foot travel was no easier in the coastal forests of mangrove or in sawgrass marshes cut by deep tidal creeks. South of Lake Okeechobee was the greatest wetland of them all: the everglades. We spent one exhausting day in the Fakahatchee Strand, slogging through ankle- to waist-deep water, welcoming any downed tree where we could sit and rest.

The Seminoles were the first substantial settlers of the interior. In 1835 the government attempted to evict them from Florida. They resisted, and war with the Seminoles continued sporadically until 1842. The final settlement granted them a reservation and other rights, some of which are still contested. Asserting sovereignty, modern Seminoles sell tax-free cigarettes and operate bingo parlors on their reservations.

The Seminole War delayed efforts to develop and settle the south, but no land rush followed the peace treaty. Settlers had been attracted to the American West by offers of good land. Most of the Florida peninsula was unfit for farming or ranching unless it was drained, and this couldn't be done one parcel at a time by individual settlers.

Drain the Wetlands!

Big ideas were now heard around the State capital: huge drainage projects, a network of railroads, sudden wealth. There was renewed talk of a canal across the peninsula, either the northern route or one through Lake Okeechobee.

The new State had little money but could offer land to entrepreneurs who would undertake drainage projects or build railroads. Some land was sold cheaply. More was granted conditionally. The General Assembly offered prospective railroad builders terms similar to those which had been offered in the West: a strip of land for the right-of-way and alternate 6-mile squares on either side--if the railroad was built. Work began on several routes in north Florida. The Florida Railroad crossing the state from Fernandina to Cedar Key was completed in 1861, the year the War Between the States began. Florida seceded from the Union.

The war put an end to great projects until Florida rejoined the Union in 1868. Its population was then about 150,000. The postwar years saw a mad scramble for land. At the capital, one set of rascals succeeded another, each bestowing huge land grants on friends and supporters. Votes were sold to the highest bidders. "Development" was always the magic word, but few politicians knew or cared what that meant.

An enterprising immigrant from Wisconsin was given the right to drain any or all of 6 million acres of south Florida swampland. For each mile of 3-foot ditch he dug, he would receive title to a square mile of land, 640 acres, for $40. Other conditional deals offered land for as little as 5 cents per acre. One grant of over a million acres was contingent on the promoters' installing one settler per 320 acres. High-stakes gambling and political shenanigans piled chaos on confusion. Some entrepreneurs failed to live up to their promises but refused to relinquish their claims. Some sold land they didn't own. Several railroads went bankrupt, leaving the State holding near-worthless bonds. In one way or another, a large share of the State's 22 million acres was sold or hypothecated at least once.

When the War Between the States ended (down here, some call it "the War of Northern Aggression"), most of Florida was still virgin. Much timber had been cut, some land cleared for farming or ranching, some wetland drained, but these were modest nicks on the land. Most of the great schemes had failed. Many of the conditional grants had expired or been canceled. By 1880, however, new attacking forces were in place and the assault on the state's natural areas gathered momentum.

Disston and Flagler

Many steamboats now plied the St. Johns, Apalachicola, Oklawaha, and other Florida waterways. Tourism had become popular. War veterans were seeking places to settle. Trade between North and South was increasing. Florida was an important link in the North's trade with Cuba and Mexico.

The new developers brought real money. They negotiated the best deals they could make with the State and had the funds to execute their projects. The biggest big-time operator was a Philadelphian, Hamilton Disston.

Disston and associates proposed to drain the Kissimmee River basin, deepen and straighten the river, drain much of the everglades, and cut canals linking Lake Okeechobee with Florida's east and west coasts, thus opening a huge region to steamboat traffic. Not satisfied with the generous contingency terms he negotiated with the State, Disston later bought outright 4 million acres of land at 25 cents per acre. The *New York Times* called it the largest single land purchase ever made by a citizen.

From time to time critics charged that Disston's progress reports were exaggerated, but those who visited his empire were impressed. The channels opened by his dredges permitted steamboats to travel from Kissimmee, his operating base, to the Gulf of Mexico at Fort Myers and beyond. Cattle were grazing on land previously inundated. Many acres of sugarcane and rice were planted. His empire collapsed in the Panic of 1893, but Disston had shown that the mysterious wilderness could be tamed. The impenetrable wetlands of south Florida had been opened for development.

Still, travel in southern Florida was by boat. When Thomas Edison, Henry Ford, and Harvey Firestone built homes at Fort Myers, building materials and guests came by ship. Along the coasts, hardy barefoot mailmen carried heavy packs, braving alligators, snakes, and pirates, struggling through swamps, sometimes overnighting in "houses of refuge" built to shelter shipwrecked seamen. Not until the 1890s was there an overland route.

The saga of Henry Morrison Flagler has been told many times. He was a man of major achievements even before coming to Florida. Here he built a railroad down the Atlantic coast to Miami, then all the way to Key West, creating great hotels along the way. The railroad was a fabulous engineering feat, crossing estuaries, rivers, swamps, marshes, mudflats, and shifting sand. Building it required thousands of workers, a hodgepodge of convicts, drifters, Cubans, blacks, poor whites--anyone Flagler could recruit by any means. Work camps were primitive, diseases prevalent. A hurricane killed 200 workers in 1906 and delayed the project for a year, but Flagler pushed on.

No rules or regulations protected the environment then, and Flagler would have been contemptuous of them anyway. Building the railroad left a swath of destruction. Forests were felled for ties, lumber, and fuel, and no one cared if stray sparks caused forest fires. Dredges excavated and filled, smothering oyster beds under spoil. Waterfowl marshes were destroyed, tidal creeks blocked.

Palm Beach, Lake Worth, Fort Lauderdale, and Miami, previously accessible only by ship, were now linked by rail to all of the United States. Flagler's hotels were immediately popular. Economic development along the railroad line was explosive.

Flagler was immensely rich and nearing age 80 when he decided to push the railroad all the way to Key West, linking the chain of keys by bridges and causeways across miles of open water. Even he had doubts that it could be done, but in 1912 the 522 miles from Jacksonville to Key West were completed.

In 1935 the Keys took the full impact of a record hurricane. Hundreds of people died, and much of the railroad was destroyed. It was never rebuilt--the need for it had passed. The Overseas Highway was already under construction, and two years later it was in service, making use of whatever Flagler bridges remained.

Boom and Bust

The steamboat era had ended in Florida. Even railroad mileage began a slow decline. Florida was now at the mercy of the automobile and the speculator. A 1926 photograph shows more than a hundred Model T Fords lined up beside a railroad station. A real estate salesman waits beside each. Soon a train would arrive with passengers from the North, eager to buy into the latest Florida land boom. Many would buy, but few would ever see the land they bought. The salesmen's maps showed dreams.

John's father was among the eager buyers in the Coral Gables land boom. He and John's mother came home singing its theme song[3]:

> When the moon shines in Coral Gables
> I will hold you in my arms.
> While the lovelight brightly shines in your eyes
> 'Neath starry skies and sheltering palms.
> When the moon shines in Coral Gables
> Hearts are ever young and gay.
> I know that we'll never roam
> We'll build a wonderful home
> In Coral Gables some day.

Like other eager gamblers, he had no thought of building a home or even keeping the land he bought. As land prices soared, some lots were resold several times in a week. Buyers came from everywhere. Some buyers never saw Florida; much land was sold by mail. Much of the land was inaccessible, much of it seasonally inundated.

[3] Words and music by Chas. Bayha. Copyright 1924.

The boom ended with a crash in 1926. Some economists say the Great Depression began here, not when the stock market collapsed in 1929. Almost overnight, land became worthless. Bank failures radiated as far north as Atlanta, and their effects to Wall Street. When the federal government began buying land for the Big Cypress National Preserve in 1974, it needed a battalion of lawyers to trace the hundreds of owners or their heirs. Many had long since forgotten the land they had bought and never seen.

Booms collapsed, but the appeal and growth of Florida did not. Population soared: to half a million in 1900, 5 million in 1960. Tourists outnumbered residents. Logging, citrus growing, cattle ranching, phosphate mining, and construction also expanded rapidly.

For the loggers, it was take the money and run. When the big pines and cypresses were gone, sawmills closed and logging towns were abandoned. From our canoe, we often see the rotting bridge pilings of logging railroads. Some modern hiking trails are built on old logging grades.

The Growth Imperative

The opening of the peninsula was swift and profitable for developers. The accepted function of State and local governments was to promote growth. Suggestions that growth might be planned or regulated were dismissed as heresy. Officials did the bidding of developers. Zoning and building codes didn't exist.

The result was sprawling, haphazard development. The newcomers needed roads, sewer systems, water, schools, police, and fire fighters. Towns and counties were hard pressed to meet the demands. For lack of collection services, trash was dumped anywhere. Newcomers who built homes on land that was dry when bought, demanded help when it flooded.

Not until the 1980s did the State government ask counties to prepare growth management plans. The first round yielded thick documents full of declarations of good intentions but empty of commitments. Alarmed by the clear portents of statewide crisis, the legislature got tough. Counties were required to produce comprehensive plans. These had to be consistent with regional and State plans and were subject to approval by State agencies. Many of the plans were sent back for revision. Some counties still resist.

The exploiters haven't quit. They contribute heavily to political campaigns, and each legislative session sees new efforts to repeal or emasculate the growth management law. Our county's officials have fought against growth management every step of the way.

Large-scale alteration of the nature of Florida began little more than a century ago. It has since been on a steepening upward curve. Only in the past 20 years have the State and some local governments recognized its threat to Florida's future. Many laws, regulations, and ordinances to protect the environment from further damage are now on the books, although enforcement is weak.

Save the Wetlands!

The 850-square-mile Green Swamp in central Florida has been the subject of much controversy. More than half of the area is wetlands, the headwaters of five major rivers. The wetlands serve as a cap that pressurizes the aquifer, and they contribute an average of 55 billion gallons a year to the underground water supply.

In the 1960s, a wave of development was spreading from Orlando, home of Disney World, toward Tampa. The Green Swamp lay between. In 1974, a State commission studied the Swamp and recommended that 322,690 acres (504 square miles) be designated an Area of Critical State Concern and given special protection. The designation was made, but the State failed to provide protection. The oversight committee didn't meet. Development continued. Sand mines were affecting the Swamp's hydrology. Loggers were fast clearing away its cypress stands. High-voltage power lines crossed the Swamp, their service roads affecting the surface flow of water. Dams were proposed to stop the natural flooding of wetlands downstream.

Most of the Green Swamp is in Polk County. Polk's developer-friendly government repeatedly asked the State to withdraw its protection but failed to provide effective protection itself. When growth management legislation required the county to take responsibility for the Swamp, the State rejected the county's plans as grossly inadequate.

The Southwest Florida Water Management District has purchased 80,000 acres for watershed protection. Another 126,000 acres have been proposed for State purchase. Developers and some landowners have vigorously opposed the purchases.

Mitigation

For most of Florida's short history, its government urged, promoted, subsidized, and facilitated drainage of wetlands. Getting water off the land quickly reduced the recharge of the aquifers. It reduced evaporation and transpiration, the supply side of the cycle that brings rain.

Now federal and State laws protect the remaining wetlands, but there are many loopholes and violations. Developers seek ways to circumvent the laws. A magic word today is "mitigation."

A developer seeks a permit to destroy a wetland. In exchange he promises to create a new one and hires a mitigation "expert" to design an artificial wetland. The State permitting agencies have issued hundreds of permits. A new wetlands policy announced by the Clinton administration in August 1993 opens the door for many more.

Artificial wetlands have short lives, simply because they aren't natural. Creating a wetland requires diverting water from elsewhere. An artificial wetland is soon colonized by some wetland plant species and the creatures they attract. Replicating natural hydroperiods, however, requires management, as does the maintenance of the dams, ditches, and other structures that brought in the water. Developers aren't required to provide management in perpetuity.

A State study evaluated 100 permitted mitigation projects in thirteen counties. Only 4 had met their goals even temporarily. Only 40 had undertaken *any* mitigation. Of these, 23 were located where present or anticipated surrounding uses of the land will soon render them worthless. And 30 projects were polluted by untreated stormwater discharges.

A better case can be made for restoration of former wetlands. More than 90 million acres of natural wetlands have been destroyed since drainage began. Some could be restored by procedures as simple as backfilling ditches. A developer could buy a former wetland, restore it, and give it to the State or a county for preservation.

Light at the End of the Tunnel?

"Bureaucracy is the hope of the future!" declared our favorite cynic. "Make the permitting process more and more complicated. Make the developer get permits from half a dozen agencies that can't agree. Send him back for changes again and again until he quits in despair."

Florida has inherited a strange State government from its jumbled past. The governor is elected and can serve only two consecutive terms. Members of the cabinet are elected independently and are not limited in the number of terms they can serve. They are not accountable to the Governor. Leaders of House and Senate name and remove committee chairmen at will and dictate what bills are heard. Few officials or legislators understand the State's weird financial system.

The Florida League of Conservation Voters publishes an annual scorecard of legislators' votes. In 1993, members of the House voted "right" less than half of the time, senators just a shade better. Only two representatives and three senators voted right even 60 percent of the time. Further, many good environmental bills were never allowed to come to a vote.

The Department of Environmental Protection[4] hires recently graduated lawyers, scientists, and engineers. Salaries are low, so, once they know the system, many are recruited by firms seeking permits from the agency.

Florida's taxes are near the nation's lowest. It has no income tax. The several million retired residents want to keep it that way. The State constitution requires balanced budgets. Roads, schools, and other services deteriorate as each legislative session confronts a budget crisis. Things have become so bad that a few brave politicians now dare whisper "income tax."

Times are changing. More laws and regulations now protect the environment. Law officers and judges are dealing more severely with violators. Permit applications are less often rubber-stamped. Florida is buying more ecologically important land for preservation than any other state. In county after county, citizens have voted to tax themselves to buy parkland. As for the legislature, citizens voted overwhelmingly for term limitation. All is not lost!

[4] In 1993, the Department of Natural Resources and the Department of Environmental Regulation were combined as the Department of Environmental Protection.

Chapter 5
What Is a Native?

When Florida began to emerge from the sea some 30 million years ago, the first land to appear was a string of small islands. Gradually the Floridan Plateau rose and was colonized by plants and animals, some species borne by air and sea, others extending their ranges from the north.

Over ages the plateau was inundated several times. For long periods only islands, the highest points of the central ridge, remained above water, and only species adapted to these island habitats survived. Then the plateau re-emerged and received a new influx of plants and animals.

Florida has been extraordinarily receptive to floral and faunal newcomers. Its long shoreline exposes it to invasion by land, sea, and air. Climate and soils are welcoming. New species still arrive in Florida. Birds and insects are blown by storm winds. Rodents from afar may be carried here on ships or floating logs. Seeds and sprouts wash ashore, and seeds are dropped by migrating birds. Some of these alien species survive and reproduce, competing with or even displacing those established earlier. Man has intensified the competition by deliberate or accidental introductions.

Members of the Florida Native Plant Society promote understanding and enjoyment of Florida's native flora, encourage its use in landscaping, and hope to reduce the spread of exotic species, especially those that threaten native ecosystems. The Florida Game and Fresh Water Fish Commission urges suppression of some species of exotic wildlife.

But what is a native? All species we now call "native" were once newcomers. The species that survived on islands when all else was submerged have the longest histories here. Their community we now call Florida scrub.

One might say native species are those that colonized Florida after its last inundation. But how long after? A narrow definition would leave a sadly impoverished "native" flora.

One scientist says a native is any species that arrives naturally and becomes established. That would legitimize many recent arrivals, some of which are displacing species we admire. That's nature, but we may not approve. Or is it nature? Would the cattle egret have invaded Florida so successfully if there were no cattle or plows to follow? Man-made disturbances of habitats, such as drainage, may penalize a native species and favor an exotic.

Another scientific view is that a species is naturalized when it reaches equilibrium within the natural community, no longer displacing species established earlier. Florida's natural communities have been so heavily influenced by man that this definition doesn't work well.

Asked for a definition of "native plant," one Florida Native Plant Society member said, "A species that was here at the time of statehood." We all became citizens together!

In 1936 a committee headed by A. Starker Leopold recommended that National Parks be managed to maintain or recreate the communities of plants and animals that prevailed when Europeans first visited. Florida's State Parks have the same mandate. This concept of "native" excludes a surprising array of familiar species.

Ever since people began crossing seas in ships, they have brought plants along. The U.S. Department of Agriculture set up a Bureau of Plant Introductions to import new commercial crops. Enthusiastic gardeners and farmers formed "plant introduction societies." Among the many pasture and range plants introduced to North America are rose, white, and red clovers; Kentucky bluegrass, common lespedeza, rescuegrass, kudzu, and blue lupine. The weeping willow was brought from China. Eucalyptus species are native to Australia. Many common vegetables and flowers are derived from foreign stock. Mangoes come from India and Southeast Asia, bananas from India and China. The gloriosa lilies, gerberas, calla lilies, kalanchoes, passion vines, and hibiscuses in our garden all derive from Africa.

New plant species are imported to Florida each year without investigation or precautions. Almost a thousand exotics have become established. The customs declaration required of people arriving in the United States asks if they are bringing plant material, but screening is cursory.

The Terrible Trio

Some new species have spread rapidly and become costly nuisances. Florida's Exotic Pest Plant Council says 23 nuisance species, widespread and fast-growing, threaten Florida ecosystems. Heading the list are the melaleuca, Brazilian pepper, and casuarina. An estimated 1.5 million acres are infested with exotic plants.

A tree book published thirty years ago spoke kindly of the melaleuca: "... much used for landscaping ... planted in rows as a windbreak along the coast ..." Now it's called "an environmental cancer," "a swamp-buster." Also called cajeput, punk tree, paperbark, and white tree, the melaleuca transpires three to six times as much moisture as sawgrass, thus lengthening dry periods and weakening wetland flora. Brought from Australia and planted in the everglades to de-water marshes, it has already usurped almost 600,000 south Florida acres and is spreading rapidly, growing thickly, as many as 10,000 trees per acre, eliminating 60 to 80 percent of native species, destroying sawgrass marshes, sloughs, and forests. The head of Florida's Bureau of Aquatic Plant Management said, "In twenty years, if nothing is done about melaleuca, there isn't going to be an everglades."

In 1992 the U.S. Department of Agriculture finally pinned the "noxious" label on the melaleuca. Now it cannot be imported or sent across state lines without a permit. The U. S. Army Corps of Engineers is seeking ways to control it.

Vigorous efforts have been made to keep it from spreading into Everglades National Park. Since 1986, with aid from state and county agencies and prisoner labor, a 4-mile-wide melaleuca-free buffer zone was established in the East Everglades. However, Hurricane Andrew may have breached the buffer zone. It flattened melaleuca forests east of the Park and scattered seeds into a huge area inside the Park.

The Brazilian pepper is a 20-foot-high upland shrub. Our 1960s book called it Brazilian pepper tree, Florida holly, or Christmas berry: "pleasantly decorative." Like the melaleuca, it has spread rapidly. We saw a huge thicket of it on Sanibel Island. A hundred thousand robins were intoxicating themselves on its fermenting berries. It grows thickly on the dikes of the Merritt Island National Wildlife Refuge. On Honeymoon Island, more than 42,000 Brazilian pepper plants were cut in one 75-acre tract.

Its greatest threat is to mangroves, the foundation of estuarine ecosystems. Brazilian pepper has already destroyed 200,000 acres of mangroves. No effective control has been found, short of cutting the plants and treating the cut stems with herbicide.

Third on the list of the "terrible trio" is the casuarina or Australian pine. Salt tolerant, it was often planted in rows as windbreaks along the coast. It, too, spread rapidly. We met it first on a Gulf sandbar and quickly learned not to walk barefoot on its half-inch cones. Soon after our visit, a tropical storm swept away both trees and sandbar, scattering seed cones afar.

An exotic plant that seems innocuous can become disruptive. Hurricane Andrew flattened many native trees in tropical hardwood hammocks. Opening the forest canopy promoted growth of understory plants. After Andrew, botanists saw a rapid growth of exotic vines competing with native species.

Exotic plant research and control hasn't been high on environmentalists' priority list, although 1.5 million Florida acres have been usurped. The state budget provides little money for research on the "terrible trio" and other exotics. Present methods of eliminating melaleuca, Brazilian pepper, and casuarina are costly, labor intensive, and seldom permanent. The Native Plant Society has a formidable task of persuasion, but its membership and influence are growing.

Aquatic Exotics

Because of farmers' and fishermen's demands, more money has been spent suppressing aquatic weeds. In the 1880s, admirers brought the water hyacinth to Florida. It spread rapidly, infesting many waterways and choking irrigation ditches. Canoeists and fishermen are plagued by masses of hyacinths barricading creeks. Herbicides and mechanical removal have cleared many infested areas, at least temporarily. There's hope that biological controls can be found for a more lasting solution.

Hydrilla, another aquatic weed, has made some lakes unfit for boating or fishing. It is often transferred from lake to lake on boat trailers and propellers. In 1992 $1.4 million was spent trying a new chemical to reduce hydrilla in Lake Istokpoga. Weed-eating grass carp may be a permanent control. In our lake, hydrilla has multiplied explosively; this year a hundred sterile grass carp were introduced in hope of controlling it.

Para grass, imported as a promising forage grass, also has a nasty habit of choking drainage ditches and creeks. It grows on banks and extends into the water. On a recent canoe outing on the Peace River, several members of our group had to go overside and drag the boats through dense growths.

Recently we tried to canoe on Lake Eaton in the Ocala National Forest. The lake was blanketed with water hyacinth, water lilies, and hydrilla. Weeds clung to our paddles. Boats with motors can no longer use the lake.

The U. S. Department of Agriculture has often introduced new species without risk analysis. Someone thought torpedo grass, an Australian native, might be a fine forage crop. Now it infests miles of waterways, displacing beneficial native species. It resists control.

Natural aquatic and shoreline vegetation is desirable and legally protected. It filters surface runoff of fertilizers from lawns and farms, provides spawning and feeding grounds for fishes and hunting grounds for wading birds, and reduces erosion by waves. Property owners often violate regulations by applying herbicides or hiring laborers to clear their waterfronts. Most residents on our lake have ignored the regulations, thus contributing to the growth of hydrilla and algae.

Some homeowner associations and resort operators hire lake management companies to kill lake weeds. Recently a dozen offices of such companies were raided by Florida State and federal officials and their records seized. They were suspected of using prohibited chemicals. In 1992 one company agreed to pay a fine of $450,000 for applying unregistered herbicides on aquatic vegetation.

Kill Them All?

Almost everyone favors removing exotic plants from weed-clogged lakes and streams and suppressing the damaging spread of melaleuca, Brazilian pepper, and casuarina. Doing so is expensive, however, and permanent elimination unlikely. It's a never-ending campaign. Most of Florida's one thousand exotic species will be tolerated because they are not causing such conspicuous damage. Gardeners accept weeding as an unavoidable nuisance, even as they cultivate and prize exotic flowers and lawn grasses.

The mandate to State Parks would seem to require elimination of all plant species not present when European first arrived. It can't be done. Suppressing just the most damaging exotic species taxes Park budgets.

Even if more money were available, wholesale elimination of exotics might be unwise. If the species has been present for decades, it may have become the preferred food source for one or more wildlife species. Rapid elimination might expose areas to soil erosion. Elimination methods requiring heavy machinery could damage native species. If the invasion by exotic species succeeded because the habitat was disturbed, plantings of former native species might fail anyway.

Most exotics are here to stay. In time, most will be accepted as naturalized citizens.

Animal Strangers

One day we met four walking catfish making their way along a sandy gutter, two blocks from the nearest water. Other alien wildlife species established in Florida include the cattle egret, European boar, armadillo, coyote, and fire ant. The African bee is expected soon.

The ages-long migrations from the north that brought so many species of land animals to Florida are now blocked by cities, roads, and other obstacles. Still, the wily coyote extended its range across Canada and south through the Adirondacks and Appalachians, finally arriving in North Florida.

Birds come from almost anywhere. Several times each year a hot line summons birders to see a species seldom if ever recorded in Florida. Occasionally a new species becomes established.

For centuries humans have accidentally or purposely brought new species to America. The Norway rat (not a native of Norway), was a nonpaying passenger on sailing ships. A few house sparrows were released in New York's Central Park in 1850; now they're everywhere.

Armadillo

Forty years later, starlings were released in Central Park, with the same result.

The spot-breasted oriole and red-whiskered bulbul, introduced in southern Florida, are now well-enough established to be included in bird guides. When we asked one birder what other exotics might be seen, his response was "Almost anything!" The chief reason is that many bird importers are based in south Florida, and birds often escape from their compounds.

Zoos once accepted budgerigars, cockatiels, and other pet birds whose owners tired of them. Now most zoos decline such gifts, and owners often release the birds instead. Tropical species set free up north die when winter comes. In Florida, several members of the parrot family have survived and multiplied.

The monk parakeet, a fruit eater, seems not yet to be an agricultural pest, but it has the potential. *Florida's Birds* (Herbert W. Kale, II, and David S. Maehr. Sarasota: Pineapple Press, 1990) lists 25 exotic doves, parakeets, parrots, mynahs, and other species known to be breeding in Florida.

One morning near Lake City, a jaguarundi — a Central and South American cat — crossed the road in front of us. We told a state wildlife biologist, who wasn't surprised. He had received other reports. Since then jaguarundis have been seen elsewhere, as well.

We talked with Frank Thompson, an animal dealer who has lived for years in south Florida. He told of many mammals that have escaped from dealer compounds or private owners. Most were single individuals, not mating pairs, and thus did not reproduce. The jaguarundi may be an exception.

One evening, Frank told us, he sat outside his travel trailer at the edge of a park near Hollywood, Florida. To his astonishment, he saw dozens of jackrabbits frisking about. Local residents told him hundreds had been there for years. They seem not to have spread.

Free-living colonies of monkeys were maintained by several Florida commercial attractions. They reproduced but didn't spread because surrounding environments didn't suit them.

Reptiles? Fishes? Frank threw up his hands.

"I couldn't begin to name them all! They're everywhere!"

He continued for some time, telling us what and why. South Florida dealers import many thousands of reptiles and fishes from all over the world, sometimes hundreds of a species in a single shipment. Specimens that seem defective or otherwise unsalable are sometimes thrown out alive, perhaps dumped in the nearest ditch or swamp. Security in some dealer compounds is lax, escapes common. Some small reptiles may be washed into ditches when pits are flushed.

Fish have been similarly dumped or flushed away. Exotic fish now abound in south Florida waters. A few years ago piranhas were caught in several streams. A few species of exotic fish have been introduced in hopes of controlling mosquitoes or exotic weeds.

Among exotic species, freshwater fish are easiest to control. Poison is dumped into lakes or streams, killing all species, native and exotic. Unfortunately, restocking is likely to be with species favored by fishermen, not a balanced assortment of native fishes.

In April 1992, agents of the Florida Department of Agriculture confiscated fourteen banana rasp snails from Florida pet shops and began tracing others shipped by the importer. This snail grows to 7 inches long, multiplies rapidly, and has a prodigious appetite. Now the Department is trying to trace illegal imports of giant hissing cockroaches.

Boas and anacondas have been seen in the Everglades, Thompson said. Walking catfish, geckos, iguanas, and other foreign species are well established, and some are expanding their ranges.

The Bahamian anole is displacing the native green anole. That is happening inside our pool enclosure. We expect geckos to arrive any day.

Gardeners who kneel in a fire ant hill may be bitten several dozen times before they can react. Even single bites are fiery. Sudsy ammonia stops the pain, but nodules still form. We sprinkle ant-killer around active hills. Other hills soon appear.

And meet the love bugs! We are pleased to call them exotic. They first appeared in Florida in 1947. Small black flies, they were so named because they mate in flight and are seldom seen unjoined. They are not loved. Twice a year, in April-May and August-September, they swarm in huge numbers, spattering moving vehicles. Unless promptly removed, which isn't easy, their remains pit automobile finishes. They clog radiators. They are a nuisance to outdoor workers, including gardeners and pedestrians. Floridians attach screens to car radiators when the first love bugs appear. The love bugs are in flight only by day. When you encounter a swarm, slow down if you can; it reduces the number of impacts.

Andrew Turned Them Loose

In 1992, when Hurricane Andrew blasted a path between Miami and Key Largo, more than 200 wild animal dealers were registered in the region. Andrew destroyed many of their buildings, cages, and pens, liberating unknown thousands of animals. Even research institutions were affected. A press story reported the escape of 2,000 monkeys and 500 baboons from one establishment. Hundreds of macaques escaped from a University of Miami laboratory.

The list of species known to have escaped included monitor lizards, iguanas, caiman crocodiles, capybaras, llamas, pythons, Gabon vipers, Gila monsters, and many more. A professional animal catcher told news reporters, "It's like a Disney World of exotic animals out there. It's beyond my wildest dreams and my wildest nightmares. This is something you'll never see again."

Officials of the Florida Game and Fresh Water Fish Commission sounded warnings: "It may be years before we are able to say how many of them made it. But if there were ever a time we were going to see establishment of a species, this is it." "It's an ecological disaster. Even before the hurricane you had things in the Miami area running around and propagating, setting up miniature ecosystems. Now they're all over the place."

Fortunately, even in South Florida most introductions fail. An exotic species may not find the climate, shelter, and food supply it needs, or it may be disposed of by competition or predation. Wildlife biologists worry that fragmentation of habitats threatens native species. Such fragmentation will limit the spread of most exotics. Of the species released by Andrew, few will reproduce. Those that do are likely to be restricted to small habitats.

Visitors to Florida won't be swallowed by pythons. They might be bitten by fire ants.

Chapter 6
The Weather's Fine

Florida is the Sunshine State. The Yellow Pages list Suncoast Realty, Suncoast Acres, Suncoast Burgers, Suncoast Carpets, and Suncoast Plumbing, as well as Sunbank, Sunniland Corporation, Sunshine Chinese Restaurant, and many more. A retirement community advertises, "About 340 days a year are mild, many of these being 'summery'." Years ago the St. Petersburg *Times* distributed free copies if the sun didn't shine.

Solar radiation is measured in langleys. Miami's December langleys are three times New York's. In December, Miami's sunshine hours are 66 percent of the maximum possible.

Rain or Shine?

Summer is Florida's wet season. There's almost a 50-50 chance that some rain will fall during a summer day, usually in the afternoon. (It's been much less than that for several recent summers.) For the rest of the year, the likelihood of showers drops to one or two days a week. Winter vacations are rarely spoiled by rain.

Average annual rainfall ranges from 50 to 65 inches in most of the state. The wettest areas are the extreme west of the Panhandle and the southern end of the peninsula.

Few years are "average." Some produce twice as much rain as others. Many weather stations have recorded 80 inches in a year, a few over 100 inches. In other years, weeks may pass with no rain. Some localities may have rainless months in the wet season. Indeed, meteorologists at the Ocala rainfall station said there wasn't even one "normal" year from 1950 to 1991.

Florida's water supplies depend on rainfall, and a succession of dry years is threatening. Spring is a crucial season for water managers. If the typically dry weather of winter extends into spring, it presages a deficit.

Most summer rain comes in local showers or thunderstorms. Motorists often meet a downpour that taxes windshield wipers, pass through it in a few minutes, then see other showers in the distance. It could rain down-beach while the sun shines on your picnic. Unless rain is brought by a tropical storm, it seldom continues for more than two hours. A frontal system may bring a few sprinkles, then a brief thunderstorm, then scattered light showers.

Winter

Florida winters are generally sunny, cool, and dry. It's usually a few degrees warmer near the coasts than at the same latitudes inland.

Florida's biggest attraction, the weather, sometimes disappoints. Members of our family came from Oregon and Maryland for the Christmas 1989 holidays, bathing suits packed. Their first few days were cool but pleasant. On the day before Christmas, forecasters warned that the night would bring frost.

At the time, oranges and grapefruit were being harvested. Freezing ruins fruit. Before air pollution was a concern, growers often burned automobile tires in the groves to fight frost. Later they used "salamanders," tall kerosene burners. Then came the oil crisis, and kerosene prices escalated. "First it became too expensive to save the crop," one farmer told us. "Then it became too expensive to save the trees."

Because cold air gathers in low places, some farmers try to dispel frost with big fans. Some use irrigation systems; spraying moderates the cold. Strawberry crops have been saved by spraying to coat the berries with ice.

That Christmas Eve brought a hard freeze. Before dawn on Christmas Day, citrus growers were competing for pickers--frozen fruit can be salvaged if picked immediately and rushed to processing. Most citrus growers lost few if any trees, but some lost all. Two years later, growers with enough capital were still replanting. Dead trees and For Sale signs marked where owners had quit.

That Christmas morning also brought electric outages. Many Florida homes are electrically heated. Because of the exceptional cold, power demand exceeded generating capacity, and our utility company instituted "rolling blackouts." Blocks of customers were cut off without warning, not knowing for how long. In many homes the big question was "Can we cook the turkey?" It was a frantic day for restaurants. Everyone was told to turn off the lights on Christmas trees and decorations.

However, freezing temperatures seldom last through a day. Cold waves seldom last more than two or three days. Killing frosts don't happen every year. A dusting of snow is extraordinary even in northern Florida. The winter after the 1989 freeze was exceptionally warm, with no frost. The next was even warmer. This past December was mostly sunny, daytime temperatures around 75°F. Water skiers didn't need wet suits.

In January, our coldest month, the mean maximum-minimum temperature range in south Florida is 75-60°F. The coldest region is the western Panhandle, where the range is 60-40°F.

Swimmers find seawater temperatures stable. Surface temperatures in winter seldom drop much below 72°F at ocean beaches, 70°F at peninsular Gulf beaches. It's colder off shore.

Summer

Even Floridians complain about the humid summer heat. Like British colonials in India, some take to the hills, often to the Great Smokies. It helps to be early risers. We do our gardening at first light. We usually turn on the air-conditioning in late morning. If a shower cools the air in late afternoon, an exhaust fan takes over from the air conditioner. At bedtime we open all sliding doors. In only 3 summers of the past fifteen have we occasionally needed 24-hour cooling to be comfortable.

For most of our years in central Florida, the daily summer weather forecasts have been almost monotonous: daily highs near 90°F, nights in the 70s; 30 to 40 percent chance of afternoon thundershowers.

As everyone says, it's the humidity. In summer Florida is almost continuously under a blanket of warm, moist sea air. Temperatures almost never reach 100°F. Last summer, when North Dakota and New Hampshire locations reported 104°F, the highest in central Florida was 95°F. Summer weather extends through September.

The temperature difference between north and south Florida is less in summer than in winter. In July, the statewide range of daily mean maximums is 88 to 91°F, daily mean minimums 72 to 75°F. Along the coasts, it's a bit cooler by day, warmer by night--just the opposite in winter.

Spring and Fall

Our favorite seasons are spring and fall. In most years no artificial heat or cooling is needed. Doors and windows are open day and night.

The wet season usually ends in late September or early October, except along a narrow strip of the east coast, where it continues through October. The occasional tropical storm may bring a downpour as late as November.

Last October we left camp in Everglades National Park, intending to go down the Keys. As we approached Homestead, we saw a storm front, checked the weather forecast, and changed our plans. Driving north, we skirted the edge of what proved to be a record downpour from Miami to Key Largo: fourteen inches of precipitation in a few hours, causing extensive flooding.

We enjoy almost any kind of weather, including Florida summers, but spring and fall are inspiring. The garden shops do their biggest business then. These are fine seasons for camping, canoeing, hiking, and bird-watching, fine seasons for enjoying the nature of Florida.

Thunder and Lightning

Florida is often called "the lightning capital of the world." The "lightning belt" extends from Brooksville south to Fort Myers and Clewiston, eastward to Orlando. Here lightning occurs 80 to 110 days a year. Our county, Polk, has the most: up to 150 days a year. Thunderstorms are most common in the rainy season.

We never heard the thunder from the strike that blitzed our first computers. We have surge protectors now, but still shut down when a storm comes close. Television repair shops do a rushing business after major storms. Our cable TV service is sometimes interrupted. Power company crews are kept busy resetting circuit breakers.

In Wyoming we attended a ranger's briefing of a summer trail crew. "Stay away from your horse!" he advised. If you have a horse in Florida, that's good advice. Many more people court electrocution by carrying metal golf clubs in the open when a storm rolls in. "Don't stay out in the open," a safety manual advises, "and don't stand right under a tall tree." "If your hair stands on end, throw yourself flat on the ground."

Warnings of severe storms are broadcast by television and radio stations. Such storms usually occur in the hottest part of the day, often with strong winds.

In April 1992 a rare hailstorm struck part of the Orlando area. Friends described 1-inch-diameter hailstones that damaged their roof and automobile, accumulating 3 inches deep on the ground. In our fifteen years here, we've seen no hail.

Tornadoes

In an exceptionally heavy rainstorm, we drove a visitor to the Tampa airport. Several underpasses were flooded, so it was a slow trip, but the plane was late, too. It was still pouring as we drove home. Later we learned a tornado had crossed the road just after we passed, wrecking a school and a factory, cutting a swath through a mobile home park. Because of the downpour, people couldn't see or hear it coming.

Tornado watches are broadcast most often in the spring. Few tornadoes actually occur, about ten to fifteen a year statewide. Most tornado paths are short and damage is usually modest. Occasionally one rips a swath through a mobile home park.

Hurricanes

The hurricane season begins in June and ends in November. The peak period is September-October. Our supermarket's shopping bags tell all about it: "Here are some tips in the event a hurricane approaches . . ." A map is printed on each bag so we can plot storm tracks as bulletins are issued.

Television weathermen show and tell when a *tropical depression*--a cyclone with winds of less than 39 miles per hour--forms in the Caribbean. Satellite pictures show a loose spiral. Floridians become attentive if the depression is upgraded to a *tropical storm*, meaning the winds are now between 39 and 74 mph. Television weathermen now show the track the cyclone has followed and report predictions of its future path. Will it come ashore, and if so where? A tropical storm, typically bringing heavy rain, can cause serious damage along the coast, especially if its arrival coincides with high tide. However, most such storms stay offshore.

Hurricane! Now the cyclone winds exceed 74 mph. If it seems a hurricane might hit Florida, forecasters and civil defense officials have tough decisions to make. What warnings should be issued, where, and when? Should evacuations be ordered or advised?

In a borrowed seaside cottage, we were awakened one night by sirens, then loud pounding on the door. A deputy sheriff told us to evacuate; a hurricane was coming in. We drove inland, slept in the car, and returned next morning. The waves were exceptionally high; wind-driven sand stung our ankles; but the hurricane had turned away.

Predicting storm tracks is far from an exact science, as weathermen freely admit. A 6-hour prediction is more accurate than a 24-hour prediction, but 6 hours may be too little warning time for thousands of people to evacuate. For example, what if our borrowed cottage had been on Key West, over a hundred miles from the mainland by a single road with many long, exposed, bridges and causeways? Evacuating the Keys could become a logistical nightmare. One automobile accident, one empty gas tank, any obstruction on a bridge or causeway, could cause hours of delay. How could emergency vehicles reach the scene?[5]

One of the most violent hurricanes on record, with wind speeds over 200 mph, struck the Keys on Labor Day in 1935. Over 800 died, many of them workers building the Overseas Highway. This was the storm that destroyed Flagler's railroad. Now that the Keys are grossly overbuilt, a similar hurricane could kill thousands. Wind-driven tide could surge over the road, cutting off escape.

When should warnings be given? Too soon and most will be false alarms. Too late and people may die. Allowing enough time to evacuate the Keys would guarantee that most alarms would be false. And should everyone in the predicted storm path be told to leave? Probably, but panic might cause people outside the warning area to evacuate.

"Our biggest problem in South Dade is getting people to stay put," says Bob Sheets, director of the National Hurricane Center at Coral Gables. Some estimates predict that a storm warning in South Florida might induce 1.5 million people to take to the roads. Highways would be paralyzed, and people stalled in their cars would be in greater danger than if they'd stayed home.

In tropical storms and hurricanes, water usually--not always--causes more damage than wind. Rainfall associated with hurricanes is usually heavy. Storm surges may send waves crashing through low-lying areas, smashing houses and other structures. Flooding and wind damage can extend far inland.

Along the coasts, tens of thousands of homes have been built on barrier islands and filled land. These homes, only a few feet above ordinary high tides, would be overwhelmed by a 15-foot storm surge such as

[5]We don't know how many residents of the Keys evacuated when hurricane Andrew approached in 1993. The exodus went quite smoothly. However, some who fled from the Keys were in the hurricane's path when it came ashore between the Keys and Miami.

destroyed Belize City, Belize, in 1961. High-rise condominiums fronting the beaches are also at risk.

Evacuation routes from Florida's barrier islands are not as long as the Overseas Highway, but the number of people to be evacuated is large, and causeways might be inundated. The causeway linking Sanibel Island to the mainland was inundated in a tropical storm a few years ago.

When a hurricane warning is broadcast, homeowners rush to buy plywood and duct tape to protect glass doors and windows. The instructions on shopping bags advise them to stock drinking water, nonperishable food, flashlights, candles, matches, and a battery-powered radio. Boats should be moved to safe places. Lawn furniture and other loose objects should be brought indoors. Campers are advised to find shelters. We've been through this exercise three times and have never seen a hurricane. It's a nuisance, but we don't complain.

Hurricane statistics are reassuring. In an average year, about a hundred cyclone patterns are carefully watched. Only about ten become tropical storms; only five become hurricanes. Of these only about half come ashore somewhere between Texas and New England.

Florida has never escaped tropical storms for more than a 2-year period. The longest period without a major hurricane has been nine years. Most hurricanes that come ashore in Florida strike the southern peninsula or western Panhandle, but they can come in anywhere. Until 1964, Jacksonville was the only large city south of Boston that had never experienced a major hurricane; then it was hit hard.

The power of hurricanes usually diminishes over land, but this is not always true. John saw what Hurricane Hazel did to Winsted and Torrington, in northwest Connecticut. The main street of Winsted was scoured down 8 feet deep by the Mad River. Many buildings were undermined. Houses were pushed down hillsides. Eighteen-wheel trucks were tumbled into streams and half buried. The city hall was bombarded by new cars swept from a sales lot a block away. Floodwaters emptied lumberyards, scattering their contents like jackstraws for miles.

In September 1926 the first major hurricane to hit Miami in twenty years devastated the city and swept inland over Lake Okeechobee, killing 370 people, injuring 6,000. Only two years later another came ashore at Palm Beach. This one created a storm surge. Water swept over the south dike of Lake Okeechobee, obliterating the towns of Belle Glade and South Bay. Estimates of the dead ranged from 1,800 to 2,400.

In September 1989, Hurricane Hugo missed Florida but did heavy damage in South Carolina. Later Bill Sadowski, then secretary of Florida's Department of Community Affairs, warned that a similar hurricane in

Florida would cost $14 billion in damages, with the State's share $3.5 billion, more than the budget could handle. He urged prohibitions on rebuilding hurricane-damaged buildings on the coast and limits on the size and height of rebuilt commercial structures.

Then Came Andrew

On Saturday, August 22, 1992, a tropical storm gathered strength east of the Bahamas and was named Andrew, the first hurricane of the year. The National Hurricane Center said it would probably strike Florida, perhaps near West Palm Beach. Emergency planning officials warned residents of south Florida counties to be prepared to evacuate. Evacuation orders were issued on Sunday, and highways were soon clogged with residents moving north.

The first hurricane *watch* was for the coast from Miami north to Titusville. Emergency relief organizations went on standby. There was little alarm. On Sunday morning stores reported no rush to buy food, plywood, and flashlight batteries.

That afternoon the hurricane watch became a *warning*. Officials of several small towns populated largely by migrant workers complained later they had received no warnings or orders to evacuate.

Before dawn on Monday, the hurricane struck the Florida coast from South Miami to the north end of Key Largo. Roaring inland, it devastated an area of 160 square miles. Homestead, Florida City, neighboring towns, and the Homestead Air Force Base were virtually destroyed. Over a million people were left without electricity, telephone service, or city water.

Newspapers called it the most destructive storm ever to hit Florida. True, the damage to property of all kinds was immense. But unlike the hurricanes of 1926, 1928, and 1935 which killed hundreds, only 10 people were killed. (One press account said 15, another 22).

Estimates of the number made homeless rose hourly, to almost 200,000 by Tuesday morning, later to 250,000. Monday's newspapers estimated the damage at $15 billion. However, with roads blocked by debris and communications limited, the chief information gathered that day was by overflights that showed mile after mile of roofless and razed buildings.

The hurricane swept across the everglades. Damage was moderate on Florida's west coast. Andrew crossed the Gulf to hit Louisiana, where the hurricane faded.

In many tropical storms and hurricanes, water causes more damage than wind: deluges of rain and great waves driven inland. Andrew dropped only modest rainfall, and the highest storm surge reported was only 12 feet--enough to have inundated the Keys had it happened there.

The first 48 hours were chaotic. Relief and rescue organizations weren't prepared, and many were left without communication facilities. Toll booths stayed open on the Florida Turnpike, causing massive backups. Emergency shelters weren't opened in Orange County. Transportation officials couldn't get helicopters to survey road conditions. At the end of the first week, homeless, sick, and hungry residents were complaining about painfully slow response to their urgent needs. Local, State, and federal officials blamed each other. Truckloads of food and clothing were sent in by people eager to help, but some spoiled for lack of storage and distribution arrangements. Profiteers trucked in chain saws, generators, plywood, and other desperately needed items, selling them off the tailgates of their trucks for many times their usual prices. Many local merchants also profiteered.

No one really knew how many families needed emergency housing. One report said 63,000 homes had been destroyed. Months later a governor's task force said 28,066. Many more structures were heavily damaged. Many people improvised shelters in the ruins of their homes, to salvage possessions and ward off looters. Among the most unfortunate were thousands of farm workers, who had always lived on the edge of poverty. Now their jobs as well as their homes were gone. The well-to-do moved to northern hotels and motels. The damage estimate rose to $20 billion.

Two weeks after Andrew hit, field kitchens were operating, tent cities were taking shape, electricity and water systems were gradually being restored, and major roads had been cleared. For most of the homeless, it seemed, at least food, water, temporary shelter, and emergency medical attention were now provided. Insurance adjusters swarmed, but many of the homeless were uninsured.

The disaster was too big for press, radio, and television to cover fully. Andrew gradually faded from front pages and evening newscasts. But six months after Andrew, we saw hundreds of ruined houses, abandoned by their owners but not yet razed. Thousands of south Florida residents were living in improvised quarters, some still in tent cities. Desperate, many fell prey to dishonest contractors. A year later one could still see ruined apartment buildings, the wreckage of homes, and great piles of debris.

The General Accounting Office reported that the Federal Emergency Management Agency had failed to prepare as Andrew approached the Florida coast, then responded with confusion and duplication; FEMA's own in-house review agreed.

Business pages predicted a great boom in south Florida as reconstruction began. "The recession here is over," one leader proclaimed. It seemed to be; contractors and subcontractors had more work than they could handle. A large problem was what to do with the debris Andrew left behind, thirty times the annual deposits in landfills. Air quality rules were bent to permit open burning, but much of the rubble wouldn't burn.

In the aftermath, engineers blamed much of the damage on poor construction. Building codes had been freely violated, and inspections were lax. Roofs were not properly attached to structures; plywood and shingles weren't securely fastened to roofs. Many mobile homes lacked storm anchors. Soon, however, builders were complaining that stricter building codes and inspection were delaying reconstruction and would drive up the cost of new houses.

Scanning our newspaper file, we found dozens of short hurricane stories: A manatee was swept a quarter-mile inland and deposited in a golf course pond. Volunteers were collecting and caring for lost and abandoned dogs, cats, and horses. Early reports said 70 percent of the rare plant species were lost at Fairchild Tropical Gardens. Concerned scientists were afield, trying to discover the fate of rare butterflies, tree snails, and other wildlife. At Miami's Metrozoo and at privately owned Monkey Jungle many animal enclosures were ripped open. However, most of the liberated animals stayed close to home and were soon rehoused.

By October we were receiving information about damage to parks and wildlife. Andrew had ripped a 20-mile-wide slash across the northern sector of Everglades National Park. Early reports had said the Park would be closed until some time in 1993, but the road to Flamingo was reopened before year's end.

At Everglades and Biscayne National Parks, 175 employees were left homeless. The Everglades visitor center, boardwalks, observation towers, and other structures were heavily damaged. As for damage to the Park's flora and fauna, one scientist said: "It's supposed to be that way." The Everglades evolved through centuries of fires, storms, and hurricanes. Andrew was just one more. "It's a rejuvenation," declared a botanist. Like the Yellowstone fire, Andrew cleared away deadwood. Other scientists are less optimistic. Years of human tampering had brought the Everglades to ecological crisis. With populations of wading birds already reduced to a twentieth of their former numbers, could they now withstand Andrew's destruction of their rookeries? With the Park already threatened by invasion of exotic plants, what will happen after hurricane winds scattered seeds over stripped land?

The panthers, bears, bobcats, and deer that had been tagged with radio collars fared well. Mangroves, hardwood hammocks, and pinelands, heavily damaged, will recover as they have before.

However, a friend familiar with Florida Bay told us that many of the hundreds of small islands had been stripped of their mangroves. Such islands are often formed when mangroves take root on sandbars and accumulate silt. "All the channels have shifted," he said. "You run aground where they used to be."

The Weather's Fine!

Andrew was frightful, but such a hurricane may not happen again for decades. North of the storm track, visitors still filled the seaside hotels and motels, sunbathed and swam. Theme parks were as busy as usual. Residents and tourists quickly returned to the Keys.

Almost always in Florida, the weather's fine!

Chapter 7
Florida's Underground

Construction was about to begin on a shopping mall two blocks from our home. Late one night, a motorist about to pass the site braked just in time to stop short of a chasm. One lane of the road had vanished. A sinkhole about 100 feet across and 35 feet deep had also engulfed part of the building site. Construction plans were canceled, and the bank withdrew its financing.

More recently, occupants of a large house felt tremors and escaped as their home began sliding into a new sinkhole. When that sinkhole stopped settling, it was 350 feet wide. Every year or so a house or automobile or highway is thus swallowed. Small sinkholes that appear in open country aren't news. In one recent year, several hundred sinkholes appeared during rainstorms in Levy and Gilchrist counties. Most were small, but highway crews were kept busy dumping fill where sinkholes opened in roads.

The cause of sinkholes is dissolution of underlying limestone. Rain is slightly acidic, and air pollution has increased its acidity. Water seeping through organic ground litter also picks up acidity. The weak acid slowly dissolves the limestone that underlies Florida. Pore spaces enlarge. Fractures widen. Cavities form, join, and become caverns. Cavern roofs become thin and collapse. Thousands of Florida lakes are ancient sinkholes or solution basins.

Sinkholes occur most often when limestone is near the surface, but caverns may collapse when overlain by a hundred feet or more of sand and clay. In the latter case, subsidence at the surface is less sudden.

"Here in Florida, especially on the western coastal lowlands, there is a layer of sand, 10 feet or so above the limestone layer," said Chris Roeder of Florida's Department of Environmental Regulation. "That limestone has become riddled with holes during the past million years because of the water flowing through it. Then what happens is you get heavy rain water percolating through the sand and into the limestone. The sand just washes into those holes in the limestone along with the water, and a sinkhole is formed."

Limestone dissolves slowly. Typically, a cavern wall or floor may lose an inch in a thousand years. The total for all Florida is impressive, however: about 13 million tons of limestone per year are dissolved and transported to the sea.

With so much water seeping through so much limestone for so many years, one might expect Florida to have caves rivaling Mammoth or Carlsbad, but Florida Caverns State Park near Marianna is the only large cave complex one can walk through. Other known extensive cave systems are submerged, accessible only to qualified cave divers. Some have not been fully explored.

Florida's only constantly flowing waterfall is inside a sinkhole. At Falling Waters State Recreation Area, visitors descend a stairway inside the 100-foot-deep cylindrical pit. Water from a stream plunges over the pit's edge. The sinkhole doesn't fill with water, so there must be an outlet below.

Another large old sinkhole, 500 feet across and 120 feet deep, is at Devil's Millhopper State Geological Site, north of Gainesville. A boardwalk and 221-step stairway descend to the bottom. Layers of embedded fossils reveal the area's geological history. It's cooler below, and plants growing inside the sinkhole are typical of Appalachian ravines. The site has other sinkholes, a visitor center, and a nature trail.

Although it is the most abundant, limestone is not the only material underlying Florida. Sand, clay, and other sediments, transported and deposited, have mixed with limestone or formed layers. A typical drill core has segments with considerable variety: several types of limestone and layers of clay, sand, sandy clay, sandy limestone, marl, phosphatic sand, and so on. Some layers, chiefly clay, are relatively impermeable to water. Above these impermeable layers, water accumulates in pores, cracks, and caverns.

Under much of the peninsula, water in a permeable limestone layer hundreds of feet thick is confined between impermeable layers. The lay-

ers are tilted slightly downward from north to south. Water moves slowly through innumerable pores, crevices, and passages in the limestone. Because the water comes from a higher level, the capping layer keeps the hydraulic system under pressure. This is the Floridan Aquifer, Florida's unique natural plumbing system, providing an immense supply of ground water, the peninsula's chief water supply.

Supposedly "impermeable" confining layers nevertheless leak. Where there is a breach in a capping layer, water gushes up. Florida has twenty-seven first-magnitude springs, each gushing more than 100 cubic feet per second. Hundreds of named springs have lesser flows. Water also comes to the surface at countless seeps.

Florida's aquifers must be recharged. About one-seventh of the Floridan Aquifer's supply flows underground from Alabama and Georgia. Most recharge comes from seepage through sandy soils and from sinkholes, lakes, and streams.

Paynes Prairie State Preserve, south of Gainesville, includes a 15,800-acre basin. During the late 1600s, this prairie was the largest cattle ranch in Spanish Florida. Rainfall drained to Alachua Sink, largest of several sinkholes within the basin. About 1870 this sinkhole became plugged, and a lake filled the basin. Soon steamboats were providing service between Gainesville and Micanopy. About twenty years later, the plug disintegrated and the lake drained, leaving the steamboats stranded. Since then the basin, as before, has drained into the Floridan Aquifer.

The Floridan Aquifer underlies the coastal plains of South Carolina, Georgia, and Alabama, and most of Florida north of Lake Okeechobee. The maximum thickness of the water-bearing Floridan Aquifer is 3,500 feet, the average 1,000 feet.

The Floridan Aquifer is not an underground lake. Except for caverns and at springs, many passageways in the limestone are small and tortuous. Movement of water through the Floridan Aquifer has been measured by injecting a dye or other tracer in one well and timing its appearance in others. The rate is usually slow, sometimes less than 1 foot per day. In more open formations, water may move several hundred feet in a day.

When water is pumped from a well, more water seeps or flows in to replace it. The yield of a well--the replacement rate--depends on its size and depth, and on the formation into which it was drilled. A typical well tapping the Floridan Aquifer yields 1,500 gallons per minute.

Ask veteran Florida conservationists to name the classic battles they have fought. They will certainly include the everglades and the Cross-Florida Barge Canal. The canal idea began when the peninsula was a wet wilderness dangerous to sail around. Linking the Withlacoochee, Oklawaha, and St. Johns rivers would provide quick, safe passage from the Atlantic ocean to Gulf. Completion of the Okeechobee Waterway almost killed the northern route, but the Great Depression revived it. Big public works projects were needed. Florida congressmen got the money to begin planning. Construction began in 1935.

Hydrologists weren't consulted when this sea-level ship canal was planned. Had it been built, salt water flowing across Florida would have percolated into the aquifer. The peninsula's water supply would have been ruined and its future habitability fatally impaired. When opponents finally made themselves heard, construction was halted in 1936. The ship canal plan was abandoned.

Coastwise shipping was almost halted by German submarines in World War II. Florida congressmen revived the canal idea. Now it was to be a shallower barge canal with locks, less threatening to the aquifer. Congress authorized the Cross-Florida Barge Canal in 1942 but appropriated no funds.

Opponents of the canal mobilized, and appropriations became an annual conflict. When $50 million was appropriated, land was acquired and the U.S. Army Corps of Engineers began construction in 1962. Canal work moved inland from the Gulf side. Rodman Dam and locks were built.

By 1969 support for the canal was disintegrating. William Partington and Marjorie Carr led the growing opposition. Many people were appalled by the swath of destruction, obliterating wetlands, forests, fields, and other wildlife habitat, as well as farms. The redesign had not removed all threats to the aquifer. Costs were soaring.

Florida politicians began to jump ship, not wanting to be linked to a canal that would carry little traffic. The governor joined the opposition. Appropriations stopped. Work was halted. Finally the opposition prevailed and Congress canceled authorization for the canal.

The land purchased for the canal route has been transferred to the State. Rodman Dam will eventually be removed. It will take decades for the scars to heal, but there will be a permanent cross-Florida greenway here.

A quite different aquifer, the Biscayne, underlies about 3,200 square miles in populous southeast Florida. It lies close to the surface, has no cap, and is recharged directly by falling rain and seepage from freshwater canals. Porous and fractured, it has been called "one of the most permeable aquifers in the world," with storage capability comparable to a gravel bed. It is the freshwater supply for the densely settled coastal strip from West Palm Beach to Homestead and Florida City south of Miami.

Two smaller aquifers are locally important water sources: the Chokoloskee, under the Big Cypress Swamp; and the Sand and Gravel Aquifer in the western Panhandle.

We once saw a resourceful camper establish his own water supply. He hammered into the ground a length of pipe fitted with a well point, then mounted a hand pump on the pipe. A few strokes of the pump handle produced a satisfying flow. When he broke camp Sunday afternoon, he took pipe and pump along.

He had tapped what hydrologists call a *surficial aquifer*, a water-saturated bed of sand, gravel, or broken shells close to the surface. In northern Florida, especially, surficial aquifers often lie above the deeper, confined, Floridan Aquifer. Surficial aquifers are recharged quickly by rainfall and are vulnerable to seasonal droughts and local pollution sources. Many homes and farms remote from water distribution systems rely on shallow wells.

The Floridan Aquifer depends on replenishment by rain. Of the average annual 54 inches of precipitation Florida receives, the equivalent of 38 inches evaporates or returns to the atmosphere by transpiration of plants. Much of the rest flows to the sea through rivers and streams.

Recharge of the Floridan Aquifer is the most crucial factor in the state's water supply. How much rainwater percolates underground depends on the characteristics of the surface and layers below. In high-recharge areas, more than 12 inches, almost one-fourth of the rainfall, reaches the aquifer. In other upland areas, less than 4 inches is added to the underground supply.

The sand ridge that extends down much of the peninsula is an important recharge area because of its permeability. The ridge is also favored by developers, whose buildings, driveways, and parking lots seal the surface against recharge. A 1971 governor's conference recommended that the State acquire recharge areas or protect them by zoning. Nothing was done. In several recent sessions the legislature has considered "blue belt" legislation, offering tax breaks to those who refrain from paving recharge surfaces, but at this writing no legislation has been adopted. Meanwhile, these high, dry areas along the ridge are being developed.

Many public water supplies in other regions, such as New York City's, are reservoirs formed by damming watersheds. Florida's topography is too flat for this. A few public supplies take water from lakes, reservoirs, or rivers, but wells are usually more convenient and the quality of wellwater is usually superior.

Nine of ten households in Florida are supplied by groundwater. Industries, many of which require huge volumes of water, get four-fifths of it from underground. Slightly more than half of irrigation water is taken from underground supplies.

Until the 1930s, it seemed that Florida had a limitless supply of water. One had only to pump it from underground. Even when massive drainage projects were undertaken to hasten the flow of water from land to sea, no one thought this would diminish the underground supply. Pumping for industrial and agricultural uses was unrestricted.

Because water supply in Florida seemed limitless, little study had been given to its underground sources. We scanned an extensive bibliography of scientific papers on Florida's water resources and found few published before 1960. Most of the research defining and mapping the Floridan and other aquifers has been published since 1970.

In the 1930s, salty water began appearing in some Miami area wells. It was one of the first signs that groundwater supplies have limits. In the years that followed, more and more wells suffered saltwater intrusion.

The Biscayne Aquifer formation extends under the sea, where it is permeated by seawater. Fresh water is lighter than salt and floats above it, with some mixing at the interface. Thus salt water penetrates inland below the fresh water. Excessive pumping of fresh water from wells sunk into the aquifer has allowed salt water to rise. Some wellwater became brackish, and wells had to be abandoned. The many drainage canals dug in the Miami area have also caused saltwater leakage into the aquifer.

Urbanization of the Miami area has been rapid and new water demands are heavy. Hydrologists were not surprised that salty water should appear in wells near the coast, although the precise mechanisms had yet to be discovered. What surprised many was finding that salt water underlies all Florida's fresh groundwater. This inland salt water is well below sea level. It becomes a significant problem only when withdrawals of fresh water in a layer above reduce pressure and permit salt water to rise. Several fast-growing coastal counties have reached the limits of their underground water resources.

Also Underground

Florida has unlimited quantities of limestone. It's quarried, crushed, and ground for cement, construction, soil treatment, riprap, and other purposes. Sand, gravel, clay, and refractory minerals are mined in modest quantities. Florida imports its natural gas and coal. (Unlikely as it seems, the *Florida Statistical Abstract* says there's one coal mine.)

The big item is phosphate. Underground Florida supplies one-third of the world's phosphate rock. In early days, rock was mined with pick and shovel. Now huge electric-powered walking draglines with house-size buckets gouge great cavities in the earth, 150 to 250 feet wide, 50 to 70 feet deep, and up to a mile long.

Water transports the material to processing plants. Water is used to separate the phosphate from sand, clay, and other materials. In general, for each ton of phosphate rock produced, one ton of sand and one ton of clay must be disposed of, an operation requiring huge quantities of water. One proposed mine would draw 37 million gallons a day from the aquifer.

Mining has left tens of thousands of acres in central Florida looking like moonscapes. State law requires mining companies to restore the land, and a tax is levied on each ton of phosphate to underwrite reclamation. Wetlands, especially, must be restored. Restoring the cavities is the easy part. The question is what the result should be. "I feel like a minor god," said a mining company official in charge of reclamation. "I can make the land flat enough for a shopping mall or industrial zone, or I can include ponds for a subdivision. I can make lakes and hills for a golf course or a natural area park."

The industry likes to call mining a "temporary use" of the land, but it has yet to solve the problem of waste clay. Dikes are built to contain "slime ponds," into which the clay slurry is pumped. A typical operation that mines 400 acres a year leaves behind 250 acres of slime ponds.

In these ponds, the fine particles of clay don't settle but remain in suspension. Evaporation soon forms a crust on a pond's surface, and this prevents evaporation from below. Years after pumping to a pond ends, a sample taken from a few feet down is as much as half water. The surface won't support buildings. We've heard that a bulldozer left overnight on a slime pond vanished by morning. Experiments are being made with growing crops on slime ponds.

Thus far it has been deemed impractical to purify the large volume of other wastewater left by phosphate processing. Much is reused, but large quantities are pumped underground.

Many Floridians are dismayed as phosphate mining devastates more and more wetlands, forests, rangeland, and pasture. Each new mine must undergo a complex permitting process. Often public opposition is strong, but for several more decades phosphate mining will be important to central Florida's economy.

The industry, sensitive to public opinion, has made substantial investments in reclamation projects. Several reclaimed areas have been donated to the State and counties for parks.

Oil

One of the few subjects on which Florida politicians, businessmen, and environmentalists agree is opposition to offshore drilling for oil. Each year, oil industry lobbyists seem close to persuading federal authorities to permit drilling. Thus far Florida's opposition has held the line. Some oil wells have been drilled on shore. A few produce modest quantities of oil, but oil geologists think the promising fields are offshore.

Opponents of offshore drilling cite the risk of spills or blowouts, which would contaminate beaches with oil, injuring tourism. Having visited the oil coast of Louisiana and Texas, we can testify that, if oil is discovered, the impact on coastal Florida could be far more extensive, devastating, and permanent than an occasional spill.

To support offshore drilling and production, the Louisiana-Texas oil industry has pre-empted harbors and estuaries. Here drill rigs and platforms are assembled. Here are shipyards, drydocks, refueling docks, outfitting yards, and berths and moorings for tugs, barges, tankers, supply ships, floating cranes, and other craft. It's no place for recreational boating.

For miles along the coast and extending inland are tank farms, pumping stations, steelyards, helicopter services, suppliers of drilling lubricants and tools, and other oil-related establishments. Refineries, too. It's a 24-hour operation, so brightly lighted we could have driven on adjacent highways at night without headlights.

When drilling and production begin, it's a boomtown setting. Workers find whatever housing they can, in crowded mobile home and trailer camps, and in shantytowns. Those employed on the platforms typically work one week on, one off. Enterprises spring up to provide entertainment for workers off duty.

Pipelines radiate from the coast. The pipeline companies have been given power of eminent domain, and pipelines slash across public waterways (now posted "No Trespassing - Keep Off"), across wetlands, pastures, and farms. Once buried, the pipelines are not forgettable. Along each route are markers, vents, expansion loops, and pumping stations.

If drilling is permitted and succeeds, miles of our sun coast could become another oil coast.

Chapter 8
What If the Well Runs Dry?

L ife on Earth depends on the hydrologic cycle. Only on Earth, of the planets within our solar system, can there be such a cycle. Other planets are too hot or too cold. Earth's ice caps modify the cycle, expanding in ice ages, then retreating.

Water evaporates from land and sea and returns as rain or snow. Of the rain falling on land, some returns to the sea through rivers and streams. Some, having seeped into upper soil layers, is taken up by plant roots and transpired by leaves, thus returning to the atmosphere. Another part, also absorbed by soil and litter, slowly migrates into streams and lakes. Some seeps underground into aquifers.

Over the ages, great changes of climate have occurred. Many of the world's deserts were once productive grasslands, forests, or even wetlands. Some say Florida's recent dry years portend the future, that we are on the downward slope of a rainfall cycle. Dry years will become the normal, they say, wet years the exceptions.

Perhaps so, but Florida's chronic water shortages can't be blamed on a few dry years. Dry-year shortages do forcefully demonstrate that present ways of using water are incompatible with continued population growth. Life in Florida depends on the hydrologic cycle, and demands for water are perilously close to its availability.

Water, simple H_2O, is a remarkable substance whose properties are not yet fully understood. For example, industry and University of Florida scientists are experimenting in a new field: aqueous organic chemistry. By defining the hitherto unknown role of high-temperature water in the formation of petroleum and coal, they foresee new ways of extracting fuel from oil shales and of liquefying coal.

More substances dissolve in water than in any other liquid. Its solvent powers can be increased by adding another chemical, such as carbonic acid. Yet water itself is relatively inert, unchanged by the many substances that dissolve in it or by their interactions. When it evaporates, solutes are left behind.

Another of water's special properties is that it absorbs and releases large amounts of heat energy in its changes of state: between ice and water, and between water and vapor. Humans and many other animals cool their bodies by evaporation. Water changing into steam expands, and this drives turbines and pistons. Condensation of the steam releases heat.

Immense quantities of water are used by industries for cooling, separating, mixing, washing, chemical processing, and transporting. In Florida, most industrial water is pumped from wells. A part evaporates. A part is discharged as waste. Little or none is returned to the aquifer from which it came.

Human withdrawals bypass a part of the hydrologic cycle. The water withdrawn returns to the cycle at another time and place. Most of the water drawn from a lake to irrigate an orange grove evaporates or is transpired. A small amount seeps underground. A tiny fraction becomes orange juice. Little or none returns to the lake.

Transportation is a major use of water. In early times household and other wastes were simply dumped into streams. Many outhouses were built over streams. Today, water transports waste matter from garbage grinders, washing machines, dishwashers, bathtubs, and toilets. Water carries off wastes from almost every factory, mill, mine, processing plant, laundry, and car wash. Water transports phosphate rock from mine to mill.

Were it not for rain, towns and cities would be impossibly filthy. Materials flushed from streets, parking lots, and driveways are carried into lakes, rivers, and estuaries. This also bypasses the natural cycle, because pavements and buildings keep water from seeping into the soil.

Draining Florida's wetlands has shortcut the hydrologic cycle. Before drainage, water in wetlands evaporated, or was transpired by plants, or seeped down into an aquifer. Now ditches and canals route water quickly to streams and rivers. The reduction in evaporation and transpiration has altered the climate; one cannot yet say how much.

Of the water pumped from the Floridan Aquifer, little or none returns. Should some return, it does not replenish the supply where it was withdrawn.

Most of Florida's urban water supplies come from wells. As populations grow, more wells are drilled, usually in well-fields. Each well lowers the pressure in its vicinity, so more water flows in. The rate of inflow determines the supply capacity of the well. When more water is needed, another well is dug.

As more and more wells are drilled in a field, inflow to the entire field eventually falls short of withdrawals. Then drilling more wells won't add to supply. Salt water may intrude.

Garald Parker was the pioneer in describing Florida's aquifers and defining their properties and functions. He made the remarkable determination that the southern half of Florida is hydrologically isolated. Groundwater and surface water flowing south across the midline roughly equals water flowing north. Thus the water supply of Florida's south half depends on rain falling south of the midline.

Here are some of the reasons why the southern half of Florida has the state's most severe water supply problems:

- It has half of the state's area but receives only 44 percent of the state's rainfall.
- It has almost 80 percent of the resident population and an equally large share of tourists, so its public water demands are greater than the north's.
- Huge irrigated agricultural projects compete for water with urban demands.
- Most development has been along the Atlantic and Gulf coasts, where wells are near saltwater interfaces.
- Saltwater intrusion has caused abandonment of many wells.
- Urban development seals land surfaces so rainfall cannot enter and replenish the aquifers.
- Dry years and heavy withdrawals for irrigation have lowered Lake Okeechobee's level, in one recent year almost 10 1/2 feet. Below that level there would be insufficient pressure to move water toward the coast.
- Massive drainage projects have disrupted the original hydrology, drying wetlands that were natural reservoirs and diverting rainfall quickly to the sea.

Water managers have tried to solve the South's supply problems by piling engineering works on engineering works, replacing more parts of the natural hydrologic cycle with their own designs. In wet years, cities and farms are protected from flooding by moving rainwater quickly to the sea. In dry years, some water needs can't be met.

By opening or closing gates and valves, the managers of these vast engineering works determine who gets water and how much. No matter what they decide, some powerful group will be unhappy. When they compromise, no one is pleased.

Short of drastic conservation measures and expensive desalination undertakings, there isn't enough available water to support further growth in south Florida.

Water Shortages Aren't New

Water supply problems first appeared in Florida in the 1930s, but twenty-five years passed before the legislature established a commission to investigate and determine whether new laws and regulations were needed. Forty years later, in 1970-1971, central and southeast Florida suffered an unprecedented drought. Gulf cities had severe water shortages; Palm Beach and West Palm Beach threatened to jail violators of water conservation rules. The State geologist reported with alarm that the water table in the citrus region had dropped 55 feet since 1920.

In September 1971, Governor Askew convened a large-scale conference. Should a limit be placed on growth in South Florida? Who should manage the region's resources, and with what powers? The conferees responded,

> There is a water crisis in South Florida today. The crisis has long-range aspects. Every major water area in the South Florida basin, Everglades National Park, the conservation areas, Lake Okeechobee and the Kissimmee Valley is steadily deteriorating in quality from a variety of polluting sources.

The conference then made sweeping recommendations, among them a halt to wetlands drainage, reflooding the Kissimmee Valley, purchase or rezoning of water recharge lands, a comprehensive land and water use plan, and a plan to limit increases in population. Twenty-plus years later, Florida's population still increases without limit, the Everglades National Park is in far worse condition, the Kissimmee River is still confined to a ditch, and only modest improvements have been made in water quality.

The legislature did enact the Florida Water Resources Act of 1972. It has been followed by thick volumes of laws, regulations, rules, procedures, and court decisions. Five regional Water Management Districts, their governing boards appointed by the governor, now have far-reaching authority over the water resources within their districts, including the purchase of land necessary to protect them.

The Water Management Districts have gathered power and money unto themselves. The South Florida Water Management District, for example, has an operating budget of about $150 million, a staff of scientists, engineers, and managers, and an impressive array of high-tech hardware. Its headquarters is a sprawling modern campus.

The Gulf coast areas of central Florida have reached the limit of well field development. Since the late 1980s, dry years have caused water levels to drop alarmingly. Pumping from wells has caused water levels in many lakes to drop, dismaying lakeside residents.

Several years ago, water managers in our central Florida county declared a limited emergency. We were allowed to water lawns and gardens only two days a week, and only before 9 A.M. and after 5 P.M. Those temporary rules have now become permanent, even when a wet year brings an apparent surplus. The era of unrestricted water use has ended.

In Hillsborough, Sarasota, and Manatee counties on the Gulf coast, salt water is advancing inland at 1 inch to 1 foot *per day* as excessive pumping removes fresh water from the aquifer. Scientists say that to save the fresh water supply, water use in the area must be cut by 50 to 75 million gallons a day.

In August 1993, the West Coast Regional Water Supply Authority adopted a stringent, although temporary, rule: A million householders were ordered to stop all lawn watering, car washing, and other nonessential uses of water.

Southwest Florida Water Management District[6] officials, having virtually stopped issuing new pumping permits in the stressed area, later prohibited additional water withdrawals 15 to 20 miles inland if they would significantly lower groundwater levels.

Now come water wars. A coalition of citrus farmers filed a legal challenge to the rule. Swiftmud expects more challenges, because the rule could deny water to new citrus groves, new phosphate mines, and new public well fields.

Counties on the central Florida Gulf coast want more water than can be pumped from wells within their borders. They seek to develop well-fields in the less populous inland counties. Inland counties resist; they want the water to support their future growth. The inland city of

[6]Folks around here always call it "Swiftmud." Staff members do, too.

Frostproof, whose water use permit is up for renewal, has been warned that its present use, 2.3 million gallons a day, must be cut to 1.12 million gallons by the end of 1996. "They're penalizing small towns like us here when the problem's on the coast," complained city manager Roger Hood. "That's unfair."

So the rule will be delayed for months by litigation, as saltwater penetrates further inland, making more wellwater unfit to drink. Swiftmud officials say even the stricter rule won't be enough.

Telling people not to water their lawns is a gesture. Less than one-fifth of the fresh water withdrawn goes into public supplies. More than twice as much is used for agricultural irrigation, three-fifths of it in south Florida. Electric power plants use about one-fourth, industry a bit more than a tenth.

The Districts have used their resources to reduce wanton destruction of wetlands, contamination of water sources, and some conspicuous water waste. Well-drilling requires a permit, but many a bootleg well is drilled. The South Florida Water Management District--under great public and legal pressure--has agreed to measures that may supply Everglades National Park with more fresh water. The District has supported restoration of the Kissimmee River and efforts to improve the water quality of Lake Okeechobee.

The WMD boards are political. Governors usually appoint their supporters, some allied with the powerful water users being regulated. In general, the recommendations of District scientific and engineering staffs are well grounded. The decisions made by the governing boards are too often influenced by the industries the Districts regulate.

Because Florida is surrounded by salt water, some optimists say there's no crisis. We can desalinate all the water we need. However, no one has found a cheap way to take the salt out. The cost of desalinated water is so high that conservation measures would be chosen first.

If Florida stopped growing, the crisis could be averted or postponed, but almost no one advocates barricading the state line. Even environmentalists advocate "managed growth," which at best would postpone the time when more and more taps go dry.

Conservation, reducing wasteful use of water, is one sensible course. Leaking pipes and faucets are often ignored. When a hot-water faucet is opened, more than a gallon of cold water runs to waste before hot water flows. Householders can save water by fixing leaky faucets, putting bricks in toilet tanks, and installing flow reducers in shower heads. Toilets that use little or no water are available. Even if every household conserved water, however, the saving would be modest.

Industry and agriculture, the big water users, can do much more. Abandoned artesian wells have been allowed to flow uncapped. We see irrigation systems spraying even after days of heavy rainfall. Spray irrigation is convenient, but much water evaporates in midair; less wasteful methods are being adopted. Much of industry's wastewater could be reused. Sewage plant effluent can be used for industrial cooling or for irrigation.

In 1993 the Southwest Florida Water Management District was considering ways to reduce water consumption by the big users: agriculture and industry. One plan was to order a flat 20 percent reduction in permitted use. Its advocates contended that this would compel users to eliminate wasteful uses and adopt conservation measures. It was vigorously opposed.

With salt water moving inland at as much as 1 foot per day, Swiftmud blocked out a water use caution area. At about the same time, what is said to be the largest continuous strawberry field east of the Mississippi was being developed within the stressed area. "We don't want to talk about the water management district," its owner told the *Tampa Tribune* [7].

"Is it really important to have a lawn or all these golf courses?" argued a farmer. "I think most people would agree that the priorities for water use should be water for drinking and water for food."

Water is used profligately because it's free. Domestic consumers pay only for pumping, treatment, and distribution, not for the water itself. European consumers pay two to three times as much for their water. Most Florida industries and farms pump water from their own wells.

Water use would decline dramatically if water cost more. Why doesn't the State charge for water withdrawn from the aquifer? Of course, farmers and other water users would resist paying for what is now free. We've heard farmers claim they own the water under their land. A Polk County official declared, "Polk County's position is water under our soil is ours."

We asked several State officials if surface and underground water is owned by the State. All were sure the State has power to *regulate* water use. They were less certain, at first, about ownership. After some research, they agreed the State does indeed own the water and thus could sell it. However, no such proposal is under consideration.

More than twenty years ago the legislature ordered preparation of a

[7] August 29, 1993.

Florida Water Plan. Several plans were dutifully produced, but not much happened. Now a new plan is about to be adopted. Will really effective measures be adopted and enforced? We are reminded of Abba Eban's words in a speech at the United Nations:

> I believe that men and nations
> Will act wisely--
> When they have exhausted the alternatives.

Chapter 9

Is It Fit to Drink?

In 1993, thousands of Milwaukee area residents became ill, with diarrhea, abdominal pain, and vomiting. The cause was found to be a waterborne parasite, cryptosporidium, in the city's water supply. Before the water was safe again, 370,000 residents had been affected.

The Natural Resources Defense Council says such epidemics could happen anywhere, charging that federal and state measures to protect drinking water aren't working. A massive report issued by NRDC in 1993 cites 250,000 violations of water-quality rules. Most of the violations were failures to make required tests.

It has been several years since we visited the federal laboratory where water samples from urban systems were being tested. At that time, cities received reports two to three months after mailing their samples!

More recently a study was made of private and municipal water systems, chiefly in the Middle West. Investigators found overhead tanks that had seldom if ever been cleaned, layers of decaying organic matter on their bottoms. They found that few water system operators had technical training.

If you are a visitor, our Florida water may be safer than the water you drink at home. Most Florida drinking water comes from underground. Many systems in other states take their water from polluted rivers and must rely on water treatment plants to purify it.

Florida has no pure water, above ground or below. Nor does any place on earth. Pure water doesn't occur in nature. Water dissolves so many substances so readily that only freshly distilled water is chemically pure.

Rainwater carries a variety of dissolved gases and particles. It is slightly acidic; some is more acidic than vinegar. Near coasts, rainwater usually carries salt dissolved from airborne crystals. Fallen rainwater dissolves many of the substances it wets, in decaying plant and animal matter and in the earth.

Moving downward toward the sea, water transports whatever it can move. A stream moving at 1 foot per second can move fine sand. Rocks are tumbled smooth in swift streams.

American colonists found streams an excellent way to dispose of their wastes. Garbage was tossed in. In many early towns, sewage flowed down streets in open ditches. Replacing those ditches with sewers made towns cleaner and healthier. They smelled better, too. However, the sewers, like the ditches, discharged the waste into streams.

There is limited truth in the old saying "Running water purifies itself." We filled a glass tank with water, tossed in assorted garbage, and let it stand. In a few days the tank was dark and stinking. Then we bubbled air through the mess. The water gradually became clear. A thin layer of solids settled to the bottom. Oxygen and bacteria had decomposed the garbage. Bubbling, as in a stream tumbling over rocks, had supplied the necessary oxygen.

When organic materials enter a water body, they create a biological oxygen demand (BOD). As long as sufficient oxygen is present, dead plant and animal matter decays. When the BOD exceeds the available oxygen, decay is halted, and the water becomes cloudy or dark. This deprives submerged plants of the sunlight they need. They die, and their decomposing remains add to the BOD. So do the remains of fish killed by lack of oxygen.

This wasn't a problem in early Florida. As settlements became towns and cities, however, their waste output overloaded more and more streams and lakes. Just as sewers had replaced open ditches, now sewage treatment plants began to replace untreated discharges.

As sewage enters a typical sewage treatment plant, a bar screen traps large solid objects. The sewage then passes into long tanks through which it moves slowly. Some solids settle. Suspended solids are precipitated by adding a substance such as alum. Next the liquid is aerated, as we aerated our glass tank, and bacteria go to work. The resulting solids are collected and dried. Dried sludge is sometimes sold as mulch.

The clarified liquid, called *effluent*, is chlorinated and discharged into a stream or lake, or into the sea. It is now inoffensive and free of disease-causing organisms, but it is rich in dissolved nutrients--essentially, fertil-izer--that promote growth of aquatic plants. Downstream from sewage effluent outfalls, rivers are sometimes blanketed with green algae. Nu-trient-rich streams are sometimes choked by weeds.

Removing the dissolved nutrients at sewage disposal plants is pos-sible but expensive. Few cities do it. Because the effluent is a kind of fertilizer, why not spray it on cropland or groves? It's an attractive idea that has been applied in some places.

However, sewage treatment doesn't remove or neutralize the many toxic chemicals that are dumped into sewers. Householders may dump used motor oil, pesticides, and leftover paint into sanitary sewers. Many industries and businesses discharge their wastes, even hazardous wastes, into sanitary sewers. Dry cleaners, printers, photo processors, metal-working shops, and others often dump their wastes into sanitary sewers for lack of a convenient alternative.

Florida has 16,500 businesses listed as generating small quantities of hazardous wastes. It's illegal to dump the stuff into sanitary sewers, but federal Environmental Protection Agency (EPA) rules require inspect-ing at least 1 percent of these small-quantity generators *each year*. By and large, an inspection happens only if there has been a complaint or if inspectors are tracing the source of a pollutant.

One such pollutant is PCE, nicknamed "perc," the most common solvent dry cleaners use. PCE is showing up more and more often in pollution tests, and it has the industry worried. "In Florida, the problem is very bad," said Jerry Levine, assistant director of the Neighborhood Cleaners Association, which has about 600 Florida members. "Florida is one big aquifer, and it doesn't take much to cause contamination . . .If the government doesn't do something about it in terms of providing some kind of relief, there are a tremendous number of dry cleaners who will be put out of business."

Sewage plant operators don't know what's coming to them through the pipes and couldn't treat it all anyway. Thus sewage effluent sprayed on crops may contain heavy metals or other chemicals toxic to plants, or to humans or farm animals that consume the crops. The spraying solution has other problems, too. Suppose a golf course is being irri-gated with effluent. Just before a tournament, a storm dumps several inches of rain, more than the grass and soil can absorb quickly. Grounds keepers would like to shut off the irrigation. If they do, the effluent must be dumped elsewhere, probably into a stream.

Construction of sewage-treatment plants has fallen behind Florida's rapid growth. Federal aid for construction of treatment plants has been curtailed, and some cities and towns can't find the money to build new plants. When the volume of sewage exceeds treatment plant capacity, raw sewage is dumped.

That's not all. Storm sewers carry runoff from streets and parking lots into streams and lakes. In dry weather, they don't flow. When it rains, the first flow flushes these sewers, and the first discharge can be as obnoxious as untreated sanitary sewage. In the past, some cities built combined systems: Their storm sewers discharge into sanitary sewers. When heavy rains overload sewage treatment plants, the excess is dumped untreated.

One expedient is to provide retention ponds to hold the storm water from the first inch or two of rain. When the storm sewers have been flushed, additional runoff goes into streams.

Pollution from still another source increases BOD in streams and lakes. It's called *non-point-source pollution*. All of the people who live around our lake have lawns and gardens. Most lawns and gardens are fertilized. Dissolved fertilizer washing into the lake promotes growth of submerged and emergent plants. Ten years ago the lake had one small patch of cattails. Because of the dissolved fertilizer, a thick stand of cattails has spread around the shoreline. As cattails die, their remains add to biological oxygen demand. Algae have become so thick few people swim in the lake. Duckweed and hydrilla proliferate. The lake water is no longer clear. In our area, new housing developments and shopping malls are now required to retain storm water on-site.

More dissolved fertilizer washes into water bodies from farmland and golf courses. Runoff of fertilizer from the 700,000-acre Everglades Agricultural Area has disrupted the ecology of Everglades National Park. Citrus groves and cattle ranches are heavy contributors. Few streams, rivers, or lakes have escaped non-point-source pollution.

Florida isn't usually thought of as an industrial state, but a Toxic Release Inventory in 1990 found 521 companies releasing toxic chemicals into the state's environment. Florida ranked eleventh among the fifty states in industrial discharges. Even large industries may dump wastes into sanitary sewers.

For some industries, lagooning was an alternative. Liquid industrial waste was pumped into artificial ponds. The theory was that the water would evaporate, leaving sludge to be dried and disposed of as solid waste. However, the liquid waste may seep underground into an aquifer, so today this disposal method is regulated in the same way as dumping hazardous wastes on open ground.

For decades, waste disposal seemed to be a local problem for local authorities to manage. Little legislative action was taken until Florida's

Water Resources Act of 1957. By then it was obvious that sewage pollution of surface water wasn't the only reason for concern. Discharges from phosphate mines and processing plants, chemical plants, paper mills, food processing plants, and other industries had contaminated numerous streams. Urban storm water was obnoxious. Colored water, fish kills, and dead vegetation were symptoms. Yet the 1957 Act offered few remedies. One reason was that most of Florida's drinking water comes from wells, which were thought to be safe.

Since then, federal, State, and local governments have made progress in improving the quality of surface waters, especially in major streams. Monitoring stations test for such pollutants as ammonia, mercury, lead, cadmium, PCBs, and radioactive substances. Health authorities check for bacteria and viruses. Quality standards have been set. Two-thirds of Florida's river mileage now has water clean enough for public recreation and for fish. Not right after heavy rainfall, however, and not for drinking.

The legal foundation for abatement of water pollution is the federal Clean Water Act. The law requires each state to adopt water pollution standards and regulations. Lobbyists and their legislators blocked action in Florida and eleven other states. As required by the law, the federal Environmental Protection Agency declared it will enforce federal standards and regulations until Florida complies.

An industry ordered to cut off or purify its waste discharge can't just close a valve. The waste must be disposed of somehow. For organic wastes, such as those from food processing, something like a sewage treatment plant may suffice. Some chemicals can be neutralized. Waste recovery may yield materials that can be reused or sold.

Some pollutants are easily traced, once they are detected in streams. The effluent of a paper mill is unmistakable. Samples taken from industrial waste outfalls can be analyzed. Each year a few companies are hauled into court for chronic noncompliance. The volume of continuous discharges of industrial wastes into surface waters has been greatly reduced.

Pollution episodes are unfortunately common. Companies are required by law to report accidental spills promptly if they cross company boundaries. Too often they report days later or not at all. A few have been known to dump noxious chemicals at night so they will be far downstream before anyone notices them. Several commercial waste haulers have been caught dumping loads into roadside ditches. Many violators have paid fines.

Although the quality of stream and river water has been substantially improved, lakes are a more recalcitrant problem. Just stopping the inflow of pollutants won't restore a heavily polluted lake.

Polluting the Aquifers

While the quality of surface water was being improved, the safety of Florida's principal water supply, the Floridan Aquifer, was almost totally ignored. Disposing of liquid wastes underground is almost as convenient as dumping it into a stream: pour it on sandy soil and let it seep down, pour it into a sinkhole, or pump it down a well.

It seemed safe enough. People believed a layer of sandy soil is a natural filtration and purification system. It is, under proper conditions, for some organic wastes.

Septic tanks are a common method of underground disposal. A well-designed and maintained household septic tank is often ecologically preferable to a central sewer system. In the tank, bacterial action decomposes wastes. The effluent is distributed through perforated pipes set in gravel.

In Florida, however, many septic tanks have been permitted in unsuitable places, such as marginal wetlands. In wet weather, the effluent has no place to go. Some septic tanks are placed above ground. In wet weather, homeowners may, in effect, be flushing their toilets into their backyards. Too many septic tanks per acre may exceed the local soil's capability. Septic systems too close to lakes may pollute them.

Further, householders who don't understand how septic tanks work dump substances down their drains that kill the working bacteria. Few if any towns or counties require periodic inspection of septic tanks. If a tank gradually fills with sludge, or if the digesting bacteria are killed, the system fails of its purpose. Two of our neighbors, both living on high, dry land, have had their ground floors flooded with sewage when their septic tanks failed.

Underground disposal of household sewage is a relatively minor problem, however. A greater threat to water quality of the aquifers is underground disposal of industrial and municipal wastes. Florida has more than 25,000 "injection wells," through which wastes are pumped underground, supposedly below the bottom confining layer of the aquifer. No one knows the exact number, because they were unregulated by the State until 1982. Many communities pump sewage or sewage plant effluent underground. All kinds of industrial and mining wastes go down the wells, including toxic chemicals. Permits are now required for some classes of injection wells, but more permits are granted every year.

The theory is that wastes confined in well casings flow down through the aquifer and confining layers into a deeper permeable bed. The casings prevent leakage into the aquifer. A confining layer supposedly prevents upward flow.

For years Florida's Department of Environmental Regulation insisted this was safe. So did engineering firms that design injection wells. But mapping the underground layers is far from complete. No one can certify that confining layers are intact. Often they aren't. Springs gush up through openings in the upper confining layer. The Florida Geological Survey studied the underground formations in Brevard County and found large fractures in the lower confining layer. Tests showed that water from the waste disposal bed was indeed migrating upward into the drinking water aquifer or was being forced up by injection pressure. In Pinellas County, too, monitor wells have shown the presence of wastes in the drinking water supply.

In 1992, the Central Florida Regional Planning Council learned that contaminated water from a cooling pond next to a gypsum stack was polluting the aquifer. The Council's own staff had warned of this three years before, but the members of the Council ignored the warning. The contamination was apparently coming from one or more of twelve injection wells. The company owning the plant promised to investigate and plug any offending well.

Some officials insist these are all minor and isolated problems. At least one member of the governing board of the Southwest Florida Water Management District is worried, however, saying, "I don't want to be a part of something that's going to create problems for future generations of Floridians. I'm really concerned. It scares me."

Only one type of injection well is no longer permitted: one that injects hazardous waste *into or above drinking-water aquifers*. Still permitted are wells injecting industrial waste, sewage plant effluent, and certain other wastes *below* drinking-water aquifers.

No one knows just how a waste discharge behaves after it arrives underground. A general theory is that it forms a "plume," fanning out from the discharge point and gradually dispersing. How rapidly it may move is uncertain; perhaps a few inches per day, perhaps a hundred feet. Nor is there adequate information on how rapidly waste from a given injection well may be diluted.

One would like to believe that public water supplies are tested for all possible toxic chemicals and that none are present in concentrations above safe limits. However, the number of known toxic chemicals exceeds 600,000, and safe limits in drinking water have been set for only about 60.

"I've been drinking the water since we moved here ten years ago and we're still alive," says an optimist.

Bully for him. But few of the potential pollutants would cause him to clutch his throat and expire on the spot. For many, including known carcinogens, the effects are cumulative over decades.

With so many injection wells pouring a variety of wastes into, above, or below a drinking water aquifer, the situation has become ominous. A 1982 legislative task force reported,

> Problems with ground water contamination have been identified usually only *after* the damage has occurred and only in seemingly isolated and discrete events. The fact that the intensified episodes appear isolated and discrete, however, does not necessarily mean that the problems in reality are not widespread.

> What if all injection wells are prohibited some day? Little is known about the hydrology or biochemistry of underground layers. Contamination of the drinking water might persist for generations.

In 1991 the Legal Environmental Assistance Foundation (LEAF), a public interest law firm, petitioned the federal Environmental Protection Agency, asking it to withdraw Florida's authority to issue injection well permits, claiming the authority had been abused and permits were issued with insufficient evidence that drinking water was not at risk.

Polluting the Aquifers from Above

As rainwater percolates downward to a drinking water aquifer, it carries materials dissolved along the way. Only recently have measures been taken to abate pollution of aquifers from the surface. Where groundwater is near the surface, it is most vulnerable to pollution by herbicides, pesticides, fertilizers, septic tanks, and spills.

Solid waste landfills, an increasing problem themselves, have received almost any kind of wastes, although the State now requires screening to exclude hazardous materials. Monitor wells have detected leaching from landfills, so new landfills must have clay and plastic liners, and some older ones have been retrofitted. The Environmental Protection Agency says such liners will eventually leak.

Huge gypsum stacks, totaling 700 million tons, have been left by phosphate mining and processing. Slightly radioactive, gypsum contains arsenic, heavy metals, and other pollutants that may leach into groundwater. The State requires new stacks to have liners to prevent leaching. It may require retrofitting old stacks.

Mounting complaints of gasoline in drinking water wells prompted a statewide investigation under the acronym LUST (leaking underground storage tanks). Thousands of underground gasoline tanks in service stations were found to be leaking. One gallon of gasoline leaking into a drinking water supply can make a million gallons of water undrinkable. Soon the legislature passed a law requiring better-designed tanks. Dealing with larger surface and underground industrial tanks seems to be more difficult, at least politically.

Almost ritualistically, the first official response to such problems is assurance that they don't exist. The Florida Department of Agriculture and Consumer Services insisted that the agricultural pesticide TEMIK was as safe as its manufacturer claimed. The then Secretary rebuffed demands that he prohibit its use. Only when the "impossible" happened and TEMIK was found in drinkingwater wells was he forced to act.

Surface dumping of industrial wastes has continued for many years, contaminating soil, leaching into groundwater. Military bases and nuclear power plants are notorious polluters. Often when a contaminated site is discovered the offending company has long since departed. Florida has many Superfund sites, those the EPA deemed hazardous enough to require cleanup. Neutralizing these sites proceeds slowly, and often at taxpayers' expense.

Many small companies are in the same position as householders: What can they do with their wastes? What can we, as responsible citizens, do with leftover paint, used motor oil, and old cans of pesticides? Until recently we had only two choices: pour the stuff on the ground or toss it in the trash. Now, as part of State-mandated recycling programs, collection points for hazardous wastes are being established. Responsible businesses and citizens will use them.

What If Fish Drink the Water?

In Holland we visited a national laboratory that monitors the water quality of the Rhine River flowing from Germany. We read no Dutch but recognized most of the pollutants listed on the daily record. We missed one and asked: "Mercury?" The manager grinned and pointed to the entry: *Kvik*.

The concentration of mercury there was low enough to be acceptable in public drinking water. It's a different matter if fish drink the water. Mercury accumulates in their bodies.

"Fish caught in mercury-contaminated water should not be eaten more than once a week by adults and not at all by pregnant women, nursing mothers, women of child bearing age, and children under 15," advises Florida's Department of Health and Rehabilitative Services. "Fish caught in certain parts of the Everglades and the Savannah Marsh should never be eaten."

The warning against frequent consumption of bass, bowfin, and gar now applies to fish caught in sixty-eight Florida waterways. Fish in most other rivers and lakes are considered safe.

How the mercury gets into lakes and streams isn't clear. Relatively high levels of mercury were found in bass taken from a lake surrounded by a private natural preserve. Air pollution is the likely source. One report said incinerators are responsible for one-fourth of the mercury emitted by man-made sources. Incinerator operators point accusingly at the sugar industry and coal-burning power plants. Florida became the first state to regulate mercury discharges from incinerators.

Can We Drink the Water?

One contaminant people detect quickly is salt. In coastal areas, pumping too much fresh water from wells allows intrusion of sea water. Soon there's no choice but to close the wells. When Swiftmud found that seawater is seeping inland as fast as 1 foot per day in three coastal counties, it warned that to stop the salt intrusion, water use would have to be cut 25 percent in a 500-square-mile critical area.

As for other pollutants, Florida has hot spots where wells have been condemned. In a few places, companies have admitted responsibility and are delivering bottled drinking water to residents. In others, residents complain bitterly about contamination of their water and accuse officials of ignoring their complaints.

Vendors of bottled water do good business. Much of it comes from local wells, however, and we doubt it's any safer than water from a municipal water supply. The Safe Drinking Water Act, which regulates public supplies, doesn't regulate bottled water. The Food and Drug Administration has jurisdiction only if the bottled water crosses a state line.

People are concerned. Many markets have installed water-vending machines. A sign on some machines says they are connected to the local water system but provide "additional filtration." Hardware stores sell filters for home installation.

Is the water safe to drink? It's difficult to be positive. Many Florida homes are served--as ours is--by private water companies. Most of these companies pump their water from wells into overhead tanks and provide filtration and chlorination.

Take a water sample to a laboratory and ask that it be tested. "What shall we test for?" is the question.

It's easy to determine that the water is free of harmful bacteria, easy to test for a few chemicals such as salt. Without much greater difficulty the laboratory can detect the presence of *something* that shouldn't be there. But industrial, agricultural, and other wastes include tens of thousands of chemical compounds, and determining just what the something is would require elaborate and costly analysis. Even if that were done, safety limits have been set for only a few chemicals.

Florida is not alone. Safe drinking water is a nationwide concern. LEAF estimates that half of America's public water systems operate in violation of the Safe Drinking Water Act.

How concerned should you be? We drink the water that flows from our faucets. We put a charcoal filter in the water line under our kitchen sink, and we sometimes remember to change the element. We should visit the water company that serves us and judge how well they're managing, but we haven't. We see progress in State and local oversight of water supplies, but it's far from admirable.

If you're visiting Florida, should you drink the water? It's probably as safe as your water supply back home. Perhaps safer. Much more must be done, however, if future generations are to have safe drinking water.

Chapter 10

The Pine Forests

E arly settlers of America's east coast called them "pine barrens." That name stuck in southern New Jersey. Farther south they became "piney woods." In Florida they're "flatwoods." When Europeans arrived, pine and pine-oak forests covered most of northern and central Florida. Although 4 million acres have been converted to other uses, pine forests still cover half of the state, although not in pristine condition.

They have inspired few poets. The flatlands seemed monotonous to people whose homelands had mountains and valleys. We were accustomed to mountain hiking and backpacking, so the flatwoods seemed dull to us at first. We were surprised to learn that a band of volunteers was building a 1,300-mile trail from the Gulf Island National Seashore on Florida's western border to the Big Cypress National Preserve in the far south. Much of the route is through flatwoods.

Founded in 1966, the Florida Trail Association has flourished. Its 5,000 members have completed and now maintain more than a thousand miles of trail across the state. Each month the 12 chapters sponsor two or three dozen hikes, overnighters, and work trips.

Our introduction to the Trail was a weekend hike in the Withlacoochee State Forest. The route put few demands on feet, legs, and lungs. Instead of watching our footing, we could look about. At the lunch break, an artist distributed sketch blocks and asked what we had seen. Each of us had seen something different.

We were reminded of a stroll in the Mexican Sonora Desert with an ethnobotanist. Again and again he pointed to small plants we hadn't noticed, identified them, and told us how Indians had used them for food, fiber, or medication. What had seemed to us a barren land was rich with living things. The flatwoods, too, have greater diversity and color than is first apparent.

The land isn't literally flat. In the Panhandle uplands, it slopes gently to the sea; in the peninsula, down from a low central ridge. A difference of a few inches can cause marked differences in plant communities. At low elevations are cypress swamps, marshes, streams, lakes, and rivers. The high ground of the ridge is occupied by sand hills and scrub.

The pines occupy elevations in between, several species with characteristic understories. The pine flatwoods are interspersed with dry and wet prairies, ponds, cattail marshes, bayheads, and hardwood hammocks.

The original forests of the eastern United States were mostly destroyed by the end of the nineteenth century. Florida's longleaf pine forests were among the first cut in the Southeast. Lumber and turpentine were then the leading industries in Florida.

Farther south, in the peninsula, virgin timber was cut beside the rivers, but most floodplain and wetlands forests remained until drainage, steamboats, and railroads made them accessible. By the 1950s, much central Florida forestland had been converted to citrus groves, cropland, cattle ranches, housing developments, and golf courses.

"Take the money and run" is a Florida tradition. Once the trees had been cut, forestland was abandoned. One can find the remains of towns, mills, bridges, and railroads that died after the trees were gone. Occasionally we come across a single huge tree the loggers missed. A few pines over 200 years old are in the Withlacoochee State Forest

Timber companies gradually acquired more than 10 million acres of forestland, managing it for pulpwood production. These timber companies now own more than ten times as much Florida acreage as State and national forests combined. Tree farms support enough wildlife to interest hunters, but to most visitors they seem little more interesting than cornfields.

Forest Restoration and Management

Florida's Division of Forestry invited a group of environmentalists to a study weekend in the Blackwater River State Forest. We toured the

Forest with eight DOF specialists and talked with them around evening campfires. We learned a lot.

These 183,000 acres were a ruin in the early 1930s: clear-cut and burned, the soils eroding. The federal government bought the land for a few dollars per acre and resettled impoverished landowners. Little was done to restore a forest until the land was transferred to the State in 1954. Then most plantings were slash pine, grown for pulpwood.

In earlier visits we had seen scattered stands of longleaf pine. Now we learned that the Division of Forestry has made great progress in restoring the original longleaf pine forest. It's not easy.

Scattered throughout the Forest are private landholdings. On our tour we passed homes, farms, woodlots, schools, and churches. The State Forest must maintain more than 250 miles of roads for use by landowners' cars, school buses, and commercial vehicles. That takes money and time, so the foresters would like to close and naturalize many of these roads. That can't be done unless the inholdings are eliminated. The legislature has provided little land purchase money. Land exchanges would be quicker, but the Division of Forestry lacks the legal authority to negotiate them.

Through many years of research at Tall Timbers Research Station (north of Tallahassee) it was shown that fire is essential to a longleaf pine forest. Without fire, oaks become dominant. A longleaf pine seedling appears first as a small umbrella of grasslike needles, its "grass stage." It seems to grow slowly while scrub oaks shoot up around it, but the pine is sending down deep roots. When a ground fire occurs, it kills the oaks but burns only the outer needles of the pine umbrella, suppressing a disease called brown spot.

Wiregrass provided fuel for natural, lightning-set ground fires. When longleaf pines were planted to restore the forest, how to reproduce the wiregrass cover was a mystery. Few modern botanists had ever seen wiregrass flowering and producing seed. How had the original wiregrass cover maintained itself?

The controlled burns used to suppress oaks weren't made in summer, lest fawns and nesting birds be killed. In 1977 Jim Stevenson, a Florida forest biologist, burned a small area in May, and was surprised to see flowering stalks on the regenerating wiregrass two months later.

"It was like discovering penicillin in a petri dish," he said. Further studies confirmed that seed production follows summer burning. Lightning is most common in summer, so that's when most natural fires had occurred. Studies also found that forest creatures are rarely harmed by slow-moving ground fires.

Although fire dependent, the longleaf pine is vulnerable to burns if fire is suppressed for several years. This allows a buildup of fuel on the forest floor. With this excess of fuel, fires burn fiercely, killing mature trees.

Largely because of the inholdings, lightning-ignited wildfires must now be suppressed. Prescribed burns are needed every two or three years, with care taken to protect private buildings and fields. Even then, residents often complain about smoke.

We watched a controlled burn. Everything must be right: the season, dryness, wind direction, and the amount of pine needles, wiregrass, and other fuel on the forest floor. A forester wearing protective clothing drove an all-terrain vehicle along a designated line, spraying and igniting fuel. Others stood by in case a wind shift required fire suppression.

Environmentalists usually condemn clear-cutting, but the foresters showed us tracts where slash pine had been clear-cut so longleaf could be planted. Once we learned to recognize longleaf pine in its "grass stage," we saw the beginnings of a new forest. Seeds are gathered from "supertrees," those that grow taller and stronger. We were shown a "tree shaker" that causes pine cones to come showering down. We visited nurseries where seedlings are produced for use in the forest and by private landowners.

Planting seedlings is labor intensive. On some cleared tracts, a number of well-spaced mature trees are left standing to scatter their seed. Either method produces an even-aged stand. Our hosts showed how, by selective cutting, they create stands with age classes from seedlings to mature trees.

The Blackwater River State Forest produces timber for sale, and needs the revenue, but management policy emphasizes biological diversity. At one stop on our tour, we saw pine trees with a dozen nest cavities of red-cockaded woodpecker and glimpsed several of the birds, an endangered species. White blazes mark the perimeter of this site, within which no disturbances are permitted. To protect streams from bank erosion, timber harvesting is prohibited within 50 yards of the shoreline of major streams. The Florida Game and Fresh Water Fish Commission and the Division of Forestry work together in developing management plans that promote wildlife.

The Forest protects several seepage bogs, one of the rarest ecosystems. We saw such a bog, with pitcher plants, sundews, and orchids.

Months earlier, at the Lower Suwannee National Wildlife Refuge, we drove on dirt roads through pine plantations. Unlike National Forests, National Wildlife Refuges aren't commercial timber producers, so we guessed these plantations were recent additions to the Refuge. This was confirmed at headquarters. The Refuge plans to restore natural forest. One method is to cut aisles through the plantations. As the openings fill with new growth of mixed species, additional rows of pines will be cut. Controlled burns will imitate natural fires.

Each Florida State Park has been required to prepare a management plan to restore conditions prevailing when Europeans first arrived. Most such areas were forested. It will take decades to restore stands of big trees, but the effects of management policy are soon seen. Here, too, fire is a management tool. Some other State-owned and federal lands also have regenerating pine forests. Some stands are now more than sixty years old.

Environmentalists tend to scorn the timber companies' pulpwood plantations. They're not magnificent; still, they're as necessary as fields of wheat. Timber companies will maintain them as long as they are profitable. If they sell the land, trees may be replaced by condominiums, shopping malls, and golf courses.

The timber company lands have pockets of diversity: bogs, marshes, and other wetlands. The companies can be persuaded to protect this diversity, keep clear-cuts away from stream banks, leave nesting trees for red-cockaded woodpeckers, and in other ways be good citizens.

Florida's Pines

These are the principal pines of Florida forests:

Longleaf Pine

The needles of the longleaf pine are bright green, 8 to 18 inches long in bundles of three. Cones are 6 to 10 inches long, with a sharp point at the tip of each scale. Mature trees are up to 120 feet tall, up to 2 1/2 feet in diameter. The typical forest floor has a cover of wiregrass.

Longleaf pinelands covered more than 85 million acres on the southeastern coastal plain when Europeans arrived. It was the principal tree north of Lake Okeechobee, dominating on well-drained sand hills and in the moist flatwoods. Less than 2 million acres remain.

Open pine forests with grassy floors are richly complex, harboring more than 350 wildlife species and 200 plant species.

Slash Pine

The needles of the slash pine are dark bluish-green and rather stiff, 8 to 10 inches long, in bundles of two. Cones are 3 to 6 inches long, with

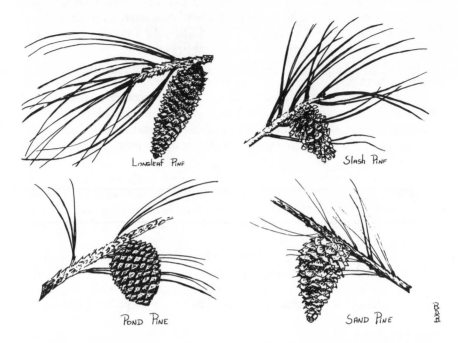

Longleaf Pine

Slash Pine

Pond Pine

Sand Pine

prickles. The bark has irregular, scaly plates. If allowed to reach maturity, slash pines may attain 100 feet in height, with diameters approaching 3 feet.

The geographic range of slash pine extends throughout Florida. It is less fire tolerant than longleaf pine, and more often found in wet sites. It is one of the fastest-growing pines and thus often chosen for pulpwood plantations.

Pond Pine

The needles of pond pine are yellow-green, 5 to 8 inches long, in bundles of three. Cones are spherical or oval, yellowish, with short stems. Much smaller than the longleaf or slash pine, the pond pine seldom attains a height of 70 feet. With closed cones and protective bark, it is fire tolerant.

Its range is from central Florida to New Jersey, in wetlands.

Sand Pine

Sand pine needles are short, up to 3 1/2 inches long, dark green, in bundles of two. Cones are up to 3 1/2 inches long, ovoid-conical, often remaining closed on the tree for several years. Its range is generally limited to central Florida.

One popular tree guide says the sand pine grows 15 to 20 feet tall. We see many sand pines taller than that, so we vote with other guides that allow it up to 70 feet.

The sand pine grows best in "wet desert," where ample rain seeps quickly through sandy soil. It's the only pine that grows well in such places. The world's largest forest of sand pine is in the Ocala National Forest.

Other Pine Species

Other pines occuring in Florida include the loblolly, common in the north and Panhandle, spruce, and shortleaf. However, recognizing the four principal pine species is sufficient for most visitors.

No Monotony Here

Monotonous? The pine forests that cover half of Florida encompass infinite variety. On a day's walk in the woods you may come on sand hills, scrub, oak thickets, cypress-hardwood swamps, freshwater marshes, live oak/cabbage palm hammocks, upland hardwood forest, wet and dry prairies, streams, ponds, lakes, and sinkholes. In places, the forest understory is dominated by saw palmetto. Elsewhere it may be a dense tangle of brush and briers or an open, sunlit expanse of grasses and wildflowers.

A typical entry in *Walking the Florida Trail*, the Florida Trail Association guidebook, describes Section 7E, Bull Creek, in Osceola County:

> The land within the Bull Creek Wildlife Management Area was once used for a variety of purposes, including timber, naval stores, and grazing. The Union Cypress Company of Hopkins operated a system of rail and tram roads to support their logging operation in the cypress swamps along the creeks and sloughs here in the early part of the 20th century. A small cemetery is found in Bull Creek, as well as a cattle dipping vat, flow wells, and cat's faces[8] on pines in the extreme northeast corner of the property. Remains of a turpentine still and sawmill also are hidden somewhere within the Bull Creek boundaries. Bull Creek is

---

[8]Cuts made to collect sap for turpentine.

owned by the St. Johns Water Management District for use as a retention area for hurricane flood waters, and is leased by the Game and Fresh Water Fish Commission for hunting and recreation. The east leg of this 17-mile trail follows the west side of Bull Creek along the old Union Cypress railroad grade. Some ties and hardware can still be found along the route. This part of the trail passes through strands of mature cabbage palms, hardwoods, and cypress. Wildflowers abound here. The south part of the trail traverses scrub oak and sand pine, and the west leg winds through pine flatwoods and prairie dotted with cypress domes. A variety of plants, birds and other wildlife can be seen amid the several ecosystems traversed by this trail.

And that's just a sample. Take a walk!

Inexplicably, there is no adequate popular guide to Florida's trees. The Division of Forestry hopes to issue a guide, but it won't include all native trees. The principal popular guides to North American trees omit some tropical species.

Visitor centers are good sources of information.

Chapter 11

Florida's Prairies

D riving south from Gainesville on our first visit to Florida, we were surprised to see an extensive grassland and stopped to photograph it. We saw no grazing cattle, but it looked like a western prairie. As we walked the roadside embankment, we met and photographed a large kingsnake, and saw sandhill cranes in the distance. This was Paynes Prairie, once a Spanish cattle ranch.

When we looked for a scientific definition of Florida prairies, we found different ones:

> Prairies are treeless flat lands covered by grasses and other low plants. Sometimes they are wet, like Paynes Prairie south of Gainesville, or they may be quite dry, as are the extensive prairies north of Lake Okeechobee, now used mostly for cattle ranching.

> The term *prairie* has a different usage in Florida than in the central or western United States. The common feature is their treeless, or nearly treeless, grass-covered nature.

> Prairies are undisturbed remnants of primeval Florida.

Dry prairies hardly differ from pine flatwoods except in the absence of pine trees. They occur on acid sands similar to those that support pine flatwoods. . . . The reason for their treelessness is unclear, but in some areas dry prairies are known to be an artifact of clear-cutting, unnaturally frequent burning, and livestock grazing.

Dry prairie is a nearly treeless plain with a dense ground cover of wiregrass, saw palmetto, and other grasses, herbs, and low shrubs.

Dry prairies are endemic to Florida but many have been converted to pasture, farm fields or citrus groves. The few remnants of dry prairie are disappearing rapidly. Because this is an important habitat for several animals that occur nowhere else in the eastern United States (such as the caracara and burrowing owl), the preservation of existing examples through appropriate management measures is critical.

Prairies are grassy shallow ponds hundreds of yards in diameter.

Prairies are shallow lakes with fluctuating water levels and wide, grassy borders.

The term "wet prairie" has been used to describe a variety of marshy habitats including deep marshes and waterlily ponds. . . . As we define it, wet prairie occurs on mineral soils that are inundated around 50-150 days per year and burn every 1-5 years.

Dry prairie: flatland with sand substrate; mesic-xeric; subtropical; annual or frequent fire; vegetation characterized by wiregrass, saw palmetto, and mixed grasses and herbs.

Florida dry prairies are open, grassy expanses--including wiregrass, bottlebrush, three-awn, arrowfeather, broomsedge, and love grasses--with sparse saw palmetto and scattered patches of low shrubs, such as fetterbush, rusty lyonia, dwarf blueberry, and wax myrtle.

Dry prairies are dotted with cabbage palm flatwoods in some areas and often grade into wet flatwoods, savannahs, or pine flatwoods in others.

These vast regions are essentially pine flatwoods without the pines.

Water, fire, grazing, and soil characteristics keep many trees from growing on prairies, and consequently much of the wildlife is different from what we find in woodlands. Animals of particular interest here are sandhill cranes, caracaras, and burrowing owls on dry prairies. Marsh hawks (harriers) are often seen flying over wet prairies in winter. Great masses of flowering plants cover wet prairies at different seasons. Even these rather uniform-appearing areas have several interesting species, many of which can be easily seen from the road.

Wet prairies and freshwater marshes are treeless expanses of herbaceous (nonwoody) vegetation. They are unusual in requiring both the regular influence of changing water levels and fire to maintain their unique structure and species composition. Marshes and wet prairies include a number of varieties such as the much reduced but still extensive saw grass everglades of south Florida to highly variable cattail marshes throughout the state.

We include these many characterizations, all from good sources, because they are illuminating aspects of a whole. The observers have grasped different parts of the elephant, but it's all one. The chief difference between wet and dry prairies is a few inches of elevation. Dry prairies aren't always dry. Wet prairies aren't always wet. Even dry prairies often have shallow ponds in the rainy season. Ponds in wet prairies are more numerous and longer-lasting. Many pine flatwoods are interspersed with prairies. Grassy prairies are most common, but some are covered by saw palmetto. Some prairies are dotted with hardwood hammocks.

So much for definitions! The glory of the prairies is their magnificent displays of wildflowers, colorful carpets that change from season to season. At any season some species are in bloom. One of the pleasures of hiking the Florida Trail in the cooler months is emerging from shadowed woodlands into the open sun of a prairie. The Trail skirts wet prairies and crosses some on old logging grades or dikes.

Here are a few places to explore and enjoy Florida's prairies. All are on public lands.

Paynes Prairie State Preserve

Paynes Prairie State Preserve, south of Gainesville, has been designated a National Natural Landmark. Since our early visits, the State has built a fine visitor center with exhibits, audiovisual programs, and overlook deck. Rangers answer questions. On winter Sundays, a ranger leads a 4-mile Prairie Rim Walk. Every Saturday there is a Wildlife Walk in the basin. An observation tower is near the visitor center, an observation platform at a wayside on US 441.

Almost 16,000 acres of the site is a basin eight miles long, a huge freshwater marsh as much as 35 feet below its rim. In some places the drop is steep, providing natural overlooks.

Visitors are free to explore the Preserve on their own. Dikes and abandoned railroad embankments provide hiking routes across the basin when it's wet.

Hiking in the basin one day, we saw a line of fire being blown our way, not rapidly enough to be alarming. This was a prescribed fire, part of management's plan to maintain the natural cycle.

The Prairie is a botanist's delight. We were shown a list of 427 species and told more await discovery. Every season has its display. The Preserve checklist of birds has 219 species. Although spring and fall are the busiest times for birding, winter populations are exceptionally large and diverse, including numerous hawks and waterfowl and the largest eastern population of sandhill cranes.

Mammals of the Preserve include opossum, shrews, bats, armadillo, cottontail, marsh rabbit; gray, fox, and flying squirrels; pocket gopher, mice, rats, red and gray foxes, raccoon, longtail weasel, striped skunk, river otter, bobcat, and whitetail deer. Bison, exterminated in the early nineteenth century, were reintroduced in 1975. The original 10 increased to 25, then declined to 7 because of disease. They have been restocked.

Faculty and students from nearby University of Florida made the first checklist of the reptiles and amphibians. It included the alligator, 10 species of turtles, 4 lizards, 26 snakes, 7 salamanders, 15 frogs and toads. We were told their numbers may have declined somewhat in the past decade.

Ocala National Forest

The 383,000-acre Ocala, established in 1908, was the first National Forest to be established east of the Mississippi. It lies east of Ocala city, between the Oklawaha and St. Johns rivers. A visitor center is just east of Silver Springs on SR 40.

The higher central portion of the forest has been called a "wet desert." Rain is ample but seeps quickly through deep sand. The Ocala highlands have the world's largest forest of sand pine. On either side are several hundred lakes surrounded by wet and dry prairies. Even the in-experienced eye can see the difference a few feet of elevation makes. Open pinelands give way to dense thickets, hardwoods to palms, prairie grasses to riparian shrubs. Wildflowers change with the seasons.

To see the prairies by car, just turn off one of the paved routes onto almost any dirt road. In the dry season one can walk on the prairies. When it's wet, one can usually find old grades or embankments.

The Florida Trail passes through all of the Forest's diverse habitats, skirting many wet prairies. Our favorite is the section that traverses the Juniper Prairie Wilderness. The Wilderness, where logging and motor vehicles are prohibited, is a mix of forest and wet and dry prairies, with over a hundred small lakes, ponds, and sinkholes. It begins at the Juniper Springs Recreation Area.

The prairies are excellent for wildlife observation, especially on their margins. More than 219 species of birds have been observed. Mammal species reported include bobcat, raccoon, black bear, opossum, cottontail, armadillo, and whitetail deer.

Prairie Lakes

North of SR 60, the Prairie Lakes site is on the east shore of Lake Kissimmee. Part of the Three Lakes Wildlife Management Area, it has few visitors except in hunting season. The State acquired the site in 1974 to protect and manage this portion of the extensive Kissimmee Prairie and the remaining longleaf pine forest.

Prairie Lakes was the nineteenth century headquarters for a rancher whose cattle grazed several hundred square miles. Logging became the principal economic activity in the early 1900s, but almost all mature longleaf pines and cypresses were gone in less than twenty years. Cattle ranching continued until the State purchase, grazing on a reduced scale thereafter.

The 3,153 acres of dry prairie are an important remnant of this dwindling ecosystem. The site also includes wet prairie and prairie hammocks, marshes, and swamps.

Volunteers of the Florida Trail Association have built 11 miles of hiking trail in two connected loops through hardwood hammocks, cabbage palm groves, prairies, and pine-palmetto woods. Hikers often see deer, bald eagle, caracara, and sandhill crane.

Myakka River State Park

Located 12 miles southeast of Sarasota, Myakka River State Park is one of Florida's largest and best-preserved State Parks. Its 28,875 acres include 12 miles of the Myakka River, a large lake, marshes, pine flatwoods, floodplain forests, oak and palm hammocks, and saw palmetto prairies. Within the Park, 7,500 acres are protected as a wilderness preserve.

More than half of the park is typical dry prairie, mostly treeless except for scattered cabbage palms, with a dense ground cover of wiregrass, saw palmetto, other grasses, herbs, and low shrubs, including many wildflowers. The prairie can be observed from internal roads or from hiking trails.

Deer are abundant and often seen along the roads even at midday. Caracara and burrowing owl are here but seldom seen. Many bird species are abundant, including wintering waterfowl.

A 33-mile loop trail is marked with the blazes of the Florida Trail Association.

Big Cypress National Preserve

The Big Cypress National Preserve lies north and west of Everglades National Park, 570,000 acres of freshwater swamps, marshes, wet and dry prairies, forested islands, hammocks, and estuarine mangrove forests. I-75 and the Tamiami Trail (US 41) cross the Preserve. The headquarters is on the Trail east of Carnestown.

Receiving an average 60 inches of rainfall, chiefly in summer, the Big Cypress is wet 6 to 8 months of the year, tinder-dry in winter.

Its diverse plant communities are on an almost flat slope rising from aquatic marshlands to wet prairies to dry prairies. Maidencane, cordgrass, beak rush, and other grasses, sedges, and rushes characterize wet prairies. The dry prairies are dominated by wiregrass and saw palmetto.

In this region are most of the few remaining Florida panthers, perhaps already doomed by inbreeding. Black bears, although reduced in number, seem secure. Other denizens include bobcat, river otter, raccoon, mink, gray and fox squirrels, marsh rabbit, cottontail, opossum, armadillo, whitetail deer. Manatees are sometimes seen in canals south of US 41.

Reptiles and amphibians find the swamp a fine habitat: frogs and toads, anoles, turtles, and alligator; as well as garter, king, ribbon, mud, and rat snakes; racers; pygmy and diamondback rattlesnakes.

Congress authorized the purchase of land for the Preserve in 1974, authorizing more acres in 1988. Buying the land tract by tract was a massive undertaking. There were hundreds of individual owners. Many had never seen their land. Many had long since forgotten they owned it.

Federal acquisition caused controversy. Owners of backcountry hunting camps were often unwilling to sell. Hunters feared the National Park Service might prohibit hunting. They wanted no restrictions on airboats and off-road vehicles. Some vociferous objections came from squatters who had built illegal hunting camps on government land; some had even built landing strips.

Visitors who want to sample the Preserve can do so from the few unpaved interior roads. Turner River Road, CR 839, runs from I-75 to the Tamiami Trail. In the southeast, a loop road, SR 94, is a scenic 24-mile drive. A few road spurs penetrate the swamp. Use caution on unpaved roads.

An excellent way to explore the Big Cypress is to hike all or part of the 38-mile Florida Trail, which crosses the Preserve. Park at the Oasis Ranger Station on US 41, check in, get a trail map, and hike north. Be prepared to do some wading.

Other Prairies

These remaining prairies are a few samples of the scattered but important remnants of what was one of Florida's primary ecosystems. The everglades are a different and extensive prairie community. Other large and small prairies occur throughout central and southern Florida.

The wildlife of these now-isolated ecosystems is at risk. Environmentalists have begun an ambitious effort to establish wildlife corridors that would linking the major prairies, enabling species to migrate from one to another, thus restocking depleted habitats and maintaining genetic diversity.

Chapter 12
The Hardwood Hammocks

The following words are often used in Florida:

xeric = dry
hydric = wet
mesic = in between

Also common is *hammock*. The dictionary equates it with "hummock," which was its original meaning. For example, the wet prairie of the everglades is dotted with tree islands, or hummocks with trees.

It is used more broadly now. *Hammock* is Florida's name for its temperate hardwood forests. Florida's Natural Areas Inventory describes five types of hammocks: xeric (including mesic), hydric, prairie, rockland, and maritime. Their common denominator is hardwoods: live oaks and mixed species.

Florida's native tree species evolved elsewhere, millions of years before the peninsula emerged from the sea. Since colonizing Florida, their distribution has been altered from time to time by changes in climate and sea level. In northern Florida, hardwoods predominated in some periods, pines in others. When the Europeans arrived, pine forests covered most of Florida. Hardwood forests--hammocks--occupied the mid-slopes between upland pine forests and wet bottomlands. They also grew around lakes and along waterways. In northern Florida, many hammocks included evergreens as well as deciduous species. They had the greatest diversity of tree and shrub species occurring anywhere in the Lower 48.

Some foresters call the hardwoods Florida's natural climax forest. Hardwoods would dominate all forests, they say, were it not for fire. But fire is as much a part of nature as sunshine and rain.

Oaks are the most numerous hardwoods, usually in mixture with hickories, magnolias, hollies, dogwoods, and sweetgums. Cabbage palms are well represented in many hammocks. Of the oaks, the most impressive are the magnificent live oaks, rarely higher than 50 feet but with huge trunks and horizontal branches. Groves of these giants can be seen at the Naval Live Oaks preserve in Gulf Islands National Seashore, at Bulow Creek State Park, in the picnic area of Lake Kissimmee State Park, and elsewhere.

Learning to identify the many oak species that occur in Florida is like learning to identify sparrows; it takes study. The oak genus, Quercus, is of the beech family. Oaks have hard-shelled acorns. Leaves are alternate, in five rows, but come in many different shapes.

The shady northern hammocks tend to have open floors. Some Panhandle hammocks are of special interest to botanists because their species mark them as biological islands long isolated from ancestral stock. We have mentioned the Florida torreya, a tree whose nearest relatives are found in California, China, and Japan.

The ranges of temperate-zone hardwoods extend south through inland Florida almost to the peninsula's tip. Tropical hardwoods, including gumbo-limbo, pigeon plum, Jamaica dogwood, wild tamarind, strangler fig, and mahogany, occur from the Keys northward in narrow strips along both coasts. A few of these tropical species occur as far north as Jacksonville.

The chief threat to hammocks is development. High, dry hammocks are good building sites, in greater demand now that wetlands are off limits. Maritime hammocks have virtually disappeared from the Florida Keys along the Overseas Highway, but survive on some islands.

Attractive hammocks are protected on federal, State, and county lands. These parks and preserves have noteworthy hammocks in addition to other natural features:

Andrews Wildlife Management Area

The Andrews Wildlife Management Area south of Fanning Springs is one of Florida's largest remaining old-growth hardwood hammocks, 3,877 acres on the banks of the Suwannee River. A small interpretive kiosk is at the entrance. The unpaved road ends at the river bluff. The site has few visitors.

The Andrews family managed it as a nature preserve. The State bought most of it in 1985 and may buy more.

Here one can see all three types of mature hardwood forest, from dry to moist. The site has three Florida Champion trees (persimmon, Florida maple, and bluff oak) and two National Champions (basswood and winged elm). All are near trails. Also present are live and turkey oak, southern magnolia, black cherry, dogwood, American holly, and redbay. Swamp species include bald cypress, red maple, black gum, water and overcup oaks, water hickory, and river birch.

It's a fine place for a cool, shady walk on a hot day.

Apalachicola River Bluffs

The steep Apalachicola River Bluffs overlooking the Apalachicola River are unusual for Florida. The bluff hammocks and ravines are also unusual in that they include species of trees and wildflowers that are at the southern limit of their ranges. A few species, notably the Florida torreya, occur nowhere else. Southern species are also present.

Access to the river is limited by its wide, often wet floodplain. This 6,300-acre Preserve of The Nature Conservancy, north of Bristol, is one of the best places to see the bluffs. The Preserve includes Alum Bluff, 180 feet high, Florida's largest exposed geologic formation.

A map of a self-guided 3 1/2-mile trail is posted at the trailhead.

San Felasco Hammock State Preserve

The 6,500-acre San Felasco Hammock State Preserve, northwest of Gainesville, was purchased by the State because of its exceptional botanical and geological features. A satellite of Devil's Millhopper State Geological Site, it has no development other than 11 miles of quiet woodland trails.

The site preserves a mature upland hardwood hammock with southern magnolia, American holly, spruce pine, and Florida maple. In the north is a large swamp forest. Also present is a good example of sand hill hammock.

Geological features include numerous sinkholes and deep ravines with intermittent creeks.

Mike Roess Gold Head Branch State Park

Often called "Gold Head Branch State Park," the 1,561-acre Mike

Roess Gold Head Branch State Park park is northwest of Palatka. Its central feature is a deep, humid ravine cut through Florida's dry central sand ridge. A hardwood hammock borders the ravine, between high pinelands and moist ravine bottom. The park has nature trails.

Tiger Creek Preserve

Beginning in 1968, The Nature Conservancy has acquired 4,500 acres east of Lake Wales on the sand ridge that extends down the center of the Florida peninsula. Two pristine streams, Tiger Creek and Patrick Creek, flow through the site. Hardwood swamps and hammocks are beside the streams. Sand pine and oak scrub, pine flatwoods, and sand hill communities are on higher ground. The Conservancy bought the site to protect twenty-four of Florida's rarest wildlife species, including the scrub jay, scrub lizard, and sand skink, and rare plants, including the pygmy fringe tree and bonamia. More than 400 plants identified include many flowering species.

A land steward is in residence.

Highlands Hammock State Park

A pristine cypress swamp and hardwood forest near Sebring, Highlands Hammock State Park is one of Florida's first state parks. It includes 3,800 acres, with additions pending. Its eight nature trails pass through virgin hardwood hammock, pine flatwoods, sand pine scrub, scrubby flatwoods, bayheads, and marsh. Most popular is the Cypress Swamp Trail, a boardwalk through wetlands and across the Little Charley Bowlegs Creek, where alligators and other wildlife are often seen. The park has many exceptionally large trees, some as old as 1,500 years.

This is the Florida the first settlers saw. A park ranger provides commentary on a backwoods tram tour.

Myakka River State Park

Myakka River State Park is one of Florida's largest state parks, 28,875 acres southeast of Sarasota, and one of the most diverse. Scattered hydric hammocks constitute only 5 percent of its area, but they add much to its scenic beauty and botanical interest. These hydric hammocks are patches in moist lowlands. Large live oaks and cabbage palms are draped with Spanish moss and decorated with epiphytes. Many branches are covered with resurrection fern, so named because it appears shriveled and dead when dry, but turns green and flourishing after

rain. Other tree species of the hammocks are laurel oak, water oak, and Florida elm. Associated are many ferns and orchids.

Hammocks can be seen from the trails and Park roads.

Jack Island

Jack Island, a 958-acre natural area in the Indian River off SR A1A, is an adjunct of the Fort Pierce Inlet State Recreation Area. The island, reached by a short footbridge, is a coastal tropical hammock mostly surrounded by mangrove swamp. A 4.2-mile trail circles the island.

Its vegetation is typical of the West Indies. Plant species include gumbo-limbo, strangler fig; red, black, and white mangroves; blolly, salt-bush, white stopper, and randia. A kiosk at the end of the access bridge has exhibits describing the island's ecology. A nature trail is on the cross-route. Labels identify the principal plant species. Tropical hardwoods can be found farther north, but we know of no better place to see, identify, and enjoy them.

Revisiting Jack Island in 1992, we found that a 1989 freeze had severely damaged many of the mangroves. Such occasional freezes establish the northern limits for many tropical and subtropical species. New growth was already abundant.

Lignumvitae Key State Botanical Area

This pristine tropical hammock is a remnant of a natural community once common on the Florida Keys. Protection is strict, and a visit must be planned, but there's no better place to appreciate Florida's Caribbean connections.

When we last checked the schedule, a three-hour round-trip boat tour left Indian Key Fill at 1:30 P.M., Thursday through Monday. Telephone reservations are advised; call (305) 664-4815. Private boats may dock at Lignumvitae Key (except Tuesday and Wednesday), but visitors must wait in the dock area for a guided walk.

Tours are on quiet trails in the shade of trees unfamiliar to most visitors: mastic, strangler fig, poisonwood, pigeon plum, and gumbo-limbo. Mangroves fringe the tidal zone. The surrounding shallows have sea grass beds and mudflats.

Chapter 13
The Scrub

At a public hearing in 1992, more than a hundred citizens, scientists, and county officials urged State purchase of the remaining fragments of Florida scrub on the Lake Wales Ridge. Polk County Commissioner Robert Connors called them "the North American Galapagos." Others called them "a string of jewels." Scientists cited many species of plants and animals that occur nowhere else in the world.

Many of the speakers at the hearings were passionate advocates of particular tracts:

"Horse Creek Scrub is the home of a newly found scrub mint," said one. "There are no protected sites for this endangered *Dicerandra*. . . Thirteen rare plant species and many rare animal species occur here. . . This site needs to be pushed to the top of the list." (It wasn't.)

"Lake McLeod Scrub and Eagle Lake Scrub may very well be the last refuges for the pink lupine. . . The pink lupine has been judged by Florida scientists as the next plant most likely to become extinct."

"Sunray Scrub . . . has long been a favorite of scrub lovers. . . The large lavender flowered Florida gayfeather is abundant here."

Marjorie Kinnan Rawlings called the scrub "unique...No similar region anywhere." It's a botanist's bonanza. Yet to the uninitiated it looks like Florida's ugly duckling. The Galapagos Islands analogy is apt. Millions of years ago these scrub areas were islands, the first bits of the

Florida peninsula to emerge from the sea, the first to be colonized by plants, the first to harbor animals. Lichens and other simple plants came first, building and holding soil. Insects and birds were early arrivals. Plant seeds were dropped by birds or blown ashore.

As the Floridan Plateau became a peninsula, it was colonized not only from the sea and air but by fauna and flora extending their ranges from the continent. The former islands were now linked along a low ridge.

The sea rose again. The former islands became islands again, and only there did terrestrial species survive. Thus did the unique natural community of the scrub evolve. Many species need large ecosystems to survive. Species of the scrub are adapted to life on small islands. A scrub ecosystem of a few acres can be viable--if allowed to be.

Unfortunately for the scrub, its high, dry land is just what citrus growers and developers want. Witnesses at the hearing warned that the fragments will soon be gone unless the State or federal government buys them. More than 85 percent of the scrub has already been lost to agriculture and housing developments. Most remaining fragments are smaller than a hundred acres.

No single definition adequately describes the scrub. On the one hand, it occupies the heights of the central sand ridge. Yet a few botanically similar areas, such as the Cedar Key Scrub, are barely above sea level.

Scrub has been called "an impenetrable mass of evergreen scrub oaks; rusty lyonia; rosemary; unusual varieties of holly, bay, and hickory; and an array of inconspicuous species, many with restricted distributions." Yet much of the scrub we see is far from impenetrable. Perhaps because of fire or other disturbances, areas of sandy floor are open enough for easy walking, patched with prickly pear and gray reindeer moss.

Scrub is often an expanse broken by patches of tall longleaf pine, but one also finds islands of scrub in longleaf pine forests. Scrub and longleaf both depend on fire. Tall pines are good lightning targets, so pine forests burn frequently and slowly along the forest floor, not damaging the pines. Low-growing scrub species offer no such targets, so lightning-set fires are less frequent. In the intervals, which may be several decades, litter accumulates, and when fires do occur they may be intense.

Scrub species are adapted to dryness, hot sun, and fire. Deep roots are one adaptation. Waxy leaves restrict moisture loss. Regeneration after fire may be from roots or seeds from heat-opened cones. Two neighboring scrub areas may look dissimilar because one burned five years ago; another fifty years ago.

Some ecologists say true scrubs are characterized by an oak-dominated shrub layer of six species: myrtle oak, saw palmetto, sand live oak, Chapman's oak, rusty lyonia, and Florida rosemary. Others recognize variety: sand pine scrub, oak scrub, rosemary scrub, slash pine scrub, coastal scrub, and scrubby flatwoods. Compositions change. For example, after a hot fire, a sand pine forest may be replaced by rosemary scrub. What all scrub areas have in common are xeric sandy soils low in nutrients.

The scrub oaks are fire adapted. "Scrub oaks" is their familiar name in Florida. However, one best-selling tree guide has no entry for "scrub oak." Another has entries for five "scrub" oak species, none of them occurring east of Texas! Ecologists name three oak (*Quercus*) species that predominate in Florida's scrub areas: sand live oak, myrtle oak, and Chapman's oak. One popular tree guide acknowledges none of the three. Another includes Chapman's and myrtle.

Ecologists describe the scrub oaks as evergreen. The guide says Chapman's is evergreen, while myrtle oak leaves may remain until new ones appear.

The guide says Chapman's and myrtle oaks may grow 40 to 50 feet tall. A much older guide describes the myrtle oak as "growing as a shrub in thickets," which it also does. Oaks of the scrub are stunted. In more favorable settings, they grow too tall to provide habitat for the scrub jay, an endangered species that can live only in scrub habitat kept open by periodic fires.

No matter; this is Florida, and Florida's oaks can be confusing. If you see stunted, acorn-bearing trees growing in dry, sandy areas, call them scrub oaks.

A compelling argument for preservation of the remaining scrub is the presence of plant species that occur nowhere else in the world and are therefore in danger of extinction. Among them are scrub plum, pigeon wing, scrub palm, and pygmy fringe-tree. Indeed, 40 to 60 percent of all scrub plant species are endemic, unique to Florida scrub.

Several threatened wildlife species inhabit the scrub. We see and recognize the scrub jay. Thus far we haven't seen the blue-tailed mole skink. Many species, including deer, bobcat, gray squirrel, raccoon, spotted skunk, armadillo, loggerhead shrike, nighthawk, ground dove, bobwhite, indigo snake, and gopher tortoise, use the scrub but are not restricted to it. On our visits we have seen many butterflies and spiders.

Early settlers called the scrub useless. Wetlands became productive when drained, but the dry, impoverished soils of scrub seemed unsuitable for crops. Now scrub areas are in great demand. Wetlands have some legal protection against development. The scrub has no such protection.

In the spring of 1992, The Nature Conservancy announced a remarkable partnership with the State of Florida, the South and Southwest Water Management Districts, and Archbold Biological Station to buy scrub tracts on the Lake Wales Ridge, as much as 30,000 acres. The U.S. Fish and Wildlife Service has announced plans to establish here the first National Botanical Refuge. The State had already purchased 1,143 acres, part of a 6,632-acre tract called Catfish Creek.

Time is short. The State can buy only from willing sellers. The federal refuge depends on Congress appropriating funds. To frustrate preservation plans, a few landowners have destroyed their scrub with bulldozers.

In suggesting natural areas to visit, we name only places that are publicly owned and open to visitors. We will not identify privately owned sites on the Lake Wales Ridge, but you'll see several scrub areas along SR 70, which crosses Florida from Bradenton-Sarasota to Fort Pierce. The two-lane road is lightly traveled. Where the land begins to rise as you approach U.S. 27, look for scrub.

The following are some other scrub areas well worth visiting.

Hobe Sound National Wildlife Refuge

For an introduction to the scrub ecosystem, come to the Hobe Sound National Wildlife Refuge. The Refuge was established in 1969 when local residents contributed 229 acres to preserve the north end of Jupiter Island from development. More tracts were added, including a second site on US 1 north of Jupiter: an area of scrub overlooking Hobe Sound.

A small nature center in the headquarters building has some fine exhibits, usually including live snakes and other animals. The Hobe Sound Nature Center, Inc., a volunteer association, operates the museum and a program of interpretive activities. The museum closes at 3 P.M.

Be sure to have the trail guide leaflet with you when you walk the Sand Pine Scrub Nature Trail.

Ocala National Forest

The 383,000-acre Ocala National Forest has mostly sandy soils. Sand pine scrub is a common ecosystem on the higher land. Although this was probably the largest publicly owned acreage of scrub in Florida, most of it is now being managed for pulpwood production. Blocks are clear-cut and reseeded. We have talked with ecologists who believe the scrub will recover if logging and seeding are stopped and periodic burning resumed.

Lake Arbuckle State Forest

Between 1984 and 1986 the State acquired 13,500 acres on the west shore of Florida's largest undeveloped lake. Lake Arbuckle State Forest is also a Wildlife Management Area.

Within the Forest is the largest remaining area of Florida scrub, showing few signs of disturbance: numerous islands in pine flatwoods. It has more identified endemic species than any other site. As in centuries past, the rare species are protected by separation. No single disturbance or catastrophe is likely to affect all.

School Bus Road traverses the property north to south, ending near the entrance of the Avon Park Air Force Range. Old dirt roads and trails invite hikers. The Florida Trail Association is developing a blazed trail.

Lake Kissimmee State Park

The leaflet for the splendid 5,030-acre Lake Kissimmee State Park mentions its lakes, prairies, marshes, and pine flatwoods, but not scrub. However, a slightly elevated sandy area called Buster Island has acres of oak scrub. You can get there by trail. Ask at the entrance.

Rock Springs Run State Reserve

The 8,700-acre Rock Springs Run State Reserve, on the Wekiva River, adjoins Wekiwa (*sic*) Springs State Park. It is undeveloped except for trails and presumably will so remain. Scrub areas are maintained by pre-scribed burning.

Sand pine scrub is one of the most extensive biological communities here, dominating the higher ground. Common shrubs here include stag-gerbush, rosemary, silkbay, and wild olive. Also present are blueberry, gopher apple, prickly pear cactus, wiregrass, and spike moss, plus a vari-ety of lichens.

Scrub jay is one of the more conspicuous wildlife species. Reptiles and amphibians include the scrub lizard and sand skink.

Any trail you choose will pass through one or more scrub areas.

Potts Preserve

Owned by the Southwest Florida Water Management District, the 8,500-acre Potts Preserve is on the west side of the Withlacoochee River northeast of Inverness. Wildlife is abundant. The site is a mosaic of riv-erine swamp, freshwater marsh and wet prairie, flatwoods, and ham-mocks.

Islands of scrub are scattered throughout. These scrub sites are domi-nated by the three oak species. The District plans to maintain them by prescribed burning at intervals of 8 to 10 years. Scrub and related eco-systems that were converted to pasture will be restored .

This is one of the most interesting natural areas in central Florida, and the District plans to keep it that way. When we visited in 1991, no vehicles were permitted beyond the entrances. Hikers could walk in, canoeists carry in. Hunting is prohibited, making this a fine place to hike in hunting season.

St. Andrews State Recreation Area

In season, St. Andrews State Recreation Area is one of the State's most popular parks. Most visitors come to enjoy the beach. After Labor Day it's a quiet place.

The SRA is on the tip of a peninsula near Panama City, between the Gulf of Mexico and Grand Lagoon. Back of the white sand beaches are rolling dunes stabilized by sea oats, interspersed with pine flatwoods and marshes. Older dunes farther inland are overgrown with sand pine, scrub oak, rosemary, and other salt-tolerant plants.

The Pine Flatwoods nature trail passes through the several habitats, including good birding areas.

Cedar Key Scrub State Reserve

Cedar Key Scrub State Reserve is a 5,000-acre undeveloped site on the road to Cedar Key. It has a small parking area, no improved roads. Hiking is on old roads, some overgrown, some muddy after rain.

The land was acquired to preserve its sand pine scrub. Other habitats include scrubby flatwoods, slash pine flatwoods, freshwater ponds, swamp, fresh- and saltwater marsh, and brackish tidal creeks.

The sand pine scrub occurs on ridges in the eastern sector. There is a scattering of longleaf pine. The understory includes Chapman and myrtle oaks and Florida rosemary. The threatened Florida arrowroot or coontie, a fernlike plant, occurs here. Wildlife includes the threatened Florida scrub jay and Florida mouse, gopher tortoise, and Florida gopher frog.

Chapter 14

Estuaries, Salt Marshes, and

Mangroves

S ea and land intermingle along the watery fringe of Florida. Here is
    one of the earth's most productive ecosystems, more productive of
    plant matter than pastures or fields of corn. Its green plants sup-
port a vast complex of living things, small and large.

Estuaries are often defined as coastal bodies of water enclosed by
peninsulas and barrier islands, where fresh and salt water mix and water
level rises and falls daily. In this sense, the 400 square miles of Tampa
Bay constitute one of the world's largest estuaries.

The definition of estuaries is too restrictive for Florida's Gulf coast.
The Gulf is so shallow above much of the submerged portion of the
Floridan plateau that shoals and oyster bars occur several miles offshore.
There wave action is slight, and the estuarine ecosystem extends far out
from land.

The ecosystem includes sea grass beds, oyster bars, tidal flats, mangroves, salt marshes--wherever fresh water runoff from the land mixes
quietly with salt water, creating zones of brackish water.

On the Gulf side, estuarine ecosystems extend from the far south to the Alabama line. On the east coast, most estuaries are back of barrier islands. The Indian River Lagoon comprises three connected lagoons extending 156 miles from New Smyrna Beach to Jupiter. It has been designated an Estuary of National Significance, largely because of its 4,315 recorded species of flora and fauna, the greatest diversity of any estuary in the United States.

The Indian River is the route of the Intracoastal Waterway. Much of its shoreline has been developed, but there are miles of natural wetlands. Tides, the mixing of salt and fresh water, sunlight, warmth, and inflow of sediments and nutrients from the land--these and other factors combine to produce a rich estuarine ecosystem unique in North America. The estuary is essential not only to the oysters, hermit crabs, mussels, and other creatures that call it home but also to the lives of many land and sea animals.

Most saltwater fishes spend part of their early lives in estuaries, finding food and safety from predators in sea grass beds, among mangrove roots, and in salt marshes. Included are mullet, menhaden, mackerel, snapper, pompano, sea trout, tarpon, drum, bonefish, and many more. Estuaries are nurseries for shrimp, stone crabs, and lobsters. Destruction of or damage to estuaries has effects extending far beyond their limits.

As fish have become scarcer, commercial and sports fishermen have been at war with each other. Sports fishermen complain that, as fish stocks decline, commercial fishermen use more sophisticated and destructive methods to maintain their catches. Both criticize the State's Office of Fisheries Management.

By arguing over allowable catches, both sides ignore the major cause of shrinking stocks: pollution and degradation of estuaries where the stocks are produced. Nine-tenths of the species sought by fishermen are dependent on estuarine habitat.

Asked to comment on the condition of Florida's fisheries, Ed Irby, Jr., of the Department of Natural Resources, said, "They're generally in a state of decline because of the impact of habitat degradation, water quality, and loss of nearshore habitat. Ninety percent of the species sought by the recreational or commercial fishermen are estuarine dependent — and our estuaries are in trouble."

Destruction of mangroves and marshes has been an important factor. As for pollution, for years rivers and streams have carried municipal and industrial waste and storm water to estuaries. Runoff from the land carries fertilizer and pesticides. Marked progress has been made in improving the quality of stream water, but problems remain. Oil spills and ships dumping wastes into estuaries have added to the decline.

Ecologists use beds of sea grasses as an indicator of estuarine well-being. Major losses of sea grasses in the Pensacola Bay estuary were followed by a marked decline in fish populations. Tampa Bay sea grass beds were damaged by pollution. As pollution was curtailed, the recovering beds were slashed by power boat propellers. Away from population centers, the damage has been far less.

Salt marshes develop in the tidal shallows of the brackish zone. Here great expanses of rushes, salt grasses, and other nonwoody plants are cut by meandering creeks. Where the terrain is close to mean sea level and the tidal range is several feet, salt marshes may extend for several miles inland from the apparent shore. Salt marsh creeks are a lively element of estuarine systems. Crabs scuttle about. We have seen dolphins, sharks, and rays in creeks.

Half of Florida's salt marsh acreage is on the Gulf coast from Tampa Bay to Alabama. On the Atlantic coast, salt marshes occur where there is shelter from waves and storms. In northeast Florida, extensive salt marshes lie behind Amelia and Little Talbot islands, others behind the chain of barrier islands that extends from Flagler Beach south to Port St. Lucie. Mosquito control dikes, dredging, and landfills for development have destroyed some salt marshes along the eastern coast, but large areas remain.

One of our fantasies is to have a cabin on stilts in some remote salt marsh. At ease on its deck we would watch pelicans and herons, listen to clapper rails, admire sunsets--and be devoured by mosquitoes and no-see-ums. Instead, we now explore marshes in our canoe or 13-foot Zodiac.

One of our early visits to Florida was by boat, a small outboard craft rigged for camping. We became fascinated by salt marshes and putted through mazes of creeks at idling speed. Our first night was spent at anchor. In the morning the tide was out, and our craft was aground.

At times marshes can be explored on foot, as we learned that morning. After an early breakfast--we held our plates because the boat was aslant--we went for a walk on the exposed mudflats. With the tide out, thousands of fiddler crabs had emerged from their burrows to feed. We recognized two species of fiddlers by their contrasting behavior. One rushed into burrows as soon as we approached. The other was indifferent to our presence; we had to step carefully among them.

Fiddlers excavate burrows, and pack the mud or sand into pellets, which are dropped several feet away. The flats we walked were littered with pellets.

Fiddler crabs practice an interesting kind of agriculture. Cordgrass is one of their chief food sources, not the living plant but its dead remains. Their burrows penetrate the root zone of the cordgrass and stimulate its growth. The crabs also feed on the rich supply of microscopic algae.

That morning we went house-hunting with a hermit crab. Hermit crabs inhabit borrowed shells. As they grow, they must find larger and larger shells. The one we met was in trouble. All nearby shells were too small. We joined the search and also found none nearby. A hundred yards away we succeeded. Feeling like real estate salesmen, we carried back our prize and presented it to the client. At first warily, then with growing enthusiasm, the crab approved our offering. Sold!

At first glance the marshes look like maritime meadows, monotonous except for the tidal creeks. The dominant plants are usually black needlerush and smooth cordgrass. Greater diversity appears near the mean high-water mark: species such as salt grass, sea oxeye, saltwort, saltmeadow cordgrass, and leather fern.

Salt marshes don't look especially productive. Their grasses and rushes aren't as conspicuous as forest trees or field crops. They aren't grazed by herds of bison or elk. Yet in fact they are enormously productive. One must look more closely.

We made a plankton net by tying a small bottle to the toe of a nylon stocking. After a few sweeps of the net in a tidal creek, we placed a few drops from the bottle on a slide. Through the microscope we saw a fascinating array of diatoms, green flagellates, and minute creatures such as crab larvae and a tiny clam so transparent we could see the beating of its heart. Sunlight on the shallow, nutrient-rich water produces a great crop of algae, food for countless marine animals.

Each drop on our slides also had a clutter of debris. This debris, *detritus*, dead organic matter, underlies the productivity of the salt marshes. Some creatures feed on the living rushes and grasses, but many more feed on their remains. Detritus decomposes, so the rushes and grasses grow in a favorable, nutrient-rich environment.

Living plants are only one-tenth of the food supply for herbivores. The detritus of dead plants supplies almost ten times as much food to a complex chain that begins with bacteria and fungi and ascends to crabs, shrimp, oysters, snails, and mussels. Algae growing in the brackish water also supply the chain. At its upper end are many creatures of land and sea that are not full-time residents but depend on the marshes for much of their food supply: birds, small mammals such as rats and raccoons, and fishes.

Chief grazers of the above-water portions of salt marsh plants are insects and spiders, some full-time residents, others that visit to feed. Only a few birds are residents: seaside sparrows, marsh wrens, and clapper rails. Many more come to feed or rest; over 40 species were observed in surveys of one salt marsh.

Salt marshes are efficient producers of mosquitoes. Birds thrive on them; humans don't. As seaside communities developed, residents demanded mosquito control. One obvious method was to destroy the marshes. Especially along the Indian River, dikes were built. By impounding water or by drying a marsh, mosquito breeding was suppressed. The DDT used to kill mosquitoes also killed some other creatures and virtually stopped successful hatchings of ospreys and some other birds. Impoundments became convenient dumping sites for sewage, garbage, and trash. Some were filled in to make building sites.

Losses have been greatest near population centers. Most of the salt marshes around Tampa Bay are gone. In Brevard County, 95 percent of the marshes were destroyed. Most of the Gulf marshes from New Port Richey to the Alabama line are still in place.

Threats to the remaining salt marshes have diminished as their value to wildlife, including commercial fisheries, has been demonstrated. Some dikes have been breached to restore marsh conditions. Some of the destroyed marshes have become natural assets of another kind. Impoundments now included within the Merritt Island National Wildlife Refuge, for example, support hundreds of thousands of migratory birds, as well as other wildlife. Wildlife managers and mosquito control officials seem to have reached an accommodation.

Mangroves

Mangroves fringe estuaries in central and southern Florida, chiefly along the Gulf coast south of Tampa, at the southern edge of the everglades, and in some estuaries on the east coast. Mangroves are tropical. At times their range extends northward, where they compete with salt marsh species, but--as at Jack Island--a severe frost kills or damages the outliers.

Our oldest (1915) guide to trees and shrubs doesn't mention mangroves. One popular modern guide includes the black mangrove, noting that three other mangrove species occurring in Florida are "outside the scope of this field guide." Another describes the red mangrove, "button-mangrove," and "white-mangrove," but gives not even a passing nod to the black.

Tropical botanists and ecologists recognize the red, black, and white mangroves, together with the button-mangrove or buttonwood, as the principal species of Florida's mangrove swamps. They are not of the same genus. The *red mangrove* grows at the water's edge, seldom more

than 20 feet tall. It is easily recognized by "prop roots" that arch out and down into the water. It has a distinctive fruit, a pencil-like tube capped by a brown berry, which floats away and may take root elsewhere. We have seen lone red mangroves sprouting on sandbars. Ten or twenty years from now these may have created mangrove islands, their tangled roots trapping sand and debris.

Black mangroves grow landward of the reds, on slightly higher ground. They are easily recognized by a thick carpet of vertical aerating branches, up to 8 inches long, projecting tubelike from the soil around them. Black mangroves grow somewhat taller than red mangroves.

White mangroves occupy the next higher zone. They are often taller than the black mangroves. Their small greenish-white flowers appear in spring and early summer.

Buttonwoods grow on dry land at the fringes of mangrove swamps.

Ecologists often use such terms as "mangroves," "mangrove swamp," "mangrove community," and "mangrove ecosystem" to describe the complex association that the four species dominate. Red, black, and white mangroves can grow in salt or brackish water, excluding or excreting the salt. The association sometimes extends inward from the brackish zone, but mangroves don't thrive in fresh water. Recently we saw this same mangrove community in Belize. The mangrove community has greater species diversity in the Indo-Pacific region.

A few years ago we impulsively bought a 15-foot boat with outboard motor, both well used. We gave the motor a test run on a local lake, then towed it to Everglades National Park and cruised from Flamingo up the canal to Whitewater Bay, then far up a remote channel. We were at anchor, eating lunch, when it dawned on me that this was a foolish enterprise. There are a dozen reasons why an outboard motor of uncertain age might not start. Another boat might not come this way for days. Paddling wouldn't be feasible. We were surrounded by mangrove islands, but scrambling through their tangled roots and swimming from one island to another would be next to impossible.

I took a deep breath and pulled the starter rope. The motor caught and ran smoothly all the way back. Three weeks later, on the St. Johns River, the motor quit and couldn't be restarted. We were passing a marina when it happened.

A complex food chain develops on and beneath the mangroves. Of the detritus that accumulates, much comes from the mangroves themselves, as leaves and fruits fall and bacterial decay occurs. Food and shelter are provided for numerous marine animals. Snails lay eggs on exposed roots. Birds nest in the mangroves. An ecologist reviewed studies of a mangrove ecosystem and found mentions of 220 species of fish, 24 species of reptiles and amphibians, 18 species of mammals, and 181 species of birds.

The destruction of mangroves has followed the pattern of coastal development. On Marco Island, for example, development wiped out 2,000 acres of mangroves. Coastal land commands the highest prices, and mangroves sometimes interfere with beach access and the view. Those who clear away the mangroves often have reason to regret their folly. Mangroves stabilize the shore and provide protection from storms; with the mangroves gone, owners are likely to lose some of their precious waterfront. Today mangroves are legally protected. A landowner who removes them may be required to replant. Fortunately, mangrove restoration is feasible.

Where to See Estuaries

In describing prairies and other inland ecosystems, we have suggested good examples. This is more difficult for estuaries, not because they are rare but because they are most accessible by small boat. For example, Florida has forty Aquatic Preserves, most of them planned to protect estuarine ecosystems. Usually there are vantage points on land, such as a bridge, causeway, or overlook, but much more can be seen by boat. A canoe or other shallow-draft boat is the best way to explore most salt marshes or mangrove islands.

Good places to begin are parks with interpretive centers. Those that explain much about nearby estuaries are:

> Gulf Islands National Seashore
> St. Marks National Wildlife Refuge
> Merritt Island National Wildlife Refuge
> Upper Tampa Bay Regional Park
> Everglades National Park

On the east coast, north of the city of Fort Pierce, many of the causeways and bridges linking barrier islands to the mainland cross salt marshes, and many offer good vantage points. SR A1A north of the St. Johns River crosses Little Talbot Island State Park and its marshes. We found a narrow, shaky boardwalk extending into a marsh. Look for interesting side roads.

On the Gulf Coast, the road to Cedar Key crosses extensive salt marshes. Much of the coastal land north and west of there is owned by timber companies. Both east and west of the St. Marks National Wildlife Refuge are county roads ending at beaches or fish camps. Try them.

Mangroves are in the south. Nine-tenths of the remaining mangrove acreage is in Lee, Collier, Monroe, and Dade counties. Excellent interpretive centers are at John D. MacArthur Beach State Park and Everglades National Park.

On Sanibel Island, the J. N. "Ding" Darling National Wildlife Refuge has a visitor center. Mangroves can be seen from Wildlife Drive, better still from a wilderness canoe trail. Much of Collier-Seminole State Park is mangrove swamp.

The tidewater of Everglades National Park is a vast mangrove swamp with miles of wilderness channels. Hundreds of mangrove islands lie offshore.

On the Keys, good views of mangroves are at John Pennekamp Coral Reef State Park and Long Key State Park, among other places.

Chapter 15

Freshwater Swamps

F lorida's rivers and streams descend slowly, a few inches per mile, often through or beside swamps. Swamp creeks offer many delightful detours where you will see many wildflowers, birds, turtles, and alligators, often otters and raccoons.

A swamp is a wet forest. Despite generations of draining, filling, and logging, freshwater swamps still occupy about one-tenth of Florida's land area. Many of the logged areas are recovering.

As we cruised down the upper Hillsborough River one morning, our canoe hit an underwater obstacle and came to an abrupt halt. What had we hit? The river at that point was 9 feet deep and no fallen trees were nearby. Paddling and rocking didn't dislodge us. John moved to the bow, but shifting weight didn't help. We were about to go over the side when another canoe appeared. Its occupants welcomed us aboard, and our craft floated free.

Now we could see the obstacle: rotting pilings of an old bridge. On shore was an old logging grade penetrating a swamp, overgrown with trees now forty years old.

Names such as "swamp," "prairie," and "flatwoods" are inventions. People found it necessary to attach names to areas with distinctive characteristics. The name-giving has continued. Scientists, seeing differences within categories, have made and named subdivisions.

The Florida Natural Areas Inventory describes nine types of forest regularly inundated or saturated by fresh water. They have such names as *bottomland forest, floodplain swamp, strand swamp, basin swamp,* and *baygall.* No two swamps are identical; one could have ninety subdivisions instead of nine. They grade into one another and into drier ecosystems.

Keep it simple. If you're standing in a forest and your feet are wet or muddy, you're in a swamp. If your feet are dry but many of the trees are cypresses or bays, you are probably in a swamp in dry season.

Many riverside swamps were originally dominated by cypress trees. Cypresses have inspired poets:

> *Know ye the land where the cypress and myrtle*
> *Are emblems of deeds that are done in their clime . . .*

> *Alas for him who never sees*
> *The stars shine through his cypress-trees!*

> *Here once, through an alley Titanic,*
> *Of cypress, I roamed with my soul —*
> *Of cypress, with Psyche, my soul.*

> *Phocion compared the speeches of Leosthenes*
> *to cypress-trees. "They are tall," said he,*
> *"and comely, but bear no fruit."*

That last quotation--not a poem--is from Plutarch, who must have meant a cypress other than Florida's. Ours, more properly called "baldcypress," isn't even a member of the Cypress family. It's more closely related to the redwoods.

Once introduced to Florida's cypress, one never forgets it. No other tree resembles it except its smaller close relative, the pondcypress. Distinctive field marks are its spreading, pyramidlike, finned base, and the conical woody "knees" projecting from the surrounding soil or water. "Bald" because it drops its needles each fall.

What's a "bay"? Dictionaries don't help; they say it's a laurel or any of several trees or shrubs related to the laurel. Once again the most popular field guides to trees haven't been kind to Florida. One of them doesn't have "bay" in its index. The other tells us the correct name is "loblolly-bay." Nature writers from the north often call it "loblolly," but to most Floridians it's "bay." (A loblolly pine, sometimes called just "loblolly," grows in northern Florida.)

Florida's loblolly-bay has thick, shiny, ovate, dark green, leathery leaves with sawtooth edges. It's an evergreen, leaves falling throughout the year. It may grow to 60 feet tall. It doesn't produce bayberries; those come from another plant: the bayberry.

What is a "bayhead?" We heard the name many times before we found a definition: "A swamp dominated by bays."

"Baygall" is less often heard. It's a swamp at the base of a slope, supplied with water by seepage. Bays are usually dominant.

Northern visitors' first sight of cypress may be slabs for sale at roadside stands, often fitted with clocks. Once there were slabs big enough for table tops. Few cypresses of that size remain. Because cypress wood is strong and resists rot and decay, it was much prized for heavy constructions such as bridges, boats, docks, and bulkheads. The most common tree in riverside swamps, it grew conveniently near water transportation routes.

Cypress seeds don't germinate in water. Once germinated, seedlings grow best in saturated soil, neither inundated nor dry. These reproduction requirements make it unsuitable for tree farming. Most cypress reproduction is by natural regeneration.

Logging was so thorough that most cypresses growing today have diameters smaller than 12 inches. Less than one tree in fifty exceeds 24 inches. Second-growth cypress lacks the rot resistance that made the original trees so desirable.

The cypress harvest is still heavy, 16 million cubic feet a year, including poaching on public land. Most of the trees now cut are so small that entire trees are chipped and sold as mulch. Conservationists are urging gardeners to switch to melaleuca mulch. We'd like to get rid of the melaleucas and let the cypresses grow.

Only two stands of virgin cypress remain: one in the Big Cypress National Preserve, the other in the Corkscrew Swamp Sanctuary of the National Audubon Society. (Only two? A recent hiking trail leaflet says a 900-acre virgin cypress swamp is within the Tosohatchee State Reserve.)

Removing tall cypresses stimulated growth of trees and shrubs that had been the swamp understory: maple, pop ash, dahoon holly, myrsine, and willow. Cypress and bay are still prominent, but what was cypress swamp is now mixed swamp forest.

We stated earlier that a few inches of difference in elevation often causes a difference in ecosystems. In wetlands, elevation determines their *hydroperiods*, the number of days each year a place is inundated. In the Big Cypress, for example, the lowest places have hydroperiods exceeding 300 days. This is too much for reproduction of cypresses and other trees. Instead, one sees *sloughs*, water areas with floating and emergent plants such as pickerelweed. Cattails, grasses, and rushes are often on the margins.

Cypresses thrive on slightly higher ground where the hydroperiod is between 200 and 300 days. The largest cypresses grow where the hydroperiod is longest within this range.

Occasionally one sees a *cypress dome* rising above a marsh or everglades, or even in rangeland. It looks like higher ground but isn't. Instead, a shallow depression provides a longer hydroperiod than prevails in the surroundings. The depression has collected organic muck. The tallest trees grow in the deepest part of the depression, often the center, thus forming a dome.

Hydroperiods between 150 and 200 days promote development of marshes where only scattered trees or hammocks rise above sawgrass and cattails. Often the next higher ecosystem is wet prairie.

The water supply of swamps and marshes depends largely on seasonal rains, although some receive water from springs and seeps. After the rainy season, water levels slowly decline. To have a hydroperiod of 300 days, a place must retain water for many weeks after the rains end.

Florida still has large freshwater swamps. Georgia's Okefenokee National Wildlife Refuge occupies a huge swamp that extends southward toward Florida's Osceola National Forest. The State's recent acquisition of Pinhook Swamp links them. The Green Swamp is in central Florida. In the south are the Big Cypress National Preserve and the Fakahatchee Strand. Many smaller swamps are scattered throughout the state.

Strand is another word with a Florida meaning our dictionaries haven't acquired. Here a strand is a narrow, elongated swamp, densely vegetated. It exists because of a long, narrow depression that has a longer hydroperiod than its surroundings. Strands are often strips of cypress swamp. We have seen cypress strands and cypress ponds in the Upper St. Johns River basin. Cypress strands and domes are both found in the Big Cypress, the Three Lakes Wildlife Management Area, and elsewhere.

Heads, basin swamps, galls, domes, bogs, sogs, bays, baygalls, strands, hammocks--these and other names are used to describe the many variations seen in swamps. While some swamps are large and easily demarcated by an abrupt change of elevations, hundreds are small with almost imperceptible intergrading. A depression in a forest becomes a small pond. Plants invade the pond; their remains accumulate on the bottom; and the pond becomes a marsh. If the hydroperiod is favorable, the process continues and marsh becomes swamp.

In her chapter, "Swamps," in *Ecosystems of Florida* (Orlando: University of Central Florida Press, 1990), Katherine C. Ewell put it this way:

In other types of swamps, however, the range of climates and mixture of biogeographic influences have produced several anomalies that make it difficult to extrapolate information about floristic patterns of other swamps in North America, or indeed in the world, to Florida.

So we're different, and in ways that give us a variety of swamps. Southern redcedar was common in swamp hammocks until most of it was turned into pencils. Florida has Atlantic white-cedar swamps in the north. Several pines--slash, pond, and loblolly--often occur in swamps, but not as dominant species. The same is true for several species of palms, laurel oak, red maple, black gum, overcup and swamp laurel oaks, and willows. The Fakahatchee Strand is said to have the world's largest stand of royal palms.

Swamps have inspired writers of adventure, mystery, and horror stories as well as poets. Sheriff's deputies with dogs have pursued escaped convicts through many a swamp. Maidens fleeing from villains into dismal swamps have been terrified by snakes, spiders, and hooting owls. Many a large swamp has its Bigfoot.

Slogging through a swamp, one is more aware of the understory than of the trees above. Limbs support resurrection ferns, colorful bromeliads, and festoons of Spanish moss. Strap ferns grow on rotting logs and stumps. Orchids are abundant, more than forty-five species occurring in the Fakahatchee.

Shrubs are prominent in the understory, often titi, black titi, dahoon holly--and on through a list of several dozen species, some of which we have learned to recognize. Vines, too: wild grapes, poison ivy, catbrier, and many more, including the strangler fig.

One day a ranger leading a group through a swamp called attention to a large strangler fig. A bird had left a fig seed high in a cabbage palm, he explained. The seed germinated. The stem grew upward. Roots extended downward, embracing the tree. After reaching the ground, the embracing roots became larger and larger. Now they were strangling the tree, he said, and it would die.

"Why doesn't somebody *do* something?" a woman cried.

Occasionally you can see a strangler fig that, having killed the tree it surrounded, now stands alone.

The Green Swamp

Some call the Green Swamp one of Florida's largest remaining wildernesses. Many people pass through it daily and see nothing remarkable. Essential to the water supply of central and southern Florida, it's in the path of development radiating from Disney World. Developers covet it.

More than half of its 850 square miles is wetlands, the headwaters of five major rivers. The wetlands are interspersed with flatwoods, low hills and ridges, and sinkhole lakes. Although these wetlands provide some water to the underground Floridan Aquifer, their chief function is that of *potentiometric high*, a cap 125 feet above sea level that maintains pressure in the aquifer, so springs flow and salt water does not intrude.

Much of the higher land is used for agriculture: citrus groves on well-drained deep soils; cattle grazing on flatwoods cleared of trees. The area has cypress swamps, pine plantations, oak hammocks, creeks, and ponds. It also has housing developments, sand mines, and scattered mobile homes.

Ever responsive to the wishes of developers, county governments did little to protect this resource. In 1974 the State intervened, designating 504 square miles — about three-fifths of the Swamp — an Area of Critical State Concern. State oversight was lax, however, and counties continued to permit commercial and residential developments. Many of these projects included drainage and land filling.

Now the State's Growth Management Act requires planning for such critical areas. The counties, especially Polk, submitted weak plans, which the State rejected. However, of late some large development proposals have been rebuffed.

The controversy would end if the State bought the entire Green Swamp or at least the 544,000 acres designated as critical. That's not likely — many landowners won't sell. However, the Southwest Florida Water Management District has purchased almost 80,000 acres in the principal watersheds, and more will be bought if Preservation 2000 funds are available.

The litany of environmental problems in the Swamp seems endless. No one in Polk County's government noticed as a landowner illegally accumulated a twenty-five-acre mountain of 4.5 million used tires. A forestry official called it to the county's attention in 1986. Immediately there was great concern. A fire in the pile, almost impossible to extinguish or control, could blanket central Florida — including Disney World — with noxious smoke for months. Burning tires give off oil, which would pollute the aquifer. And the tires were breeding habitat for mosquitoes.

These were great reasons for concern. After much bureaucratic maneuvering, waffling, and buck-passing, the pile was still there six years later. Finally it was subdivided, guardianship was provided, and reduction began.

Because of the high water table, ordinary septic tanks won't work in many parts of the Swamp. Builders have been allowed to put them above ground; in wet weather, sewage may flood yards or enter homes.

The Southwest Florida Water Management District says it welcomes public recreation on its lands in the Green Swamp but can't provide necessary facilities and management. Hillsborough and Pasco counties have developed fine parks on SWFWMD land. Offered the same opportunity, Polk County didn't. Most of the SWFWMD holdings are now a Wildlife Management Area, managed by the Game and Fresh Water Fish Commission, so the road gates are open only during hunting season. The Florida Trail crosses the area, and the hiker entrance is open except in the early days of hunting seasons.

In 1991 the State bought a 28.5-mile abandoned railroad line, from Lakeland to Mabel. It crosses the east side of the Green Swamp. A private group took the lead in developing the Polk County Rails to Trails for hikers, bikers, and equestrians.

Swamp Animals

Despite — or because of — the alternation of wet and dry periods, swamps have a rich and varied wildlife. At the base of the food chain are *benthic* creatures, bottom-dwellers, such as worms, leeches, insects, snails, clams, and crayfish. Mosquitoes are among the insects that begin their lives in water. Dragonflies, damselflies, and many species of beetles and spiders depend on water. Also at the base of the chain are grasshoppers and other insects that graze on foliage. Mosquito fish, minnows, and darters in the swamp are food supply for herons, ibises, snakes, and raccoons.

Raccoon

Wildlife populations differ from one type of swamp to another. Swamps with permanent pools provide habitat for more species of snakes, frogs, and turtles than do swamps with little or no water in dry periods.

Birds and mammals, seasonally abundant in swamps,

Wood Stork

adapt to changing conditions by moving from one habitat to another. Many bird species are migratory, spending a part of each year, often winter, in southern swamps, especially riverine swamps. The limpkin feeds chiefly on snails, which swamps provide. Many wading birds feed on fish, crayfish, and frogs.

Wood storks require shallow water with concentrations of fish. Breeding is timed so their young will have ample food. Although they have traditional nesting grounds, they won't nest if the water level is too high or too low. Loss of suitable habitat has caused wood stork populations to decline alarmingly. Some are finding new nesting sites further north. Those that visited our lake didn't stay.

The raccoon, one of the most omnivorous mammals, is at home in swamps. The black bear, its numbers greatly reduced by habitat loss and hunting, uses swamps as refuges. So do the last of the panthers; only the Fakahatchee Strand is said to have a resident population.

Visiting the Swamps

Boardwalks through swamps are available at Highlands Hammock State Park, Arthur R. Marshall Loxahatchee National Wildlife Refuge, Fakahatchee Strand State Park, and Hillsborough County's Lettuce Lake

Park, among others. Many state and county parks have swamp trails with boardwalk sections. The Florida Trail crosses the Big Cypress and continues north, skirting many swamps or passing through them on old grades.

The Corkscrew Swamp Sanctuary of the National Audubon Society has a two-mile boardwalk through its 10,560 acres. Staff members are usually out there, answering questions and pointing out things a visitor might overlook. More than 200 bird species have been recorded. Most visitors come between Christmas and Easter, but we enjoy a visit at any time. On one visit we saw--and heard--a record wood stork nesting.

In 1989 the Corkscrew Regional Watershed Program was formed, linking local, regional, state, and federal governments with Audubon, other nonprofit groups, and private landowners. The objective is to acquire and manage a 40,000-acre preserve connecting the water sheet-flow systems of Southwest Florida with the Everglades National Park. By 1991, 13,500 acres had been donated or were under contract. The Audubon Sanctuary is at the heart of the new preserve.

Most Florida rivers and streams flow through swamps. Maps show where many of them are and what roads penetrate them. In our view, an ideal way to enjoy the swamps is by canoe. Many rivers with adjacent swamps are served by outfitters who provide canoes, equipment, and shuttle service. Canoe camping is an unforgettable experience: finding a bit of high ground for your tent, cooking dinner on a pocket stove, listening to the swamp sounds as darkness falls.

Chapter 16
The Many Lakes

W e live beside a lake. Every room faces it. We see the lake as we lie in bed, from the breakfast table, from our desks. It's never the same. At times it's mirror-smooth, marked only by the wakes of wood ducks. Then, perhaps suddenly, rain squalls sweep across it.

Lakeshore property is plentiful in Florida. The relatively flat terrain, limestone base, and 50 to 65 inches a year of rainfall have combined to form more than 30,000 lakes and ponds. Of these, 7,800 lakes have surface areas of 10 acres or more. Five natural lakes are larger than 25,000 acres. By far the largest is Lake Okeechobee: 448,000 acres. Lakes are scattered statewide, but their greatest concentration is on either side of the peninsula's central ridge. Our county has 550. Most Florida lakes are less than 20 feet deep. The average depth of Okeechobee, the largest, is less than 15 feet.

Our lake was created long ago when a limestone cavern collapsed and overlying layers of sandy clay, mudstone, and peat subsided, forming a basin that filled with water.

It has no inflowing stream, nor is there a surface outlet. In our years here, the lake's water level has fluctuated by only 2 feet. Rain falling on the lake and runoff from surrounding land are roughly balanced by evaporation, seepage underground, and pumping for lawn and garden irrigation.

Only a minority of Florida's lakes enjoy such stability. Some drop so much in drought years that docks are left high and dry. For about 80 percent of the state's lakes, the normal range of fluctuations is about 5 feet. A few have been known to fluctuate as much as 30 feet, exasperating waterfront residents.

Brooklyn Lake, near Keystone Heights, has dropped 22 feet in twelve years. The cause appears to be leakage into the aquifer. At the time when Brooklyn Lake and several others were at their lowest, some lakes were at near-record highs.

Crooked Lake, in Babson Park, gradually dropped 17 feet from its all-time high. The decline was attributed to excessive pumping by citrus growers and residents. Since then, citrus growers have reduced their water use by adopting surface rather than spray irrigation. That and higher rainfall have caused the lake to rise 5 1/2 feet.

When we saw that our lake has no exiting stream, we wondered why it remains fresh. Utah's Great Salt Lake, too, has no outlet. Unlike our lake, it receives a constant inflow of fresh water from several rivers. However, because of its altitude and the prevailing climate, evaporation is rapid, leaving salts and other minerals behind.

We know a Maine lake that is fed by a rushing stream and has a cataract at its exit. That lake is continuously flushed; its water is replaced about five times a year. Our lake loses some water by seepage, but the turnover is much slower. In comparable lakes it exceeds two years.

Because of their slow turnover, such Florida lakes are especially vulnerable to pollution. Runoff from farms, groves, pastures, streets, driveways, and lawns carries pollutants and sediments into the lakes. Shoreline vegetation can intercept much of it, and this vegetation is a necessary nursery for fish. Therefore State regulations permit landowners to clear no more than twenty-five feet of their waterfronts (or 25 percent, whichever is less). Too many landowners seem unaware of the rules and there's little enforcement.

As noted earlier, an excess of nutrients produces an excess of plant growth. We saw cattails spread from a small patch to surround our lake. Now we have hydrilla, an obnoxious exotic weed that has grown explosively. Several times a month we pull masses of it from the screen of our irrigation intake.

The lake is still pleasant. Children swim. Water skiing is popular. We enjoy canoeing. The lake's scenic quality is high. Wildlife is abundant. The fishing is good. Few residents are alarmed by the insidious changes. When the degradation finally becomes obnoxious, it will be too late for prevention and restoration will be expensive, even if possible.

A River Runs Through Them

The St. Johns and Kissimmee rivers flow through a number of lakes. One might assume that lakes with inlets and outlets are less vulnerable to pollution because of flushing. It's not so. For generations, rivers were used as convenient waste removal system. Municipal sewage, industrial chemicals, waste from food processing plants, and other materials were dumped into streams. Animal wastes, pesticides, and fertilizer drained from farmlands. This pollution was tolerated because few Florida communities use surface water for drinking.

When a stream enters a lake, the rate of flow drops to near zero. The lake is a settling basin, trapping whatever the stream brings. Silt is deposited. The burden of organic sludge settles and accumulates on the bottom. The exiting stream merely decants surface water.

A Million Creatures

Say "fish!" to a landlocked Floridian, and he'll answer "bass!" Most small boats are advertised as "bass boats." Small electric motors are used to maneuver while fishing. We wondered why many bass boats have huge motors. Then we saw the beginning of a bass tournament. Contestants drew lots and sat in their boats, motors idling. When the referee called his number, each fisherman took off at high speed, racing to claim his favored fishing spot. Fishermen don't scorn black crappie, catfish, and pickerel, but bass is king.

Lake Okeechobee, surrounded by a high dike, has little scenic value, but it's known nationwide as a premier fishing lake. Sport fishing is the principal activity on many lakes.

Bass are at the top of a complex aquatic food pyramid, each level dependent on those below. Nutrients, water, and sunlight produce the lake's green plants, from microscopic algae to emergent weeds and grasses, water lilies, cardinal flowers, and cattails. Floating with the microscopic algae are microscopic animals, consumers of algae. A water sample may also contain larvae of insects and freshwater shellfish. Other micro-organisms and worms inhabit the lake bottom. When we walk out on our dock, we see a sudden flurry of tiny fishes. If we toss in a bit of bread, they quickly surround it, nibbling. They are prey for larger fishes and wading birds. Neighbor boys catch shiners on tiny hooks, then use the shiners to catch bass.

Occasionally a patron of our bird feeder leaves an empty snail or clam shell as payment. Snails attach their egg masses to plant stems above the water line. Frogs chorus at night--or did until recently. Turtles poke heads above water.

Countless insects breed in and around lakes, a feast for egrets and wood ducks, and then, as they take to the air, for swifts and purple martins.

Lakes are a rich food source for creatures of the land and air. Dragonflies prey on gnats, flies, and mosquitoes. Forster's terns plunge into the water for minnows. Ospreys prefer larger fishes. Once we heard a loud splash and a louder squawk: an alligator had tried for a mallard and missed.

The food pyramid is a wonderfully intricate structure. The stuff of life is constantly recycled. As one ecologist puts it, living things are composed of materials borrowed from the environment. When plants or animals die, micro-organisms, the agents of decay, decompose them into their ingredients, ready for reuse.

A lake is not a permanent ecosystem. Even in a wilderness lake, sediments and organic debris accumulate. The lake basin fills until the lake becomes a wetland, perhaps later a forest. Pollution accelerates and distorts the process.

Who Owns Them?

Newcomers to Florida may hear an unfamiliar term: "meandered lake." It has an interesting story, although court decisions have minimized its original importance. Soon after Spain ceded Florida to the United States in 1819, surveyors were deployed. One of their instructions was to survey each lake they considered navigable. The survey method, called "meandering," was to frame each such lake with connecting straight lines.

In 1945, federal law affirmed the State's title to the beds of navigable lakes. "Navigable" by steamboat, or Indian dugout? Each surveyor had decided for himself. The surveyors had meandered only 236 lakes. One of them covered only two acres!

As waves of development swept over Florida, State ownership of lake beds became increasingly important and was often challenged in courts. Thus far courts have agreed that meandering is sufficient proof of navigability, but the fact that a lake wasn't meandered doesn't prove the opposite. Courts now decide what is navigable.

Most controversies concern the boundary of State ownership. The original definition was a lake's ordinary high-water mark "at the time of statehood." Largely because of drainage projects, the levels of many lakes have changed in 150 years, and the historical high-water mark is obscure. Landowners are irked when the State asserts ownership to waterfront land they have long assumed was theirs. The Kissimmee River restoration project will require raising the level of some lakes closer to their historic high water marks. Landowners don't like the idea.

Restore Damaged Lakes?

Today our ever-changing lake is quiet, not a ripple on its surface. At midday, few birds are active. It is difficult to imagine the immense amount of activity by countless billions of organisms that is keeping this ecosystem functioning. If one component is damaged, all are affected.

Lake Hancock, in our county, is fed by a creek that for years transported great quantities of municipal and industrial wastes. State and federal rules prohibit such dumping now, but when we canoed on Lake Hancock every paddle stroke stirred up clouds of nasty sludge. The sins of the past remain. Deep beds of muck containing noxious stuff may remain in lakes for decades.

As more and more people became lakeside residents, concern grew for the condition of Florida lakes. Neighbors formed lake associations, and associations joined federations. New laws and regulations were adopted. New housing developments and commercial establishments must now be set farther from shores and must provide on-site retention of storm water by such means as holding ponds and berms. New roads are designed to keep the first flush of storm water out of lakes.

Can a polluted lake be salvaged? One step is reducing or eliminating the excess plants produced by the surplus of nutrients. Herbicides kill weeds, at least temporarily, but the chemicals may kill desirable species. Killed weeds decay, releasing more nutrients.

Mechanical harvesting removes emergent or floating weeds that interfere with boating and fishing. Harvesting is useful, but weeds return, and removing a sun-blocking surface layer increases plant growth below.

Biological remedies are being tested. Grazing species of fish have been introduced. As noted earlier, our lake recently received 100 sterile grass carp, which may eat the hydrilla. Certain insects, plant diseases, or parasites may affect only an unwanted species.

Drawdowns have been used at several lakes: the water level is lowered, exposing and drying the bottom in shallow areas. This may kill nuisance plants and benefit desirable species. Detritus oxidizes. Later the lake is refilled. This treatment alone benefits habitat and fishing.

Sludge can be removed from lake bottoms by dredging, but this is too costly a remedy for large lakes. Another method is to drain much of the water, let the exposed bottom dry, then remove sludge with mechanical shovels and dump trucks. Where to dispose of sludge is not the least of the problems.

Banana Lake was one of the state's most polluted. Here the first test of hydraulic dredging was made. The lake covers only 256 acres, but dredges removed almost a million cubic yards of organic bottom sediments, about 85,000 tons! Several months later the test was pronounced a success. Water clarity had greatly improved. The cost was $1.6 million, or $61,500 per acre. At that rate, not many lakes can be restored.

Another suggested method is aeration. Organic bottom sediments don't decompose because oxygen doesn't reach them. We have seen our fish tank experiment applied successfully to a one-acre duck pond. Powerful jets of water entraining air bubbles stirred and oxygenated the muck, which soon decomposed. The pond bottom was cleaned, the water clarified. The nutrient-enriched water was replaced. However, the method seems impractical for large lakes.

The St. Johns River Water Management District is testing a novel method of lake improvement. A former vegetable and sod farm has been made into a marsh. Sediments rich in phosphorus and nitrogen will be removed as lake water flows slowly through the marsh. If the method works, the marsh will be expanded until it can filter the lake's total water volume twice a year.

Enjoy the Lakes!

Lake water quality has been improved year by year. Most lakes are suitable for boating, birding, swimming, water skiing, sailing, and fishing.

Visitor who have their own canoes or outboard boats will find no lack of lake launching sites. They are well marked on the maps of the *Florida Atlas and Gazetteer*. Renting a boat is more difficult. Most canoe outfitters serve rivers rather than lakes. Marinas with boat rentals are on a few of the larger lakes and chains of lakes. Some fishing camps have boats for rent. Ask at bait and tackle shops.

How do you choose a lake that retains most of its natural qualities? Local advice is best, of course. Maps such as those in the *Atlas and Gazetteer* show land uses. Look for lakes largely surrounded by woodlands or wetlands. For canoeing, we prefer relatively small lakes linked with rivers and creeks that wind through marshes and swamps. As our canoe slips silently along, we feel a kinship with the Indians who called this lovely land their home.

Chapter 17

Floating Down the Rivers

River travel was the only way to explore interior Florida in early times. Steamboats began operating on the Apalachicola River in 1827, on the St. Johns in 1831. Hamilton Disston began dredging the Kissimmee River to make Orlando an inland seaport. A small steamboat carried sightseers to Silver Spring, passengers shooting at alligators and herons.

Cities such as Jacksonville and Pensacola developed as transshipment centers where river and ocean steamers exchanged cargoes. Logging, mining, farming, and other developments concentrated near navigable rivers.

We think river travel is the best way to explore Florida today. Many great natural areas are accessible only by boat. Drifting quietly, we pass within a few feet of limpkins that would take flight if we approached on foot. Some of the turtles basking on logs slip into the water; others ignore us. Some alligators hit the water with great splashes, while others sleep on. Raccoons look up curiously. A kingfisher scolds us each time our approach puts him to flight. An anhinga drying her wings plunges headlong from an overhanging branch. Two dozen white ibises are feeding in a shallow backwater.

The lives of many animals are linked to rivers. Some fishermen are attracted by the species that frequent the upper reaches. Others prefer to fish the brackish waters near the mouth. Fish are prey for alligators, turtles, water snakes, raccoons, otters, black bears, wading birds, ospreys, bald eagles, terns, and many other hunters. Snails, clams, and other freshwater shellfish are also a food supply. Spiders spin webs from overhanging branches. Deer come to rivers to drink. In and around the river live frogs, salamanders, and newts.

Leaving the Withlacoochee River, we paddled up Gum Slough. The stream wanders through hardwood swamps and freshwater marshes. Cardinal flowers bloomed brilliantly. Patches of water hyacinth floated by. We passed a few riverside cottages, but the State has bought the land for a preserve and they may have been removed by now. Anticipating the return trip, we tried to remember the route; it's a braided stream, and only one braid may offer clear passage.

Near noon we reached our destination, the stream's source. From a distance it appeared to be a modest pond about 150 feet in diameter. Entering, we floated on crystal water over two large, deep, blue springs. The pond seemed quiet, but all the stream's water was gushing up from these twin orifices below us. We were reminded of Yellowstone's Morning Glory Pool.

A *first-magnitude spring* is one that flows at 100 cubic feet per second or more, about 3 million gallons per hour. Florida has twenty-seven first-magnitude springs, about one-third of all such springs in the United States.

The state has 320 visible springs and countless seeps. Water from seeps trickles down river banks. Many unseen springs supply rivers, lakes, and wetlands from below. Several springs are associated with underwater labyrinths, some so extensive they have yet to be fully mapped.

Manatees are attracted to several of the large springs in winter, because the upwelling water has a constant temperature all year. Once, as we canoed on the St. Johns River, a huge manatee surfaced just beside us. We noted the colors of his collar and reported to the scientists at manatee winter quarters in Blue Spring State Park. They were expecting him.

Some of the large springs are available to swimmers. "Tubing" on a few short rivers flowing from springs has attracted so many floaters that natural settings have been degraded.

Cruising

Power boats can be used on the larger rivers. For a day's outing on the Suwanee or St. Johns, a rented pontoon boat is a good choice; one can walk about, set up a camera tripod, lunch at a table, nap on a bench,

Black Bear

take shelter if it rains. Houseboats can be rented, some of them luxurious craft with staterooms, observation decks, full kitchens, even clothes washers and dryers. One evening, soon after we dropped anchor for the night in a lonely backwater, more than two hundred white ibises glided in to roost in nearby trees.

Small boats with motors, such as our 13-foot Zodiac, can explore creeks too narrow and shallow for larger craft. Best of all, we believe, is the canoe. Few days are as rewarding as one spent floating down a river. Camping overnight on a remote river island or sandbar is an unmatched delight.

Most Florida rivers flow slowly. The U.S. Geological Survey says the average velocity of Florida streams is about 1 mile per hour. Most canoeing streams run at 2 to 3 mph, meandering through forests, swamps, marshes, and prairies.

We call trips "canoe runs" because almost all are made downstream. Paddling upstream is laborious. Outfitters serve some of the best canoeing rivers. They provide canoes and shuttle service, as well as camping gear for overnight runs.

Private shuttling requires a minimum of two cars, a nuisance when we're alone. Instead, we clamp a small electric fishing motor at the stern. When we head upstream, the propeller is lowered and locked in straight-ahead position. The quiet motor needs no further attention. Its thrust just overcomes the current, so we paddle normally. The battery is good for more than four hours.

Flow in some rivers is highly variable. Along the lower Apalachicola River, we saw recent roof-high flood marks on weekend cottages; the river had since dropped 12 feet below its bank top. On another occasion, at a launch site where the Withlacoochee River is usually 30 feet wide, we found only a trickle one could step across. A Wildlife Officer said it had been weeks since he could make his boat patrols. Spring-fed rivers, such as the Wekiva, have less variation.

Much has been accomplished to abate river pollution. A State study of the fifty principal rivers found that two-thirds of their 3,300 miles have good water quality, half of the rest fairly good. Only one river, the Fenholloway, near Perry, is so heavily polluted as to be rated "industrial."

The State's Save Our Rivers program is one of several funding sources for purchase of riverside land. Several private organizations, notably The Nature Conservancy, have also been buying.

The Rivers

Eleven Florida rivers are longer than 100 miles. Because of the flat terrain, some have huge drainage basins. The Apalachicola and its tributaries drain 11 million acres within Florida, several million more in Alabama and Georgia.

The State Division of Recreation and Parks publishes leaflets for 36 canoe trails. Each leaflet describes a trail, has a map showing put-in and take-out points, estimates travel times, tells what level of canoeing skill is necessary, and warns of any hazards.

The State's 36 designated canoe trails are only a fraction of the possibilities. One of our favorites, Arbuckle Creek, isn't on the list. For most of its 26 miles, a cypress swamp is on the east side; this is a buffer zone of the Avon Park Air Force Range. Most of the west side is ranchland. In the day-long run one passes less than a dozen houses and under only two bridges. Birding is excellent.

The Suwannee

Thanks to Stephen Foster, who never saw it, the Suwannee River is regarded affectionately. Threats to its integrity cause roars of public outrage and official action. The state's second longest river is first in the hearts of Floridians.

The Suwannee flows from Georgia's Okefenokee Swamp to the Gulf of Mexico. Sources disagree on its length. We'll choose the longest: 245 miles. No dams interrupt the river's flow, and there is remarkably little riverside development. The river meanders pleasantly through pristine cypress and oak swamps. Adding to its flow are numerous springs, some emerging as trickles from limestone outcrops along the banks, others deep enough for a dip. The two principal tributaries are the Alapaha and one of Florida's two Withlacoochee rivers.

One can canoe the river's entire length, camping on white sandbars. It can be done in a week, but why hurry? Birding is excellent, and one will see turtles, alligators, opossums, raccoons, otters, and at least the signs of beaver. The only obstacle, Big Shoals, is the only real whitewater in Florida; portaging is recommended.

When threats to the river's beauty and water quality appeared in the early 1980s, The Nature Conservancy proposed a massive effort to save it. Pollution has been abated. State agencies, the Suwannee River Water Management District, and the Conservancy have bought about 60 tracts of riparian land.

Along the river corridor you can see examples of many Florida habitats. The river and its floodplain support at least 54 species of fish, 39 species of amphibians, 73 of reptiles, 232 of birds, and 42 of mammal species. We have yet to see an alligator snapping turtle, the world's largest freshwater turtle.

St. Johns River

Florida's longest and largest river has its source in a huge freshwater marsh interspersed with hammocks, swamps, and creeks. Common trees are cypress, red maple, bay, live oak, and cabbage palm. To protect the marshes, which were threatened by drainage, pollution, and development, the St. Johns Water Management District has bought 80,000 acres in a strip 50 miles long. A cooperative project with the U.S. Army Corps of Engineers will ultimately restore 125,000 acres of marshlands.

Wildlife is abundant. Birders are attracted by the many waterfowl, wading birds, other marsh species. Bald eagle, hawks, wood stork, caracara, and swallow-tailed and snail kites are often seen. Common mammals include bobcat, cottontail, swamp rabbit, armadillo, squirrels, river otter, raccoon, wild hog, and deer. Reptiles include lizards, frogs, alligator, turtles, and water snakes.

Within the marshes are lakes popular with fishermen for their largemouth bass, crappie, and panfish. The largest are Blue Cypress Lake (6,555 acres), Lake Washington (4,362 acres), and Lake Poinsett (4,334 acres). Smaller lakes and waterways are accessible only by small boat. The river is navigable by small craft from a few miles south of US 192.

Until recently, fishermen and hunters were the chief users of the area and its primitive campsites. During hunting season, boaters are advised to carry a blaze-orange flag on a 6-foot staff .

From the marsh the river flows northward through a series of lakes to the Atlantic Ocean at Jacksonville. Lake Poinsett, also a favorite of fishermen, is largely surrounded by marshes. Beyond the lake, the river passes through more wetlands, largely State-owned. The river flows slowly, descending at only about 1 inch per mile.

After passing under SR 50, the river trends northwest through a complex of marshes, backwaters, and small lakes to 6,058-acre Lake Harney, turns west through still more wetlands, and enters 9,406-acre Lake Monroe. Beyond the lake the river is wider and deeper. The city of Sanford on Lake Monroe is an inland port. Beyond here boaters should be on watch for barges and other cargo carriers. Beyond here is more shoreline development: waterfront homes, marinas, and trailer parks; but there are miles of wetlands that can never be developed.

We like the section between Lake Monroe and Lake George because of the many tributaries and backwaters. Launching at Blue Springs State Park or Hontoon Landing, you can paddle up the Wekiva River, explore miles of meandering creeks and oxbows through vast cypress swamps, camp on Hontoon Island.

At Palatka the river becomes wider than most of the lakes along its course. Finally it becomes a busy commercial avenue, intersecting the Intracoastal Waterway. Tidal marshes on both sides offer miles of twisting channels for exploration by canoe or other shallow-draft boat.

The Apalachicola

We don't recommend canoeing the Apalachicola, Florida's eighth longest river. There are few put-ins and take-outs. The river's flow, controlled by releases from Seminole Dam, is variable and often swift.

Boat traffic is heavy. The river has carried commercial traffic since the steamboat era. Seminole Dam and locks extend commercial navigation far into Georgia.

A good way to see the river's bluffs, ravines, and riparian forests is by power boat. The floodplain is broad, and land access points are few. Scientists call the bordering land a *paleorefugium*, a place where ancient species have survived long after disappearing from elsewhere in the region. It has greater diversity of flora and fauna than any other place on the coastal plain.

On land, Torreya State Park offers a rare panorama of the river, trails through forest and ravines, and over a thousand species of wildflowers, shrubs, and trees. The park is named for the Florida torreya (as noted earlier, a tree that occurs only here).

The Nature Conservancy has a 5,845-acre preserve along the river south of the state park.

Kissimmee River

Restoration of the Kissimmee River has begun. It is the first attempt to restore a major ruined river to its natural condition. It will be the first time the U.S. Army Corps of Engineers has dismantled one of its large projects.

In its natural state, the Kissimmee meandered slowly from near Orlando through several lakes to Lake Okeechobee. Its floodplain, 2 to 3 miles wide, was almost flat. Above Lake Kissimmee the river drained over 1,400 square miles. Below Lake Kissimmee, it descended at 7 inches per mile, draining over 700 square miles. The channel was often braided. Oxbows developed and vanished. The extensive wetlands were habitat for a rich diversity of flora and fauna.

Between 1961 and 1971, in the name of flood control, the Corps dug a ditch 200 feet wide from Lake Kissimmee to Lake Okeechobee. The 52-mile-long ditch, known as "C-38," dried 98 miles of river and 35,000 acres of floodplain.

The Corps has been blamed for the environmental disasters that ensued, but it did not come to Florida uninvited. At the behest of Florida's governor and many influential citizens, Florida's congressional delegation got the money for the ditch. The State's South Florida Water Management District, long in the ditch-and-drain business, worked companionably with the Corps. A few environmentalists cried havoc.

Neither the Corps nor the Water Management District foresaw the effect on Lake Okeechobee. This 700-square-mile lake supports the water supply of southern Florida. Fresh water, flowing from the lake through hundreds of miles of canals, seeping through porous limerock and coral into the aquifer, holds back saltwater intrusion. The system supplies drinking water to the state's most populous region and irrigation water for thousands of acres.

The Kissimmee wetlands had served as a giant storage and filtering apparatus. With this filtering destroyed, the ditch soon polluted the lake with over 300 tons of nitrogen nutrients daily. Without the wet weather storage, quick runoff was followed by alarming declines in Okeechobee's water level during droughts. Developers and other business people were soon calling for help.

Floundering, engineers proposed new projects that wouldn't have helped and could have made matters worse. A few impractical environmentalists proposed an obviously impractical remedy: *Restore the river!* No such river restoration had ever been attempted. No one knew how to do it. But beginning in the early 1970s the idea took root and began to grow.

In the words of *Ballad for Americans*, "Nobody who was anybody believed it. Everybody who was anybody, they doubted it." Corps spokesmen ridiculed the idea. The South Florida Water Management District wanted no part of it. Among many opponents, ranchers whose holdings bordered the Kissimmee basin were fiercest. The dried-out land had also attracted developers.

The campaign for restoration was fought on many fronts with politically powerful opposition, few dedicated allies, frequent defeats, and rare triumphs. Such a campaign can succeed only if at least one determined crusader carries the flag. In the defeat of the Cross-Florida Barge Canal, it was Marjorie Carr; in preserving the Everglades, it has been Marjory Stoneman Douglas. The Kissimmee's constant advocate has been Richard Coleman of Winter Haven, chairman of the Sierra Club's Kissimmee Restoration Committee and now President of the Florida Lake Management Society.

An important convert was Bob Graham, then Florida's Governor, now U.S. Senator. Early in the 1980s he appointed a committee to study the problem and consider remedies. In its final meeting, the committee recommended an experiment: restoring a few miles of the lower river. The South Florida Water Management District agreed, skeptically, to try it. The Corps objected, tried to block the experiment, then stood aside.

In 1984 three sheet-metal weirs were placed across the C-38 ditch, diverting a portion of the canal's flow into 12 miles of the old oxbows. In 1987 we canoed the 12 miles with Richard and Frances Coleman, camped on an island, and were impressed. One would think the river had never left. Riparian vegetation was lush, birds abundant. Veteran naturalist Harlan Herbert, who had opposed the ditch from the outset, said, "It looks the way it did." The demonstration seemed to be a success.

It wasn't a true restoration, but it showed how quickly the natural environment would repair itself. The weirs divert water to the old river channel only when there is a high rate of flow down C-38. In drier periods, water in the oxbows stands stagnant, oxygen is depleted, and fish die. The natural system was not fully restored.

Richard Coleman wrote of the restored section:

> Neither the whisper nor the feeling of a flowing river is here. And still, the odors of subtropical vegetation, the whir of beetles and chatter of nesting waterfowl, mingle with the splashing and popping of predatory fish on the oxbows of the old Kissimmee River. These pleasantries remind us not only of what was a wonderful old river but what it will be again.

In many ways the Corps of Engineers' destruction will be of no more significance to the riverine system than an exceptionally long winter or dry season during which the marshes dried and the river was reduced to a narrow channel. Even changes in some of the old channel will not be significantly different than thousands of changes nature herself has wrought on this riverine system.

An engineering study compared four restoration methods. The best was the costliest: backfilling the ditch. This became a consensus of State officials, landowners, environmentalists, and the Corps, a consensus that had seemed impossible, a triumph of persistence, innovative policies, capable engineering, and skillful negotiating.

Difficult problems remained. Accelerated drainage in the upper basin had lowered lake levels, and riparian landowners asserted ownership of the dried borders. Yet restoration could succeed downstream only if the natural storage capacity of these lakes was restored. Below Lake Kissimmee, ranchers who had appropriated the dried floodplain now asserted ownership of thousands of acres that would be inundated by restoration.

Now convinced of the need, the South Florida Water Management District decided to appease the ranchers by buying the land they claimed. The courts might have upheld State ownership, but only after years of costly litigation. Upstream, the State is paying riparian owners for the right to bring lakes up to the old high-water mark during wet seasons.

The original price tag for restoration was $267 million. By 1992 it had increased to $400 million. The State committed $100 million and begun purchase of land and easements. The U. S. Congress appropriated an initial $6.8 million for the Corps' work, but the Corps delayed requesting the full amount.

New objections arose, and there seem to be endless hearings and reports. The Water Management District yielded to protests from a group of downstream residents and canceled one section of the project. Still, no one doubts that the Kissimmee will some day again flow free.

Oklawaha River[9]

Second only to restoring the Kissimmee, in both ecological significance and drama, is reclamation of the Oklawaha River. Originally, it flowed 96 miles from near Lake Apopka to the St. Johns River. For

[9] The name of the lake behind Rodman Dam is spelled "Ocklawaha," and this spelling is often — mistakenly — used for the river. Local residents have urged agreement on "Oklawaha."

generations, politicians and promoters campaigned for a canal across the Florida peninsula. The U.S. Army Corps of Engineers began contemplating the possibilities in the 1890s. In the 1920s, the J. D. Young canal bypassed and dried a section of the Oklawaha. In 1935 work began on a ship canal route from the Gulf of Mexico up the Withlacoochee River, thence to the Oklawaha, and on to the navigable St. Johns.

Opposition arose before the first shovel bit the soil. The U. S. Geological Survey warned that a canal deep enough for ships would let salt water enter the Floridan Aquifer, ruining the peninsula's water supply. That stopped the work for a time.

By 1958 proponents had a revised plan: a shallower Cross-Florida Barge Canal. Congress authorized it, and the first construction money was appropriated in 1962. It was obvious that the canal would attract too little traffic to pay its cost, but pork barrel projects were not uncommon.

Land was purchased for the right-of-way. Some channels were dug and dredged. Rodman Dam was built, its 9,000-acre impoundment destroying hardwood swamps. Buckman Lock was constructed.

More and more people were outraged by the swath of destruction. The Florida Defenders of the Environment, led by Marjorie Carr, campaigned against the canal in Tallahassee and Washington. About one-third of the canal had been completed when President Nixon ordered the work halted in 1971. In 1976 Florida's governor and cabinet withdrew their support. Congress stopped appropriating money for the project, but not until 1990 was its authorization repealed. Congress then directed that the land purchased for the route become a greenway park across the state.

In the summer of 1992, water was returned to a section of the river that had been dry for more than seventy years. The river and associated marshes which had been bypassed by the J. D. Young canal are coming back to life.

Much restoration remains to be done. It now seems probable that Rodman Dam will be removed. Its impoundment, Lake Ocklawaha, shallow and thick with weeds, has little to commend it. Over coming years, the 110-mile cross-Florida greenway can become a splendid addition to the state's natural areas, a wildlife corridor with foot, horse, and canoe trails.

Blackwater River

The Blackwater River in the Florida Panhandle is a favorite with canoeists for day runs or canoe camping. Of the river's 53 miles, almost

50 are remote and undeveloped. The water is reddish, not black, tannin-stained but pure. The designated canoe trail is through Blackwater River State Forest, ending at Blackwater River State Park.

Atlantic white-cedar, wax myrtle, maple, cypress, and longleaf pines shade the river. A number of rare or endangered plant species are in the understory. Some sections are between high bluffs. Floodplain swamps are along the lower reaches.

Deer, turkey, and bobcat are often seen. Numerous bird species include the Mississippi kite, waterfowl, osprey, shorebirds, and warblers. The rare red-cockaded woodpecker is sometimes sighted.

The current is moderately swift in the upper reaches, requiring some skill. The difficulty rating is "easy" for the middle and lower sections except after heavy rains. Canoes can navigate even at low water.

Several outfitters serve the route with canoes, shuttles, and overnight trips. Camping is permitted at any suitable place, and many who make the run camp on the white sandbars.

Wekiva River

The Wekiva, near Orlando, is an easy paddle through wetlands, hardwood hammocks, pine flatwoods, and sand pine scrub. Wildlife is abundant, human intrusions few. It has been designated an Outstanding Florida Water, a Wild and Scenic River, and an Aquatic Preserve. Land at both ends of the river is now State-owned and more State acquisitions are planned.

The river rises at Wekiwa Springs, in Wekiwa Springs State Park. About 3 1/2 miles downstream, the Little Wekiva River enters. Then it's about 9 miles to the St. Johns River. The flow is largely spring fed, so it can be canoed in periods of drought.

The river was once deep enough for small steamboats. Now there are places where we pole instead of paddling, but this is a minor nuisance compared with the blessed absence of motor craft.

About once a year, often with visitors who are novice canoeists, our outing begins at Katie's Wekiva River Landing and Campground. Canoes are transported to a private put-in on the Little Wekiva. With a stop for lunch on one of the small islands, it's a 5-hour paddle back to the Landing.

Just below the put-in, the Little Wekiva is narrow and winding. Sometimes we push through masses of water hyacinth. Except for a few homes, the bordering land is wild, with good stands of cypress, oak, and pine. Once on the main river the run is more open. Paddlers should save some energy for the last two miles, where the river is wide, the current slow, and we always seem to meet a head wind.

Flowering plants make the run colorful, in season such species as Florida bonamia, spring coralroot, butterfly and other orchids, spider lily, cardinal flower, and swamp honeysuckle.

We always see many birds, including an exceptional number of limpkins, as well as various herons, osprey, wood stork, egrets, sandhill crane, and bald eagle. It's black bear country, but we've never seen one. Always basking alligators and turtles.

Many More Rivers, Streams, and Creeks

Except south of Lake Okeechobee, one is never far from a canoeable river or stream. Delightful canoe runs are on the Alafia, Aucilla, Chipola, Econlockhatchee, Little Manatee, Loxahatchee, Ochlockonee, Peace, Perdido, Sopchoppy, St. Marys, Tomoka, Wacissa, Wakulla, Withlacoochee, and Yellow rivers. We have our favorites, but each year we try an unpublicized stream our canoeing friends have recommended.

Florida has canoe clubs as well as outfitters. Local groups, such as those of the Sierra Club, often announce canoe outings open to non-members.

Tidewater

Some tidewater creeks are called rivers, but the ebb and flow of tides is stronger than stream current. In the hundreds of miles of creeks that wander through coastal marshes, the current is barely perceptible. There's no quicker way to experience isolation. Paddle around the first bend after launching and you may see what the first European explorer saw.

On the Atlantic side of the peninsula, it's easy to find a put-ins on tidal creeks. On much of the Gulf coast, map study and local knowledge are helpful. Some creeks become almost dry at low tides. We once exited from a marsh on the last inch of water.

Canoeing Strategy

It was a weekend canoe outing, and we participants were assembling at the put-in. A van arrived with two young men in heavy jackets and hunting boots. They launched a 12-foot apology for a canoe. Once they climbed in, it had about two inches of freeboard. We saw trouble coming.

"I hope they capsize here!" someone muttered. That was our heart-felt consensus. If they capsized a mile or two into the cruise, we'd have a problem.

The prayer was answered. They swamped and capsized ten feet from shore. We rescued them and their gear and left them behind to dry in the sun.

Once we were rammed by a canoe paddled by two men dressed like bank tellers. They capsized and came up sputtering.

"Damn!" said one. "That's the third time today!"

Many Florida streams are suitable for novice canoeists, but there are requirements. Capsizing is rarely dangerous, since most Florida streams are shallow. Even so, nonswimmers should wear life jackets. Novices shouldn't canoe alone. Novices should read a book about canoeing and practice in quiet water. The most common mishap for novices not in full control of their craft is being carried by the current into brush or a fallen tree and capsizing.

If you've had only limited experience, paddle upstream from the launch site, drift back, then paddle up again, until you feel sure you can control the canoe. Until you're sure, don't commit to a run where the first take-out is several miles downstream.

Inexperienced canoeists should have no serious difficulty on most canoe trails except at flood stage, if — and it's a large "if"— the run has been scouted recently. Reliable outfitters scout their runs often, certainly after every storm. Twice, on runs that hadn't been scouted, we have encountered downed trees and masses of weeds blocking channels. Again and again we had to manhandle our canoe over slippery tree trunks or portage through swamps. To force passage through the weeds, we had to go over the side to push and haul.

An unexpected hazard for the inexperienced is head winds. Twice, on broad reaches, we have seen novice canoeists making little progress against stiff breezes. They needed help.

Such unforeseen delays extend travel time. Possible take-outs may be as much as twenty miles apart. Allow extra time or you might spend a night in the canoe or on a sandbar. Bring insect repellent!

Chapter 18
Along the Seacoast

In the clutter of our souvenir shelves are limpets from the Isle of Jersey, jade from a New Zealand beach, cuttlebone from the Ivory Coast, brain coral from the Virgin Islands, a conch shell from the Florida Keys--dozens of rocks, fossils, shells, corals, bones, and other trophies gathered in days of pleasant beachcombing on the edges of five continents. Once we thought of moving to Arizona, but decided it was too far from the water. One reason we chose Florida is its thousand miles of sandy beaches.

Dr. Stephen Leatherman, of the University of Maryland's Laboratory for Coastal Research, studied and ranked America's best 650 beaches. Five of Florida's made the top 10; the other 5 were Hawaiian. Five more Florida beaches were high-ranking. The beaches Leatherman chose are popular. We prefer those where we can sometimes be alone; they can be found.

Except where broken by inlets, sand beaches extend along the Atlantic Coast from the Georgia line to Key Biscayne. Sand beaches extend along most of the Gulf Coast from Alabama to Ochlockonee Bay, then south from Anclote Keys (north of Tampa) to Cape Romano.

Most outer beaches are on barriers: islands, capes, and former islands now joined to the mainland. Most unaltered beaches are backed by sand dunes. On the Atlantic Coast, sand is constantly being carried southward by ocean current. This is conspicuous where jetties have been built to protect inlets. Sand accumulates on the north side of jetties; on the south side, beaches erode. Water currents along the Gulf coast are weaker, and most changes are effects of storms.

A sand beach is a truly natural area, at least transiently pristine. Tides and visitors leave trash, but storms sweep it away. Beaches are ever-changing, ever renewed.

The best beachcombing is at low tide after a storm. Not all of our trophies are natural. We have acquired a Russian fishing float, an undamaged dairy crate, an excellent knife, fifty feet of good nylon rope, and a bottle with a note inside ("Thanks for letting me out!"). Our shelves are so crowded we now collect only the irresistible.

Dogs are banned from most Florida beaches, which annoys us. True, an ill-mannered dog--or owner--would be a nuisance on a crowded beach, and no dog should be allowed to run where terns nest in the sand. We'd punish owners who don't control their dogs or who fail to kick sand over their droppings. We go to beaches where our black Labrador can run and retrieve in the surf, playing joyously with any children present.

Always just ahead of us are flocks of gulls and shorebirds. If we approach the dunes, terns may try to drive us off by diving at our heads, screeching, pulling up just before striking. Warned, we retreat. Pelicans glide just above wave tops, a phenomenon that inspired the inventor of the hovercraft. Sometimes we see coquinas, tiny colorful clams, vanishing into wet sand as a wave recedes. Once we made coquina chowder; it took about a hundred of them to make two cups. Sand crabs scurry into their holes. Always there is something fresh, new, and different.

When the ice of the latest Ice Age began melting about 13,000 years ago, the sea level was about 350 feet lower than it is today. The North America coast was 20 to 75 miles east of where it is now. Inundation and erosion have continued since then.

Before we moved to Florida, the tip of a barrier island in South Carolina was one of our favorite places for solitary beachcombing. We arrived one spring to find access to the tip barricaded. Only residents and guests of the newly built condominium could pass through the gate.

We aren't really nasty people, but we returned two years later with ungenerous hope. Sure enough, the ocean beach in front of the condo had almost disappeared. High tides were washing at the foundation. We understand the condo has since been abandoned.

Virginia's beaches are eroding at 10 to 25 feet a year, North Carolina's 3 to 5 feet. Florida's ocean beaches, too, are washing away. The sea is moving landward at an average of 1 foot or 2 a year. On one 2-mile section of beach at Cape Canaveral, the sea has been moving inland at 10 to 15 feet a year. Cocoa Beach and Melbourne Beach are retreating as much as 2 feet per year. A single storm tore away 50 feet of beach near Ponce de Leon Inlet.

People who have built beachfront homes, condominiums, and hotels close to the water demand government protection from the sea. Legislators have been all too willing to oblige, subsidizing a succession of remedies that failed. Groins, like jetties, create a scalloped shoreline, trapping sand on one side, increasing erosion on the other. Barriers of riprap or concrete-filled bags are soon undermined. It is not unreasonable for people to expect government help, since government promoted beachfront development by building roads just back of the dunes, and bridges and causeways to barrier islands.

In 1968 the U.S. government offered a deal to communities with areas vulnerable to storms and floods. The National Flood Insurance Program would sell low-cost guaranteed insurance to cover flood damage if the communities would adopt building codes, zoning, and floodplain regulations to keep new development out of flood-prone areas. The insurance was provided, $5 billion in policies covering structures in high-hazard zones along coasts, rivers, and lakes.

The communities, influenced by developers, builders, and property owners, haven't kept their part of the bargain, and the federal government hasn't insisted. The number of homes in high-hazard zones has increased by 40 percent!

Hurricane Andrew wiped out the fund and bankrupted several insurance companies. As usual, taxpayers are paying for the government's laxness.

Three questions are hotly debated. Should property owners be prohibited from building (or rebuilding after damage) in high-hazard areas? Would a prohibition violate their constitutional property rights? If they are permitted to build, should government insure them against subsequent losses?

A few jurisdictions have adopted ordinances requiring that new structures be set back from the beach. Some ordinances provide that a structure within the setback zone cannot be rebuilt if it is destroyed or heavily damaged by storms.

Beachfront property owners argue that government cannot deny them use of their property. The U.S. Supreme Court, in a decision too complex to report here, limited the power of communities to prohibit construction in high-risk areas without compensating the owners. Property owners and developers also insist that government insure them against loss, even if they build in a known high-hazard zone.

Coastal engineers attribute some accelerated beach erosion to the opening and maintenance of new navigable inlets. Inlets trap southward-moving sand. When the St. Lucie inlet was cut, conspicuous erosion occurred for seven miles below the inlet. Developers call for more inlets. Sand washed in from barrier islands once nourished many beaches, but development on islands interrupted this natural process.

Many Florida beachfront hotels are losing their beaches. At high tide there's little space for guests to sunbathe. Hotel owners and local chambers of commerce demand that government rebuild the beaches.

Always willing to challenge nature at the taxpayers' expense, the U.S. Army Corps of Engineers offers a remedy. If nature takes sand away, the Engineers will replace it. They call it "beach nourishment." First they find a source of sand. Then sand is transported by dredging and pumping to a vanishing beach. The nice thing about this remedy is that it must continue forever. Taxpayers in Kansas and Montana are doubtless delighted to contribute to the welfare of Florida resorts.

Beach nourishment sometimes threatens sea turtles. Each year the turtles come ashore to lay and bury their eggs in the sand. Volunteers patrol turtle beaches at night to protect the eggs from poachers and predators. Recently the Corps of Engineers planned to pump sand over one of the principal turtle beaches. This would prevent some nesting and destroy eggs that were laid.

"We'll move the eggs!" they offered, but with no evidence that their nesting skills equal a turtle's.

It's convenient if the sand for beach nourishment comes from nearby, but that can have unexpected consequences. When Pinellas County beaches narrowed, a sandbar west of Egmont Key was dredged to provide sand for nourishment. There followed a startling erosion of the south side of Egmont Key, an island at the mouth of Tampa Bay, home of thousands of gopher tortoises. In one year 30 feet was lost. Just coincidence, said county officials, calling for more sand.

Much offshore sand is too silty to use. It washes away quickly. Delray Beach tried it once, fouling the water and killing fish. Broward County was offered Bahamian sand at $2 million per mile.

The engineers are not yet pumping sand 400 miles from south to north so it can repeat its journey endlessly. Where inlets trap sand, however, dredging and pumping can put it back on its normal route. It's all a losing game. Not only is beach erosion a natural phenomenon, but the sea is rising. Not even the Corps of Engineers can hold back the sea.

Public Beaches

Despite signs and barricades indicating otherwise, beaches are public property below the high-water mark. That doesn't guarantee access, because you can't cross private property to get there, and at high tide there may be no public land.

For example, near Flagler Beach route A1A is just back of the dunes. Private homes are on the landward side of the road, but the dunes between road and beach are also private property and so posted. For several miles there is no public beach access.

Some residential communities have a simple way to keep their beaches free of crowds: They prohibit parking along the coast road. There may be a public beach, but a small parking lot provides effective crowd control.

Florida has more than 160 public beaches. Some, such as Daytona Beach, are intolerably crowded in season, but we can usually find quiet places. Because dunes are damaged by foot traffic, many seaside public parks restrict crossings to boardwalks over the dunes from parking lots. Beach visitors cluster near the ends of these crossings, which may be a mile or more apart. To get away from crowds, you need only walk a while.

Early on a sunny Sunday morning we drove slowly along the coast road north of West Palm Beach. Palm Beach County has been buying undeveloped beachfront tracts. We stopped at one that has parking for two dozen cars, dressing rooms, and toilets. At that hour only one car was parked. We met its occupant on the beach, a surf fisherman. Soon thereafter, north of Juno Beach, we stopped at an unmarked parking area and crossed the dunes. The beach was empty of visitors. A few miles to the north, on Jupiter Island, we came to the Hobe Sound National Wildlife Refuge. This provides the only land access to 4 1/2 miles of wilderness beach between the Refuge and St. Lucie Inlet.

We mention these examples because you might not expect to find unpopulated beaches in populous Palm Beach County. They can be found here and there along both coasts.

The Canaveral National Seashore is Florida's longest wilderness beach, one of the few places where beach backpacking is permitted. One of our favorite beaches for solitary hiking is along St. Joseph Peninsula, near Port St. Joe, on the Panhandle.

You needn't travel far. Just go where–or when–other people don't. As we mentioned earlier, the seasons are reversed along the Panhandle coast. Just after Labor Day the weather is often fine, the sea warm, and beach visitors few.

Swimming

Swimming from Florida's Atlantic beaches is delightful. The surf is usually moderate. Tricky currents occur chiefly around inlets and groins.

Only a few places have submerged rock outcrops, holes, old pilings, or other underwater surprises. Shark attacks are exceedingly rare, although the presence of harmless shark species may cause lifeguards to close a beach. An occasional unwelcome visitor is the Portuguese man-o-war, a complicated jellyfish with a blue float and long tentacles with batteries of stingcells. An encounter can be agonizing.

Gulf beaches are a mixed lot. Some are excellent, among the best, although surf is often mild to absent. In some places you must wade half-way to Mexico to reach shoulder-deep water. Some of the best beaches are on barrier islands.

Because Florida is warmed by the Gulf Stream, winter seawater temperatures on both coasts average in the low 70s, according to the National Climatic Center. "Average" is the key word; the water is sometimes cooler. The water temperature in Tampa Bay is occasionally in the low 60s.

We swim twice daily, all year, in an unheated pool. In winter, water temperature drops to the low 60s. "Your blood will thin," say Florida friends who like their water hot. It hasn't yet. On the coast, we see children playing happily in the surf while their parents huddle in sweaters.

BRENDA DEAL BAKER
4-6-92

The Dunes

Dunes are formed of wind-blown sand. Their sizes and shapes depend on the direction and velocity of the prevailing wind, the width and slope of the beach, and the presence of salt-tolerant plants such as sea oats. Florida's Atlantic beaches face the prevailing easterlies, which promotes dune formation.

On windy days, you can make a heap of sand and watch the process. On the windward side, sand grains are propelled up the surface of the slope. At the crest they appear as a spray, then drop on the lee side. As sand is transported up one side of the heap and deposited on the other, the heap migrates. Thus do the dunes. At the Oregon Dunes on the Pacific Coast, migrating dunes are burying a forest and intruding on the highway. At the Great Sand Dunes National Monument in Colorado, dunes several hundred feet high have moved across a creek and into a forest. (We're told that when huge dunes invaded a Venezuelan town, the enterprising residents offered dromedary rides to tourists.)

"Let's pick up some money," a friend said after a strong wind had swept a popular beach. As we strolled, he saw a penny perched on a tiny sand hill. Later he found a dime. The wind had blown sand from around but not under them.

Dunes are stabilized by plants that grow in sand. The plants intercept, slow, and stop the moving sand, which accumulates and buries them. Burial would kill most plants, but the dunebuilders have unique qualities: They can take root in sand, tolerate salt, and extend their growth upward as sand gathers around them.

The chief dunebuilder is the sea oat. As sand accumulates around the oats, they send out higher and higher layers of roots. The plants grow upward, intercepting more and more sand. Because sea oats are ornamental, they were often harvested for sale to florists. Now sea oats are protected by law in all eastern states. Railroad vines hold sand by spreading along the surface. Several other species survive burial and moderate storm damage by adaptations of their seeds.

"Live" dunes are those closest to the sea, the frontal dunes, where sand blown from the open beach accumulates. Behind the frontal dunes may be older stabilized dunes, now well covered by vegetation. When people cross these dunes, they trample and kill this vegetation. A path becomes a notch. Wind widens and deeps the notch, which becomes a "blowout." Dune buggies racing over the old dunes do even greater damage. Tropical storms and hurricanes often obliterate dunes and their colonizing plants. Panhandle dunes are still rebuilding after hurricanes in 1979 and the 1980s.

Dunebuilding can be promoted. One of the simplest methods is bull-dozing sand to form a low dune and erecting snow fence where a foredune had been. Snow fence traps sand more rapidly than vegetation. ("What's snow fence?" a Florida native asks. Light slats wired together.) As the first snow fence is buried, another is erected above it. Sea oats are often planted.

Back of the Dunes

Foredunes shelter what lies behind them from wind and salt. Often what lies behind are old stabilized dunes, maritime forest, and salt marsh. Here may be found a variety of grasses and wildflowers; wax myrtle, oak, and palmetto scrub. Maritime forests have live oak, redbay, magnolia, and sabal palm.

One good place to see this zonation easily is the Blowing Rocks Preserve of The Nature Conservancy, where exotic species have been eliminated and native species labeled. But at countless places along the coast you can do what almost none of the other beachgoers do: cross the outer dunes and see what's behind them.

Many of Florida's Atlantic beaches are on barrier islands separated from the mainland by open water. Along most of the Atlantic side, this is the route of the Intracoastal Waterway: the Tolomato, Matansas, Halifax, and Indian rivers. Sections of the Waterway are heavily developed, and boat traffic is considerable. On a morning's cruise we have encountered shrimp trawlers, a Chinese junk, barges under tow, million-dollar yachts, and modest jon boats. Other sections are wonderfully wild, with countless meandering tidal creeks and lagoons to explore.

Dredge and Fill

Looking down from a plane flying into Tampa or Miami, you will see an artificial coast. Housing developments crowd every square inch of mainland. Dead-end canals with many branches provide boat channels for houses built on the fill from dredging. Causeways extend to artificial islands.

When Florida became a state, it was given title to all intertidal and submerged lands, including those along the coast. To encourage development, the State gave away or sold most of the coastal land. A law adopted in 1856 gave waterfront owners and developers the right to extend their land by filling submerged areas as far out as the edge of navigation. It was a hundred years before reason prevailed. Then the legislature reaffirmed State ownership of submerged lands, prohibited further sales, and required permits for all future dredge-and-fill projects. That sounded just fine, but for years neither the U.S. Army Corps of Engineers nor the responsible State agencies did much more than rubber-stamp requests for permits.

Serious regulation began in 1967, when the Florida legislature adopted the Randall Act. It made dredge-and-fill permits subject to environmental impact study. If fish or other wildlife would be adversely affected, permits might be denied. This was significant progress, but developers still covet real or artificial waterfront.

Offshore

Oil companies want to drill for oil off the Florida coast. Time and again, federal government officials have been on the verge of letting them. For years, Florida's governors, legislators, businessmen, and citizens have resisted successfully.

Their objections to drilling have stressed the risk of oil spills that could wash up on beaches and ruin the tourist trade. Having seen the oil coasts of Louisiana and Texas, we can testify that, if oil is discovered, the impact on coastal Florida may be far more extensive, devastating, and permanent than an occasional spill.

To support offshore drilling and production platforms, the oil industry requires harbors and estuaries where drill rigs and platforms are assembled. Along miles of waterfront are shipyards, drydocks, refueling docks, outfitting yards, berths and moorings for tugs, barges, tankers, supply ships, floating cranes, and other craft.

For miles along the oil coast and extending inland are tank farms, pumping stations, steelyards, helicopter services, suppliers of drilling lubricants and tools, and other oil-related establishments. Refineries, too. Oil is a 24-hour operation. We could have driven at night without headlights, so brightly lit are these facilities.

It's a boom-town setting. Workers find whatever housing they can, in crowded mobile home and trailer camps. Those employed on the platforms typically work one week on, one off. Enterprises spring up to provide entertainment for workers off duty.

Pipelines radiate inland from the coast. Legislatures usually give pipeline companies power of eminent domain. The pipelines slash across public waterways, wetlands, pastures, and farms. Even when buried, the pipelines are not forgettable; you can see, along each route, markers, vents, expansion loops, and pumping stations.

Whatever was on the Louisiana-Texas coast before has been displaced.

Should resistance to drilling falter, our sun coast could become another oil coast.

Saltwater Cruising

Florida is the yachtsman's paradise. Florida has more and bigger seagoing craft and more marinas than any other state. Million-dollar yachts seem almost as common as sand fleas.

We have friends among the many couples who retire and try full-time living aboard. They may find a sheltered cove on a Caribbean island and spend their winters sunning and scuba diving. Recently friends stopped off for a visit as they cruised homeward from Louisiana to Maryland. We see 50-foot yachts being hauled south on commercial trailers in the fall, back north in the spring. Larger yachts are shuttled seasonally up and down the Intracoastal Waterway by hired captains.

You needn't own a boat to join the boating clan. Power boats can be rented by the day at marinas on both coasts. Sailing and yachting magazines advertise bare-boat charters.

We admire and sometimes envy the offshore boaters. Perhaps we'll join them some day. For now, we prefer to be close to the nature of Florida.

Chapter 19
The Everglades

There was nothing like it elsewhere in the world. Water from the north funneled into huge, shallow Lake Okeechobee. The lake overflowed in the rainy season. Beyond, flat land tilted imperceptibly to the south. Flood- and rainwaters spread over this land in a sheet, moving too slowly to cut channels. A unique ecosystem developed on this moist plain, a river of grass, an endless expanse of tall sawgrass with scattered tree islands. Only as the sheet approached Florida Bay did open water appear: Whitewater Bay, shallow lakes, and countless tidal creeks and rivers with innumerable mangrove islands.

The assembly of wild creatures was as unique as their habitat: deer, panther, bobcat, black bear, porpoise, manatee, foxes, opossum, squirrels, raccoon, mink, weasel, skunks, muskrat, otter, shrews, bats, mice, alligator, crocodile, lizards, a dozen species of frogs and toads, fifteen species of tortoises and turtles, two dozen species of snakes, more dozens of fish and shellfish.

Birds! Almost 350 species, great clouds of spectacular birds, resident and migratory. White and brown pelicans, bald eagle, osprey, roseate spoonbill, black skimmer, swallow-tailed and snail kites; great blue, little blue, tricolored, and green-backed herons; black- and yellow-crowned night-herons, white and glossy ibises, wood stork, and hundreds more.

The web of life was complex, its elements interdependent. As every-

165

where, it was supported by photosynthesis of green plants, from micro-scopic algae to sawgrass to tall palms. Millennia of growth and decay had produced a deep layer of peat under the sawgrass.

"Drain the everglades!" cried developers, promoters, adventurers, and speculators. "Drain the everglades" was a campaign theme of gover-nors and legislators. When Flagler's railroad opened the Miami region to explosive growth, the cries became insistent.

Drainage would bare fertile peat for cultivation. Drainage and dikes would divert floods from burgeoning towns, cities, and resorts. Early drainage ventures failed, but the lure was irresistible. Serious disruption of the great natural system began in the early 1900s. Once the engineers were on the loose, the draglines and bulldozers couldn't be stopped.

"Everglades" is not synonymous with "Everglades National Park." There was no Park then, nothing to check the draglines or the whole-sale slaughter of birds by plume and market hunters.

Conservationists urged Congress to save this vast natural wonder, but developers had greater influence. Not until 1934 did Congress au-thorize the Secretary of the Interior to acquire over 2 million acres of the everglades for a park, and then it gave him no money to do so. Florida's legislature provided the first land purchase money in 1946. Although Congress "established" the Park in 1947, federal funds weren't appropriated until 1958. In the next several years, 1.4 million acres, the southernmost part of the 7 million acre everglades, finally became a National Park. Its death certificate may have been written before it was born. Drawing a boundary-line did nothing to assure the Park of the water on which it depends.

The Park boundaries include Florida Bay and its numerous islands and keys, extensive mangrove swamps, a part of the Big Cypress, and the Ten Thousand Islands. The Park's heart is in the everglades, how-ever, and the heart has been gravely damaged.

The massive works that destroyed the upper everglades can be seen by astronauts without visual aids. On the east, spreading metropolitan development stops as if it had met a barricade. From Lake Okeechobee to the Park boundary, the original everglades have been carved into great polygons by dikes, canals, and roads.

The marshlands north and west of Lake Okeechobee have been drained, chiefly for cattle and dairy ranches. Their wastes drain into the lake. South of the lake, 700,000 acres have been drained for agriculture, chiefly sugarcane production. Phosphorus and other nutrients from here drain southward into the wetlands.

The everglades south of the lake are penned by canals and dikes into three huge blocks euphemistically called "conservation areas." The storage and diversion of water is controlled by massive floodgates and pumping stations. Water flows where and when the operators decide.

The chief operator of the ecosystem, the South Florida Water Management District, has the unhappy task of trying to reconcile the irreconcilable. Farmers want water for irrigation, but in wet weather they backpump excess fertilizer-bearing water into the lake. The metropolitan areas on the east must be protected from floods, but they also depend on the underground aquifer for water, and decisions of the Water Management District affect aquifer recharge. Already some wells along the coast have been abandoned because of salt water intrusion.

For years powerful interests dictated the water regime. When floods threatened, excess water was dumped into the National Park. When the weather was dry, the Park was cut off. When Congress ordered that the Park be assured of water, the District delivered water when it thought best, not on the schedule the Park ecosystem required.

The plants and animals of the everglades are adapted to natural hydroperiods, seasonal alternations of wet and dry. For some species, disruption of hydroperiods was a death sentence. Cattails were replacing sawgrass. When the flow of fresh water was curtailed, salt water intruded deeper into the Park, killing plants that could not tolerate saltiness. Too much water at the wrong time drowned the eggs of alligators and apple snails. Wildlife populations declined alarmingly. The disaster has gradually wiped out 95 percent of the herons and egrets.

Such a catastrophe would be frightening anywhere. Why was it allowed to happen in a unique National Park?

Who spoke for the Park? As recently as 1948 the only Park road was unpaved and often muddy. In that year only 7,500 visitors came. Thereafter, with good roads, visitor centers, waysides such as the Anhinga Trail, campgrounds, guided tours, cruises, and other inducements, visitors came by the millions. The Park Superintendent and Rangers have been outspoken about degradation of the Park. Visitors have become a constituency.

Who spoke for the Park? Above all, Marjory Stoneman Douglas, at first a lone crusader, then with a growing army of support as she spoke, wrote, testified, accused, pleaded, and demanded. She marshaled and presented evidence. She made it popular for Florida governors to assert leadership in efforts to save the National Park. Now 102 years old, she is still active. Her army is now the Everglades Coalition, a powerful alliance of citizen organizations.

What once seemed just a matter of sharing water has become more and more complex. The Everglades National Park ecosystem is being damaged by pollution of the water allocated to the Park.

It has been invaded by exotic plants. Alarming concentrations of mercury are found in wildlife; a primary source seems to be exposed peat, the route of the mercury's travel less certain.

The Everglades National Park has repeatedly been "saved" in press conferences. In 1988 the federal government sued the State of Florida for failing to protect the Park from polluted farm runoff. The State's lawyers fought back. In 1990 Governor Martinez boasted that he had negotiated a deal with the sugar companies to create a 76,000-acre area where sugar's waste water would be treated before discharge. It didn't happen, and the lawsuit continued. When Lawton Chiles became Florida's governor in 1991, he ordered a halt to Florida's defense against the suit and forced a settlement. The sugar companies protested that paying for the cleanup would put them out of business. They filed more than thirty lawsuits to limit their responsibility.

In fact, the sugar industry has long been the beneficiary of government subsidies and import quotas which cost consumers and commercial sugar users $1.4 billion a year, according to the General Accounting Office. GAO estimated that $560 million a year go to a relatively few companies. Farms representing only 1 percent of the country's sugar production received 42 percent of the benefits.

"They should pay for the cleanup in proportion to the damage they have caused," said Tom Weis of Clean Water Action, a citizen group. But some officials of the South Florida Water Management District said the sugar industry isn't entirely to blame; they pointed the finger at the U.S. Army Corps of Engineers, builders of the water-management system.

A federal judge ruled against the sugar companies but ordered all parties to work out their differences. Governor Chiles convened a well-publicized Everglades Summit. This produced an agreement with the sugar industry that called for a 34,700-acre treatment area, less than half of the Martinez scheme. It made headlines, but the deal was toothless and unfunded.

Still hanging over the failed deal was the threat of action by the federal court. In July 1993, President Clinton's Secretary of the Interior, Bruce Babbitt, called a press conference to proclaim salvation. Now the taxpayers, not the sugar industry, would pay the lion's share of the cost of cleaning sugar's mess, and the 1997 deadline fixed by the earlier "agreement" was put off by five years or more.

Charles Lee, senior vice-president of the Florida Audubon Society was disgusted:

It does not seem to make a lot of difference whether the

politician is a Bob Martinez, a Lawton Chiles, a Bob Graham, a George Bush, a Bruce Babbitt, or a Bill Clinton . . . the reality is the same. Sugar's mess in the Everglades is still something political figures just have press conferences about. . . . The courage, candor, and moral strength necessary to look across the table into the eyes of the sugar industry lobbyists and tell them they are going to have to significantly change their ways isn't there.

George M. Barley, Jr., columnist for the *Tampa Tribune*, wrote[10]:

> Now, government has given up. Declaring a new era of friendship with the sugar industry, federal officials suspended the Everglades litigation and agreed to limited sugar growers' initial liability for Everglades cleanup. . . . The appalling die-off of Everglades wetlands and wildlife and Florida Bay sealife continues. . . . The sugar growers are still guaranteed astounding subsidies and profits.

It is at least technically possible to clean the water flowing from the sugar industry's lands. Almost 3,800 acres of former sugarcane land have been flooded and quickly became a marsh. Herons, alligators, and other wildlife soon returned, along with marshland plants. But even 35,000 acres might prove insufficient.

The quantity of water supplied to Everglades National Park is an even less tractable problem. Miami's water supply can't be cut off to restore water to the Park. Could the South Florida Water Management District refuse additional water permits, thus halting growth in southeast Florida? Environmentalists shudder at the idea of more engineering "solutions," piling on more vast water control works.

Only recently has much attention been given to Florida Bay, most of which lies within Park boundaries. Fishermen sounded the alarm several years ago when clear water turned green and shrimp catches plummeted. Fishermen call it the "dead zone." The cause was no mystery. The flow of fresh water through the everglades to the Bay had been reduced by 90 percent. Lack of rain plus evaporation in hot weather had made Bay water twice as salty as seawater. Sea grasses died and decayed, darkening the water, driving fish away.

Fishermen had good reason for concern. Commercial and recreational fishing in the Bay has generated more than $500 million per year. Con-

[10]August 18, 1993.

servationists had reason, too: a large share of the populations of roseate spoonbill, great white heron, and American crocodile depend on the Bay, as does a huge population of wintering shorebirds.

In October 1992 a gigantic algal bloom appeared near the dead zone. It also was fed by nutrients from dead sea grasses. It devastated 300 square miles of the Bay. Where it passed, sponges and sea grasses died. "There's not a sponge left in Everglades National Park," said Tom Mathews, State biologist. The devastated area included Florida's principal lobster nursery. Later in 1992 the bloom, still covering 80 square miles, drifted from the bay toward the chain of living coral reefs. The sickness of the Bay can't be cured unless the everglades are saved.

In 1993 Hurricane Andrew ripped through the Park, doing great damage to visitor facilities. Many hurricanes have swept through the everglades in past centuries, and its natural systems have quickly recovered. This time, however, the ecosystem was weakened and vulnerable. The storm promoted growth of invading exotic vines and trees. The long-term effects aren't yet known.

Is a Visit Still Worthwhile?

Emphatically yes! Just as we deplore smog over the Grand Canyon, commercialization of Yosemite and Glacier National Parks, and helicopters flying low over the Badlands, we are sad to see five great egrets where once there were a hundred. But despite its wounds, the Everglades is still a great park with the largest Wilderness Area in any National Park south of Alaska.

A Wilderness Waterway, 99 miles of creeks, rivers, and open bays, extends from Flamingo to Everglades City, a week's trip by canoe. Camping is limited to a few beaches and "chickees," 12-foot-square platforms, about the only places one can step out of a boat. Bring your own water. Gnats and mosquitoes are fierce, intolerable in summer. October-May is the only reasonable season. Friends who have made the trip say they're glad they did — but never again! Small outboard craft can travel the Waterway, but one should expect such hazards as downed trees, snags, and oyster bars.

Many visitors come to the Park just for the day. They tour the visitor center, walk the Anhinga Trail, stop at a few other waysides, park at Flamingo, and go home. They have seen about 1 percent of what the Park offers. Other entrances are at Shark Valley on US 41 and at Everglades City.

Plan your visit! Write for information before you go. When you write, specify your interests. Possibilities include camping and primitive camping; canoeing and canoe camping; hiking (although the longest trail is only 14 miles); sightseeing cruises and backcountry tram rides; boating and cruising; houseboating; and fishing.

The Park is open all year. Most visitors come between December 15 and April 15, when the weather is best. Campgrounds and the motel at Flamingo are often full then, but hurricane-damaged commercial camps and motels at Homestead, near the entrance, are being rebuilt.

Summer is the rainy season. Downpours are frequently heavy but seldom last all day. We were there last year in the first week of October, a good time to avoid crowds. The campground at Flamingo was almost empty. It rained one afternoon. Especially in summer, bring a good repellent!

To see and understand the upper everglades, visit the Arthur R. Marshall Loxahatchee National Wildlife Refuge, one of the three large water conservation areas, west of West Palm Beach. It has an excellent visitor center and trails, with good birding.

Chapter 20

Keys, Reefs, and Islands

In most of Latin America the name is *cayo*: "A low island or reef of sand or coral." In Belize, it's *caye*. In Florida, we call our coral islands "keys."

When people say "Florida Keys," they usually mean the chain of islands linked by the Overseas Highway from Key Largo to Key West. These Keys separate the Straits of Florida on the south from the Gulf of Mexico and Florida Bay on the north. About a hundred other keys are scattered over Florida Bay within the boundaries of Everglades National Park. Several dozen more are in the Gulf of Mexico, some included in the Florida Keys National Wildlife Refuge, others in a cluster long known as the Dry Tortugas.

The Florida Keys parallel the edge of the continental shelf. The corals of the keys, formed under the sea, are fossilized. A living tropical coral reef 200 miles long lies at the bottom of a narrow strip of shallow sea between the Florida Keys and the shelf's edge.

Shallow-water tropical corals live and grow only in warm seas. The corals of the keys built reefs for millions of years. About 15 million years ago sea temperature and sea level began to decline. The range of the reef corals shifted southward. The corals now incorporated in the keys died. Not until about 7,000 years ago was the sea again warm enough here for tropical reef building to resume.

In the ancient past, tropical conditions extended well north of the keys. Submerged fossil reefs occur along the Florida peninsula, but those coastal waters are now too cool for living tropical corals.

To call the Keys "coral islands" is to over-simplify. Underlying them are several thousand feet of limestone, the consolidated remains of ancient sea creatures large and small. The layer of fossil corals above this floor is generally less than 200 feet thick. Incorporated in the layer are remains of plants and animals that lived and died among the corals or that were deposited here.[11]

Much has happened since the reefs died. The keys have been exposed, submerged, and exposed again, washed by currents and tides, torn by hurricanes. When they were submerged, marine plants grew on the dead coral and sea creatures found shelter in its crevices. When the keys rose, terrestrial plants colonized and soil formation began. Shallows became marshes.

Most places on the Florida Keys are less than four feet above high tide. The highest point, on Windley Key, is 18 feet above. Most are — or were — surrounded by mangrove swamps. Few have natural sand beaches.

The history of the Florida Keys is fascinating, colorful, dramatic, romantic, tragic, and dismaying. Since completion of the Overseas Highway, the Keys have been overwhelmed by development until only patches of natural green remain, threatened remnants of a unique ecosystem. Water must be piped in from the mainland. Wastes have no place to go but the sea.

Driving the Overseas Highway with its long bridges and causeways across open water is an adventure. On the Keys, long lines of motels, shops, restaurants, marinas, and condos are broken by a few State Parks.

The best reason to visit the Keys, in our view, is to see Lignumvitae Key. It's what the Florida Keys used to be, a lush assemblage of tropical and subtropical plants. You can get there only by private boat or tour boat. [12]

Other keys scattered over Florida Bay and the Gulf of Mexico

---

[11] Shakespeare wrote, "Full fathom five thy father lies;/ Of his bones are coral made." In fact, modern reconstructive surgeons are using coral as a substitute for bone. "Certain species of coral have almost an identical configuration to bone, with numerous channels that are interconnected," says Dr. Timothy Miller at the Los Angeles Medical Center.

[12] Tour boat from Indian Key Fill, Thursday through Monday. For schedule call (305) 664-4815. Private boats may dock (except Tuesday and Wednesday), but visitors must wait in the dock area for a guided walk.

are uninhabited, many girded by impenetrable mangroves. In the past few years, many mangroves have appeared to be dying because of higher water temperatures and saltiness in the Bay.

The Marquesas and Dry Tortugas are popular with scuba divers and birders. Visitors go ashore on Garden Key to see Fort Jefferson, an extraordinary National Monument occupying most of the island.

The Living Reefs

From Sharm esh Sheikh, then occupied by Israel, we took a glass-bottom boat over the wonderful coral gardens of the Red Sea and saw why divers come there from around the world. We have snorkeled over reefs of the Virgin and the Hawaiian islands. Oddly, we have yet to see the reefs off our own Keys. On two occasions when we might have, seas were choppy and the water turbid. Our urge to see them is dampened by the crowds they attract, more than a million a year.

Coral is formed as various tiny animals, chiefly polyps, extract carbonate of lime from seawater and store it in their tissues. The polyps are members of a large group that includes sponges, sea anemones, sea fans, and jellyfish. Of the many species of coral-building polyps, not all are tropical. Some grow in cooler coastal waters more than half a mile deep. Polyps are carnivores, stinging, capturing, and ingesting animals of the plankton. Fixed in place, the polyps depend on food brought to them by currents.

These polyp species are distinguished by colonialism and the characteristic structures they build. Hard corals include *brain, elkhorn, staghorn, mushroom,* and *rose;* others are known only by their Latin names. Soft corals include sea fans and sea plumes.

The specimens people gather on beaches are mostly bleached white, but a few have red spots. Living reef corals are made colorful by symbiotic algae living in the polyps, and some fluoresce brightly under ultraviolet light. The red corals of the Mediterranean and black corals of the Red Sea have been prized for jewelry and other ornamentation. Red and black corals have also been collected in the Hawaiian Islands.

Charles Darwin hypothesized that the coral atolls of the Pacific formed as fringing reefs around islands. The islands sank. The reefs grew upward, becoming a barrier and eventually an atoll. It's still the accepted theory.

Corals reproduce asexually by budding and sexually by production and fertilization of eggs. The eggs become free-swimming larvae that soon--if lucky--attach themselves permanently to hard surfaces. Growth rates differ from species to species and according to the qualities of the environment. Some massive corals, such as the large brain corals, may add just a fraction of an inch a year to their diameters; some branching species may extend by several inches in a year. Living polyps occur only on the growing surfaces.

Coral reefs are bustling communities. Divers are fascinated by the colorful fishes that inhabit the reefs, by the waving of sea fans and the tentacles of anemones. Like almost all communities, its base is the photosynthesis of green plants. The sea grasses on the floor around the reefs are highly productive. So are the single-cell plants that thrive within the tissues of the polyps and others that float free. This ample food supply supports countless herbivores and carnivores, predators and prey: worms, sea cucumbers, crabs, lobsters, shrimps, starfish, shellfish, and more, from microscopic to large. The Florida reefs harbor more than 150 species of tropical fishes. The reefs also support predators of the land and air.

Doomsday for our coral reefs has already been announced. Our only living barrier reef may be near death by the end of the present decade. Frightful damage has been inflicted, and more occurs each year.

It began on the Keys, where development has been a juggernaut. Wherever resorts and homes were built, mangroves were ripped away and waterfronts "improved" by dredging and filling. Tons of coral were dredged and used as fill. That was illegal, but it wasn't stopped. Most of the Keys' wildlife habitat has been destroyed; the habitat of the endangered Key deer becomes less habitable each year.

With the soil-holding mangroves gone, silt made the reef waters increasingly turbid. When dredge-and-fill activity was at its peak, nearby coral growth virtually ceased. The mangroves had been nurseries for many marine species, which now declined.

The Keys are bathed in sewage. Residential sewage is treated, but the effluent is nutrient rich. Some is pumped underground, only to seep into the sea. The nutrients cause algae blooms, darkening the water and slowing photosynthesis. Much of the sewage from the flotillas of boats, including moored houseboats, is dumped raw, although this is gradually being brought under control by requiring live-aboard boats to have sewage holding tanks which can be pumped into onshore sewage lines.

Therefore, high concentrations of coliform bacteria occur in the water around the Keys. Pesticides used on lawns and gardens and to kill mosquitoes also enter the sea, and chemicals used to preserve wharf pilings add to the brew.

Assaulted from the land, the coral reef is also attacked from the sea. Among the worst attackers are the very people who come to enjoy its beauty. The damage begins as boats roar out to the reefs, propellers stirring silt clouds, killing sea grasses in the shallows. Small power boats leave traces of oil and gasoline. Larger ones often pump oily water from bilges. Antifouling paints leach. Anchors that are dropped improperly tear at the corals.

Wherever a diver's fins or hands touch living coral, polyps die. Accidentally or purposely, divers break off sections of coral. Although it is now illegal, some divers still collect coral specimens, and illegal commercial collecting hasn't stopped.

As if this were not enough, off-course ships have grounded on reefs, grinding through the corals as they strike and as they are pulled off.

In 1990 a dredging company was fined $1 million for damaging 2.2 acres of coral reef. The following year two companies paid $200,000 for dragging a chain across a reef while towing a dredge.

Sewage and garbage from passing ships is dumped. In 1991 a passenger on the cruise ship Royal Princess videotaped an employee jettisoning twenty large bags. The Coast Guard investigated. The cruise line agreed to pay a $500,000 fine.

To complete this tale of woe, scientists fear the overheated and overly salty water of Florida Bay is flowing to some of the living reefs, whose organisms can't withstand such a change.

Can the Reefs Be Saved?

The reefs are doomed if the developers and politicians of Monroe County continue to have their way. They greet proposed restrictions with screeches of "property rights!" The reefs must be saved from the wastes of passing ships and from captains steering too close to shore. They must be saved from commercial and hobbyist coral collectors. And they must be saved from those who admire them most.

The John Pennekamp Coral Reef State Park, established in 1959, was America's first underwater park. Scuba diving was not yet popular, and no one foresaw the reef would attract so many people. The Pennekamp experience was instructive. Biscayne National Park, which includes another large portion of the reef, was planned for preservation. It has no facility for boat launching. A single concessioner operates two tour boats that carry sightseers and divers to the reefs. Private boats visiting the islands and reefs are monitored to assure compliance with safety and resource protection regulations. Pennekamp is tightening its controls. Mooring buoys have been provided, and boats may no longer drop anchors on the reefs.

The Keys and reef do have defenders. The National Audubon Society has maintained a presence here since 1939, its scientists studying and calling attention to the degradation. The Nature Conservancy opened its Keys office in 1987 as a base for developing management plans. One of its research workers is studying the underwater behavior of divers. The Wilderness Society has added its support and influence.

In 1991 Congress established the Florida Keys National Marine Sanctuary, 2,600 nautical square miles on both sides of the Keys, extending from Key Biscayne to the Dry Tortugas. This gives the federal government greater authority to regulate what is happening inside the Sanctuary. The National Oceanic and Atmospheric Administration is preparing a management plan, which was to be ready in 1993. Ships are now forbidden to pass near the reefs, and the penalty for running aground on a reef is severe. Ships are also forbidden to throw wastes overboard, but enforcement is next to impossible. Boats with toilets may be required to have holding tanks if they are operated near the reefs.

NOAA was not given authority over the county, state, and federal agencies that have overlapping and conflicting policies and jurisdictions. These agencies have powers they could have exercised long ago to manage growth on the Keys and protect the reef, but the reef brings hundreds of millions of dollars to the Keys, and money buys political power.

The Florida legislature acted in 1991, adopting the broad Pollution Discharge and Prevention Act. It includes a scale of penalties. For example:

- $10 for each square foot of coral reef impacted
- $1 per square foot for damage to mangroves, seagrass, or beach
- $10,000 for each endangered animal

A 500-gallon diesel oil spill that damaged 3 acres of seagrass could cost the offender $134,000, plus his legal fees.

Ten Thousand Islands and More

We come at last to a part of Florida where almost nothing seems to be happening and where much has happened for the better. Look at a good map, such as those in the DeLorme atlas[13].

From Naples, look southward along the coast. Notice the only large intrusion into the coastal wilderness: Marco Island. Local citizens--a different breed from those of Monroe County--were appalled when devel-

[13]The *Florida Atlas and Gazetteer* (Freeport, ME: DeLorme Mapping, 1989) has 103 maps on the scale of 1 inch = 2.3 miles.

opers began maneuvers around the mangrove islands. They wanted their coast kept the way it was, not like Florida's east coast. They organized to block development of Marco Island–and lost. Roads were built through the swamps and across creeks and estuary. Dredging and filling made building lots. Marco Island was lost, but more has been saved. The citizens have drawn a line: No more!

Organized as the Collier County Conservancy, they succeeded in blocking a road that would have opened the Rookery Bay region to development. With allies such as the Conservation Foundation, National Audubon Society, and The Nature Conservancy, they demonstrated the ecological importance of Rookery Bay and raised money to buy the critically strategic land around it for the Rookery Bay Aquatic Preserve. At their instigation the complex was designated a National Estuarine Sanctuary. Local support also maintains the Briggs Memorial Nature Center, accessible from SR 951. It's worth a visit.

Beyond Marco to the south and east is mostly wilderness, including Collier Seminole State Park and the Cape Romano Ten Thousand Islands Aquatic Preserve. Other islands of the Ten Thousand Islands lie within the boundary of Everglades National Park.

We first saw this area forty years ago when we turned south from US 41 past Everglades City to the island town of Chokoloskee. It was a little fish camp then. We had lunch at the ramshackle diner and listened. Some famous people came here regularly to wear old clothes and fish with local guides, we heard. Local residents seemed to enjoy their reputation for lawlessness: rumrunning during Prohibition, alligator poaching in the 1950s and 1960s. Today it's said to be drug trafficking. They still enjoy telling the stories, true or not.

We visited again before Hurricane Andrew and parked our motor home at the water's edge in a commercial campground. The town is bigger now. More boats are in slips. There are more places to sleep and eat. Wells on the island yield only salt water, so drinking water is trucked in.

From Rookery Bay through the National Park, the coastal region is predominantly mangrove swamp. Access is almost entirely by water. Boat tours are available at the National Park's Gulf Coast Ranger Station at Everglades City and at Collier Seminole State Park. Boats can be rented or launched at Everglades City, Chokoloskee, and Collier Seminole. The west end of the Wilderness Waterway is here.

The Ten Thousand Islands lie west of Chokoloskee. These are mangrove islands: red mangroves in the water, black and white mangroves on shore, buttonwood slightly higher. Hammocks grow on islands with patches of higher ground. The islands are peaceful sanctuaries, nesting and feeding grounds for countless birds, including snail kite, anhinga, white-crowned pigeon, mangrove cuckoo, wood stork. Magnificent frigate birds soar above. At low tide, fiddler and hermit crabs scurry on mud flats dotted with worm castings. The shallow waters around the islands teem with marine life: oysters, crabs, shrimp, lobsters, and fishes. Fishing is the main attraction for many visitors to the Ten Thousand Islands--snook, snapper, and more. We photographed an osprey with a sheepshead in his talons.

A few campsites are available, by permit, in the National Park portion of the islands.

Cruising the Ten Thousand Islands is delightful, if one is reasonably prudent. Even with chart and compass, it's possible to get lost. The Park has marked some routes. (Charts dated before Hurricane Andrew should be discarded; the channels have changed.) If you have experienced this mangrove wilderness even once, just looking at a map of it is refreshing.

Hurricane Andrew left a swath of destruction, but mangroves recover after hurricanes. The greater threat is that the salinity of Florida Bay has increased because the flow of fresh water to and through the everglades has been reduced. Red mangroves can tolerate about 35 parts of salt per 1,000 of water. Some samples from the Bay show twice that concentration. National Park scientists report a gradual die-off of the island mangroves. The Bay's complex of living things depends on them.

Conservation campaigns begin slowly. A few scientists, or fishermen, or local residents see what's happening and try to sound the alarm. No one seems interested. Government officials say it isn't so. The break may be a newspaper expose or a feature article in some national magazine. Perhaps a congressional committee holds hearings and calls witnesses. We're reading more about the keys, reefs, and islands today. Perhaps they can be saved.

Chapter 21
The Gulf of Mexico

───

S lip space is at a premium in the countless marinas along Florida's Gulf coast. The Gulf waters are inviting for craft from jon boats and sailing dinghies to multimillion-dollar yachts. For fishermen, sailors, and swimmers, Florida's Gulf coast has been one of America's favorite playgrounds. The coast has provided great feeding, resting, and nesting grounds for resident and migratory birds.

Florida shares the natural resources of this 582,000-square-mile sea with Alabama, Mississippi, Louisiana, Texas, Mexico, and Cuba. More than 100 million people live along the U.S. Gulf coast. Half of our nation's coastal wetlands are along the Gulf. It is crucial habitat for more than 500 species of migratory birds. Two-fifths of the nation's fish and shellfish harvest comes from here.

Until recently, its condition seemed to be no one's concern, not even that of the Environmental Protection Administration. Yet quantities of industrial waste, sewage, and storm water were discharged daily into the Gulf. More than 2 million tons of solid waste were dumped into the Gulf each year.

Shrimpers and other fishermen were among the first to recognize a disaster in the making. Closures of oyster and clam beds, for health reasons, became increasingly common. The rapid development of a 3,000-square-mile "dead zone" off the Louisiana coast was frightening. Citizens became vocal about trash-littered beaches, oil spills from offshore wells, and destruction of marshes.

The Environmental Protection Administration unwittingly brought matters to a head. Some EPA officials thought it a good idea to dispose of hazardous wastes by incineration on a ship anchored in the Gulf. They held a public hearing in Brownsville, Texas, in 1988. More than 6,000 residents came to protest. The incineration plan was scuttled, but now the citizens were in full cry. Under mounting pressure, EPA organized a Gulf of Mexico Program, the first of its kind. Nine EPA employees were assigned to work with federal and state agency representatives and a citizen's advisory committee. The objective: to protect, maintain, and restore the Gulf's productivity.

Florida participates, although Florida's contribution to pollution of the Gulf is small compared with that of Louisiana and Texas. Florida has made progress in cleaning up such polluted waters as Tampa Bay. Florida's Gulf estuarine ecosystems have suffered less than those of Louisiana and Texas, and the state is among the leaders in protection and restoration of coastal wetlands. Florida's governor, legislature, and congressional delegation have thus far blocked oil drilling off Florida's coast.

But Florida's commercial and sports fishermen are gravely affected by the Gulf's rapid deterioration. Fish and shrimp catches have declined. In 1993 a general warning was issued against eating oysters from the Gulf. So Florida has good reason to support the Gulf Coast Program.

Chapter 22

Florida's Wildlife

Mastodons, rhinoceroses, camels, giant sloths, saber-toothed tigers; herds of wild horses. Many remarkable mammals roamed prehistoric Florida.

Today, on East African plains, a single pan of a video camera may capture several hundred mammals of more than a dozen species. What of Florida? A guest wants to see mammals. What can we promise him or her?

Gray squirrels come to our door daily. If it's winter, manatees are at Blue Springs. Our guest could probably see raccoons roaming the picnic grounds at Highlands Hammock State Park. He or she could visit a bat cave.

We sometimes see marsh rabbits on our lawn, otters in our lake, but not every day. We could tell the guest where he or she could probably see deer and armadillos. Deer at Myakka State Park aren't shy. Armadillos occur along many rural roadsides. Bottle-nosed dolphins, striped skunks, and wild boars are common, but the chances of seeing one would be less.

Rats eat our grapefruit, but in the dark of night. We glimpse voles too briefly for positive identification. Opossums are common roadkills. We have yet to see a fox squirrel, perhaps because we're not golfers; these squirrels have adapted to life on the links.

Key Deer

One morning on Big Pine Key we saw a herd of the little Key deer, considered a race rather than a subspecies of the abundant whitetail. Hunted and poached until the 1950s, they were reduced to fewer than eighty individuals. Under protection they recovered. Now they are threatened by loss of habitat and road kills.

About 94 mammal species occur in Florida or Florida waters. Of these, 16 are bats; another 16 are rats, mice, or voles; and 28 are whales or dolphins. Only 34 species belong to other families.

About half of the 94 are rare and seldom seen. Only 18 are considered abundant, and in this context "abundant" doesn't mean one can count on seeing them. For example, 2 of the 18 are the eastern flying squirrel and the pilot whale, rarely seen by us or visitors.

Another 31 mammal species are considered "common," a term more useful to wildlife biologists than to visitors. Biologists base their population estimates on tracks, scat, and other indicators as well as sightings.

Visiting the African plains is like going to the theater. In Florida, you must be alert, looking left and right, driving slowly, paddling or walking quietly. Jane's hand grips my arm. She points and whispers, "There!"

Manatees

Manatees are marine mammals, vegetarian, slow-swimming, weighing up to 3,000 pounds. Hunting the manatee has been outlawed in Florida since 1907, but the species is gravely endangered, largely because of human carelessness.

Browsing on sea grasses, manatees range widely along the Gulf and Atlantic coasts in summer. Degradation of estuaries, especially damage to sea grass beds, has reduced their feeding grounds.

Manatees

As the water cools in winter, manatees gather at natural springs such as Blue Springs and Crystal River. Spring water is about 72°F all year. Some manatees are attracted by the warmth of power plant outfalls. As they swim up rivers, creeks, and canals, many are killed or injured by speeding boats. Collisions with watercraft cause 25 to 30 percent of manatee deaths. Many survivors carry deep wounds from propeller slashes.

Florida waters are manatee sanctuaries. Boat speed limits are posted along manatee routes. Many boaters, chiefly sport fishermen, ignore the regulations and warning signs. As we idle along in our Zodiac, their boats roar past. We have yet to see one apprehended.

At a fish camp off the St. Johns River, a glass bowl beside the cash register was half full of $1 and $5 bills. A sign said the money would finance a campaign to repeal boat speed limits, an infringement on the civil rights of fishermen!

Panther

Some wildlife biologists believe the Florida panther is doomed. The reasons for the big cat's decline include loss of habitat, roadkills, poaching, and mercury poisoning. The U.S. Fish and Wildlife Service and the Florida Game and Fresh Water Fish Commission didn't act in time. Hunting panthers wasn't prohibited until 1958. Poaching wasn't made a felony until 1978. Panther research wasn't undertaken until 1981. With the panther at last declared endangered under the federal Endangered

Panther

Species Act, a recovery team was named. By then the remaining population was about fifty, too few for an adequate gene pool. Because of generations of inbreeding, 90 percent of panther sperm is abnormal.

Wild panthers have been fitted with radio collars. Scientists track them, note when males and females meet, find them when they die, and determine causes.

After opposing it for years, the recovery team finally recommended captive breeding. Artificial insemination works. Captive-born kittens are twice as likely to survive as those born in the wild. Captive animals receive mercury-free diets. A captive population is insurance against an epidemic. Cats can be reintroduced.

Animal rights activists delayed action by lawsuits and negotiations. At last the program got under way. In 1991, collar signals indicated a probable mating in the wild. After an appropriate interval a team tracked the female, then found and captured her kitten for the breeding program. In 1991 six kittens were in breeding pens. Recently one of the last two panthers in Everglades National Park found and mated with a female outside the Park.

Look for "panther" in one popular mammal field guide and you won't find it. The entry for "mountain lion" mentions "cougar," "puma," and "catamount" as synonyms, but not "panther." All, including panther, are of one species: *Felis concolor.* Rather than have the species extinct in Florida, breeding stock could be translocated from other habitats. Like captive breeding, that's controversial. Some urge that the Florida strain should not be mixed with others. Proponents say the Florida strain is doomed by inbreeding now, and new blood is necessary. In the summer of 1993, thirteen western cougars were released into the Pinhook Swamp wilderness area. They'll be studied for three years.

Reported panther sightings far outside the cat's present known range are surprisingly frequent. Wildlife officers investigate but have found no tracks, scat, or other confirmation. Oddly, many people say they've seen "black panthers." Florida panthers aren't black.

Black Bear

The black bear isn't endangered nationwide, but many wildlife biologists believe it is endangered in Florida. Numbers declined so alarmingly it was listed as "threatened" in 1974. An adult male needs about 60 square miles for his home range; a viable population of bears, perhaps ten times as much. As habitat is fragmented, those remaining are more vulnerable to hunting. About two dozen a year are killed by vehicles.

In 1991, environmentalists petitioned the Florida Game and Fresh Water Fish Commission to ban bear hunting. The hunter-dominated Commission refused, ignoring the recommendations of its own professional staff. When the season opened, one of the commissioners shot a 315-pound male bear after it was cornered by dogs.

One might think the ensuing public outrage would make a difference. In 1992 the Commission staff publicly recommended that all bear hunting be stopped. Again the Commissioners rejected the staff's advice. A furious legislator said he'd introduce a constitutional amendment abolishing the Commission. At last the U.S. Fish and Wildlife Service was goaded into action, listing the black bear as threatened. Now the Florida bear hunt has been stopped.

Wild Hog

Hogs were brought to Florida by Spanish explorers. Some escaped, and settlers soon realized they needn't confine and feed them. On the loose, they multiplied rapidly, living on the land. When a settler wanted meat, he went out with dogs and gun. As the hogs became wilder, they also became fierce, ripping many a dog with their tusks.

The hogs aren't native, but they've been here for a long time. The domestic pig and the introduced wild hog are both *Sus scrofa*. So is the European wild boar, introduced widely in the United States after 1890, but apparently not in Florida, although our wild hogs are often called "boars."

Settlers caught, castrated, and released young males because the meat of "bars" tastes better. They notched ears to show ownership and cut tails for quicker identification of bars in the field. These practices continue on hunting preserves.

State Park managers would like to eliminate the hogs because they're not natives. Park managers and some nonhunting landowners object to them because their rooting churns up the land. The Florida Game and Fresh Water Fish Commission manages them as a game species, setting hunting seasons and size limits.

River Otter

Days pass without a sight of the otters who live in our lake. Then we see one sunning on our dock, or one surfaces near our canoe. We see otters at the Merritt Island National Wildlife Refuge and in cypress swamps. Usually they're shy, but one who was munching on a two-pound bass dared us to come closer.

Behind a motel at Yeehaw Junction, a chain-link fence encircles a small sewage effluent pool covered with a mat of green algae. As we walked by, a black head rose through the algae. The otter, fish in mouth, glided up the bank. Another otter slid under the fence and into the pool. Evidently the fishing was good.

Everyone likes otters. Years ago Emil Lears traveled with a troupe of otters. We saw them on a lawn at the Bronx Zoo, surrounded by visitors. On Lears's signal, they raced across the grass, down a flight of steps, into a small auditorium, and up on the stage. After they had performed in a tank of water, Lears showed a film of the otters and his golden retriever in Florida. As he canoed along a creek, otters and dog slid down mud banks, romped in and out of the boat.

Lears raised otters and would sell them to buyers who met his strict standards. We and our black Labrador would be pleased to have free-living otters who enjoyed our company. Still, we prefer things the way they are.

As we rafted down the Snake River in the Tetons, the oarsman told of otters brought there to perform in a Disney film. Trained at what was then Disney's animal farm at Sequim, Washington, they performed flawlessly until the filming ended. Then they quietly disappeared. "They liked it here," the oarsman said. "Can't blame them!"

Bottle-Nosed Dolphin

One afternoon Jane was swimming in the ocean. I was on the beach. Someone yelled "Shark!" I started running, then stopped and laughed.

Whitetail Deer

No shark. Several dolphins were circling around her, and Jane was delighted.

We see dolphins more often than we see otters, but with no less joy. When the Refuge Manager took us out to the Cedar Keys, three dolphins played in the wake of his boat. One day, in our own boat, we dropped anchor off the Intracoastal Waterway. As we ate lunch, several dolphins, one a baby, swam lazily nearby. We see them most often from causeways over the Waterway.

Dolphin legends have been recounted for centuries wherever there are dolphins. Dolphins have rescued swimmers, piloted boats through narrow passages, driven off sharks. We believe them all. In Europe we were horrified to see performing dolphins kept in tiny tanks of stale water. We are no less horrified to read of the nefarious skills the U.S. Navy teaches them.

Experimenters have tried to expand communication with dolphins. Those who know them best believe the limitations are more ours than theirs.

It's delightful to see performing dolphins at Sea World. We have watched training sessions, and the bond between trainer and dolphin is akin to ours with our Labrador. Autistic and other handicapped children respond wonderfully to swimming with dolphins. Still, the dolphins are captive, and their mortality rate in captivity is high. Were it our decision, we'd veto further captures of dolphins for public entertainment.

Whitetail Deer

Whitetail deer are abundant. No wolves or panthers remain to prey on them. They adapt to almost any habitat, including farms, ranches, and golf courses. They are most often seen early and late in the day and near woodland shelter. Does are bolder than bucks, easily accustomed to hand feeding and petting.

In some Florida habitats, poaching by local residents keeps deer numbers low. In favorable habitats, deer populations increase beyond what the food supply will sustain. Wildlife managers regulate hunting to keep populations in balance.

Coyotes

On our first trip to the Tetons together, we had been camping for a week when Jane complained she had yet to hear coyotes singing. After high-altitude hiking each day, we would have slept through a rock concert. That night we set the alarm for midnight, and she heard them, one mournful chorus seeming to answer another. A chill, clear night with a million stars seems incomplete without them.

Coyotes in Florida? We knew they had extended their range eastward to New England, then south to New Jersey and the Blue Ridge. They reached northwestern Florida in the 1970s. In 1981 they were reported in eighteen northern counties. Seven years later they were in forty-eight counties. In the meantime, western coyotes had been illegally imported and released. The Florida Game and Fresh Water Fish Commission predicts coyotes will become established statewide.

Their role in western ecology is disputed. Many ranchers say they kill livestock, especially sheep. Ranchers shoot them, trap them, poison them with baited cyanide guns. The U.S. Fish and Wildlife Service Animal Damage Control unit kills about 100,000 coyotes a year. A few ranchers consider coyotes beneficial and post their land to protect them.

"The coyote has always been a pretty good scapegoat," said John Wooding, Florida Game Commission biologist. "It may occasionally take calves, but not very often." Coyotes get the blame for stock losses caused by wild dogs, he added. Other biologists say coyotes are a bigger threat to goats and chickens than to calves. Coyotes also like watermelons.

Although reports of stock losses are scanty and suspect, many Florida cattlemen shoot coyotes on sight. One such rancher acknowledges that the coyotes on his ranch seem to have enough rabbits and raccoons to satisfy their hunger.

Red Wolf

The last red wolf in Florida was shot in the 1920s. When the species was declared endangered everywhere, questions were raised about its genetic purity. Some thought red wolves had interbred with coyotes or feral dogs. Some of the remaining wolves were trapped. Sophisticated tests established their purity, and captive breeding began. Now, with well over 150 wolves available, it's time for reintroductions. St. Vincent's Island in Florida is one of the sites where red wolves have been released.

This island, near Apalachicola, had been stripped of most timber and wildlife when the Loomis brothers bought it and began restoration. The recovery of the ecosystem was a heartening demonstration of Florida's resiliency. The owners introduced exotic species: eland, black-buck, sambar deer, zebra. Years later it was acquired by the U.S. Fish and Wildlife Service, and most of the exotics were eliminated.

The Birds

Here are thirty-one reasons birders come to Florida. Some of these species are seldom seen farther north. Others are easier for visiting birders to find here than at home. [14]

White-tailed Tropicbird	Sooty Tern
Magnificent Frigatebird	Brown Noddy
Great White Heron	Black Noddy
Reddish Egret	White-crowned Pigeon
Roseate Spoonbill	Eurasian Collared-Dove
Wood Stork	Mangrove Cuckoo
Greater Flamingo	Smooth-billed Ani
Mottled Duck	Burrowing Owl
Masked Duck	Antillean Nighthawk
American Swallow-tailed Kite	Red-cockaded Woodpecker
Snail Kite	Gray Kingbird
Short-tailed Hawk	Cave Swallow
Crested Caracara	Florida Scrub Jay
Limpkin	Red-whiskered Bulbul
Spot-breasted Oriole	Black-whiskered Vireo
Cape Sable Seaside Sparrow	

Birders coming from South America would have a different wish list. For some species, Florida is at the southern limit of their ranges, for others the northern limit. Peninsular Florida is on the Atlantic Flyway; the Panhandle is on the Mississippi Flyway; and vast numbers of mi-

[14] From Herbert W. Kale, II, and David S. Maehr. *Florida's Birds.* (Sarasota: Pineapple Press, 1990.)

Burrowing Owl

grants pass through in spring and fall. Florida's diverse habitats support a great assortment of full-time residents. Some, the sandhill crane, for one, have both resident and migrant populations.

We have met birders whose only interest is their life lists. Having once seen and recorded a new bird, they have no further interest in the species. For our birder friends, however, bird study is an endless challenge. They study behavior and trends in populations. They have compiled checklists for several parks and a Breeding Bird Atlas. Several times each year, responding to a hot line summons, they drive half a night to see a species seldom if ever seen in Florida before. In 1991 birders flocked to the Keys to see two unusual visitors from the Bahamas: La Sagra's flycatcher and the thick-billed vireo.

Every birder we know is a conservation activist. Indeed, birders were the pioneers of the environmental movement in Florida. As early as 1898, hunting had drastically reduced populations of many bird species. The Carolina parakeet was extinct. Flamingos no longer nested in Florida. Herons, egrets, roseate spoonbills, and white ibises, slaughtered for their plumes, were near extinction, many of their rookeries empty.

A few laws were passed but not enforced. Guy Bradley was the first game warden in south Florida, hired by the newly created Audubon Society. He was murdered near Cape Sable in 1905. Three years later another Audubon warden, Columbus McLeod, was also killed by poachers. Citizens everywhere were outraged, and the Society's membership grew, but it was another decade before the plume trade was finally suppressed and populations of many species began to recover.

Today even an army of game wardens couldn't stop the catastrophic decline of egrets, herons, and other wading birds in the Everglades. Destruction of habitat, not poachers, is the enemy now. Birders and other conservationists lay aside their binoculars to fight the good fight in Tallahassee and Washington.

We can offer little advice to visitors who are experienced birders. They will have equipped themselves with checklists and field guides that tell when and where each species can best be seen. They will have learned that some birding bonanzas here are episodic. For example, hordes of

Wood Stork

spring migrants crossing the Gulf of Mexico sometimes meet a cold front and "crash" on coastal islands, feeding and resting before flying on. They can call the Florida Rare Bird Alert at (813) 984-4444 to learn what's present and where to look.

We are among the many amateurs for whom bird-watching is a pleasant part of the natural experience. Last year we went to Belize to see Montezuma oropendolas, guans, and jacanas, but also to hike in the rain forest with its giant fig and ceiba trees, cohune palms, lianas, orchids, bromeliads, wild ginger, leaf-cutting ants, termite nests, and much more.

We often go to the Everglades in winter, Fort DeSoto in spring, the Merritt Island refuge in the fall. Whatever the season in Florida, birding can be rewarding.

In late February the first purple martins arrive at our martin house. In April the moorhens and purple gallinules have chicks. Forster's terns are fishing in the lake. A pair of wood ducks have occupied our new wood duck box. A great blue heron stands patiently on our dock. A flock of red-winged blackbirds swirls about our trees and waterfront. Bald eagles sit motionless on the highest available perches, as if surveillance were their chief occupation. The red-tailed hawk favors a branch at mid-height. Boat-tailed grackles sit on our deck railing, complaining until we make an offering. A pair of northern cardinals remind us of species we left behind in Maryland. At night, chuck-will's-widows and limpkins sing us to sleep.

Reptiles and Amphibians

The most alarming news we've heard for some time is the worldwide disappearance of many species of frogs.[15]

Great Blue Heron

The disappearance has been noted by herpetologists who have been observing frog habitats for many years. In ponds where millions of eggs once hatched, mortality has neared 100 percent. Many once-familiar species are no longer seen. Such reports have come from every continent and a great variety of habitats. We had wondered why we no longer hear the evening chorus.

Local declines might be caused by local changes. The French passion for frog legs has doubtless helped deplete populations of Asian bullfrogs. But frogs have also vanished from many wilderness ponds. Scientists intimately familiar with sites where drastic declines have occurred have as yet found no explanation.

Any serious break in the food chain is cause for concern. Frogs consume countless billions of insects and, in turn, are essential to the diet of various reptiles, birds, and mammals. Most alarming is the suggestion that "amphibians are the canaries in a global coal mine." The frogs may be succumbing to environmental changes that will, if they continue, affect other species--perhaps us.

The International Union for the Conservation of Nature (IUCN) has organized 40 teams of scientists in thirty nations to seek answers. They will investigate several possible causes: acid rain, increased ultraviolet radiation, global warming, and as yet unidentified pathogens. Frogs have permeable skins.

Alligators

There were alligators in the age of reptiles, 100 million years ago, before there was a Florida. An early Florida explorer, William Bartram, wrote of huge alligators attacking his canoe "roaring terribly and belching floods of water over me." He described a river so thick with alligators he could have crossed by walking on their heads.

Alligators and crocodiles have pursued legions of movie actors. Some people, knowing they can't swim as swiftly as Tarzan, won't swim in Florida lakes and rivers. Some are nervous about canoeing. One of our visitors gripped a thwart when he saw an alligator slip from a bank into the water as our canoe approached. He feared the alligator might capsize us.

The facts: In a state where millions of men, women, and children swim, wade, and play in lakes, ponds, and rivers, about six alligator attacks on humans occur per year. Only one attack in twenty is fatal.

[15]Beth Livermore. Amphibian alarm: Just where have all the frogs gone. *Smithsonian*, October 1992, 113-120.

Alligator

Most attacks occur when someone intrudes on an alligator's territory, especially a nest. One fatality occurred when a young woman climbed a fence at night and swam where signs warned of a nesting female. More recently a 10-year-old boy on a family canoe outing was killed while swimming or wading in the Loxahatchee River. It was the first fatal attack in the 43-year history of Jonathan Dickinson State Park.

On our first visit to Florida in the 1950s, we wanted to photograph an alligator. We saw one in a pond and experimentally tossed a marshmallow into the water. The gator swam and grabbed it. The next marshmallow brought him closer, and soon we had a closeup. We were ignorant then, not realizing that the most dangerous alligator is one taught that people are a source of food. Feeding alligators is now illegal.

"One thing we do know about alligators is those that are not afraid of humans are more likely to attack," says Dennis David of the Florida Game and Fresh Water Fish Commission. The Commission receives about 7,000 nuisance alligator complaints a year. About half lead to trapping and removing a gator. A typical case was a 14-foot alligator that had been fed fish scraps tossed from a fish-cleaning station.

We see many alligators while we canoe. Recently a 12-footer surfaced just beside the boat, exhaled, and sank. None has ever roared or belched water over us. Lustful male gators do roar. We're told they sometimes roar at low-flying jet planes.

Alligators rarely attack a human on land. Dogs are a different matter. A dog allowed to roam or play near the water's edge is at risk. A friend was bank fishing on a lake near our home. An alligator surged up from the water and grabbed his black Labrador.

Alligators may seem slow-moving, but we saw one breaking speed records. On a blazing hot day, it was crossing a road that would have blistered our bare feet. The gator was on tiptoe, belly arched up, tail curled over back, in a great hurry.

The Endangered Species Act

In the mid-1960s, the alligator was on the way to extinction in Florida. Killing alligators was against the law here, but trade in alligator hides was legal elsewhere. Poachers killed alligators at night, skinned them, and trucked them across the border. Once out of Florida, the skins could be sold legally. The trade flourished, and alligators became rare.

Alligators dig holes or dens in wetlands. In Florida's periodic droughts and dry seasons, these holes, sometimes as large as small ponds, are often the only wetland places still holding water. Aquatic animals, insects, birds, and mammals depend on them. As the alligator population dwindled, natural processes filled in gator holes, and other species suffered. Alligator poaching had undermined whole ecosystems.

In 1966, John S. Gottschalk, then director of the U.S. Fish and Wildlife Service, attended the General Assembly of the International Union for Conservation of Nature (IUCN) in Lucerne, Switzerland. One evening he met with delegates from several nations and was told about the huge trade in endangered wildlife species, both live animals and their skins and hides. Many species, such as the orangutan and snow leopard, were protected by laws in their homelands, but smuggling is easy when international markets are open. The biggest open market was the United States.

U.S. animal dealers were importing thousands of wild animals captured and exported illegally from other countries. The import trade in ivory, reptile skins, and furs was far greater.

The U.S. Lacey Act prohibited importation of any wildlife exported illegally from another country. I (John Perry) learned how ineffective it was when I asked a U.S. Attorney to act in the case of an orangutan smuggled from Indonesia. First, the attorney explained, he'd need a certified translation of the relevant Indonesia law and regulations. He would also need certified declarations from Indonesian authorities that this particular orangutan, positively identified, had been captured in Indonesia and exported illegally. He might require a court appearance by an

Indonesian official. He knew of no successful prosecution under the Lacey Act and didn't believe there ever would be one.

At the meeting in Lucerne, Gottschalk listened and promised action. On his initiative, an endangered species act was introduced in the U.S. House of Representatives in 1968. Hearings were held. Opposition by the fur trade industry killed the bill. Their chief concern was that if the fur-processing industry were outlawed in the United States, it would move to Europe, bankrupting U.S. companies without benefiting wildlife.

Negotiations between proponents and opponents followed. I had participated in the Lucerne meeting; now I was a member of a delegation that met with leaders of the International Fur Trade Federation at the impressive old headquarters of the Hudson's Bay Company in London. The outcome was a remarkable agreement: the fur industry would *support* the endangered species act if Congress also directed the Secretary of State to call an international convention to adopt an international ban on trade in endangered species!

In 1969 the Endangered Species Act became law. The international meeting was held, and a Convention on International Trade in Endangered Species (CITES) has been ratified by many nations. The trade in endangered wildlife and their products hasn't stopped, but it is much reduced.

However, the U.S. Fish and Wildlife Service has been appallingly slow to add species to the endangered list, and lax in enforcing the Endangered Species Act. So few agents are assigned that wildlife and wildlife products are smuggled through Miami and other ports daily without interference.

With respect to the alligator, however, the Act was a great success. Now that alligator hides and products were contraband everywhere in the United States, poaching virtually ceased. Alligator populations have recovered so rapidly that a regulated annual harvest is now authorized. Wildlife officers are kept busy removing "nuisance alligators" from urban lakes, golf courses, and backyards.

Crocodiles occur only around the Keys and the southern tip of the peninsula. Less than a thousand remain. Biologists of the Game and Fresh Water Fish Commission have tagged about 400 on Key Largo.

Snakes

So many people fear snakes! They kill millions of harmless ones. They can't be persuaded that most are beneficial and that it's easy to identify the few poisonous species.

John's mother couldn't abide even looking at a picture of a snake. In Florida, she never dared walk across a lawn in the dark. One of our neighbors calls Jane to remove snakes that wander into her patio. Another neighbor shoots any snake he sees.

At the National Zoo, where John worked for several years, a visitor told the curator of reptiles he was terrified of snakes. The curator invited him back of the line of cages. On the second visit he was persuaded to hold a small ball python in his hand, finding it wasn't cold, slimy, or aggressive. As his confidence grew, he handled larger snakes. To demonstrate his new-found courage, he brought his family to see him drape a fair-size python around his neck. Just then the curator's small daughter arrived, scampered over, and patted the python familiarly on the head-- "Hello, George!" At our local Audubon Nature Fair, children are eager to touch and hold snakes exhibited by a local fancier. Florida has forty-four species of snakes. Six are venomous. Of these, the copperhead (whose bite is almost never fatal) occurs only in northern Florida, and there infrequently. In years of hiking, camping, and canoeing throughout Florida we have seen numerous snakes, but only four were venomous.

The coral snake's venom is potent, but this small reptile is shy and seldom seen. It is difficult to be bitten by a coral snake, because its mouth and fangs are small. Bites have occurred, usually on fingers or toes.

The cottonmouth or water moccasin occurs throughout Florida, almost always in or near water, often basking in the sun. Some grow to 5 feet long, but the Florida average is about 3 feet. Its bite is very painful but seldom fatal.

The most common bite of a venomous snake in Florida is that of the pygmy rattlesnake. Common because this species is small, hard to see in grass and brush, and sometimes aggressive. Bites cause pain and swelling, but we know of no deaths.

The diamondback rattlesnake is our nastiest: big, aggressive, swift to strike, with venom that destroys tissue. It occurs throughout Florida and in most well-drained habitats. Don't go crashing blindly through brush. The canebrake rattlesnake, related to the timber rattlesnake, occurs chiefly in northern Florida.

If you should be bitten? We've seen and heard too much conflicting advice from nonmedical people to offer any ourselves. Except to ask, Are you sure it was a venomous snake that bit you? Many harmless snakes bite or nip if threatened. Do you see puncture wounds? Do you see swelling? Some venomous snake bites are dry; no venom is injected.

Relax! It may be painful but you won't die. Hie thee to a hospital, promptly but not in panic. Ask if they have antivenin in stock and if any doctor on staff has had experience with snakebite. Few Florida doc-

Brown Anole

tors have ever seen a snakebite. The reptile curator or veterinarian of the nearest large zoo will know where to get antivenin; there's a national data bank. He or she can recommend a doctor with snakebite experience.

Lizards

The lizards we see daily around our pool are the green and brown anoles (pronounced *a-no-lee* in our dictionary, usually *an-ole* by Floridians). Both inhabit our garden and hunt insects on the screened pool enclosure. The green anole was the more common ten years ago. The brown, an introduction from the Caribbean, now predominates. We also see the crested anole. Anoles grow to about 7 inches long, but most are smaller. They "threaten" us and each other by head-bobbing or doing pushups and by extending red or orange throat fans. They lay single eggs every couple of weeks, and we frequently see tiny lizards scampering. The smaller, scaly scrub lizard inhabits the Florida scrub and is threatened by habitat loss.

The southeastern five-lined skink, slender and up to 8 1/2 inches long, has five light stripes and a blue or gray tail; males have red-orange heads at breeding time. They seem to prefer shade and dampness and don't climb our screens, so we see them less often.

Sea Turtles

The leatherback, green, loggerhead, Kemp's ridley, and hawksbill sea turtles spend most of their lives at sea, but crawl up on sand beaches to lay their eggs. This has been their undoing. Indians gathered turtle eggs for subsistence. Then came market collectors, who raided every nest they could find. Turtle meat was also in demand.

So were beaches. Traditional turtle beaches were pre-empted by resorts. Eggs were crushed by beach buggies. Thousands of turtles going to or from their beaches were caught and drowned in shrimp trawls.

If sea turtle species survive, much credit must go to the late Archie Carr, who devoted his life to studying and saving them. This quiet, modest man hated meetings and formality. He patrolled turtle beaches at night, squatting on the sand to talk with egg collectors. At Kino, Mexico, on the Gulf of California, he left a conference to wander the wharf where fishermen were bringing in captured turtles. He bought turtles, brought them back to the hotel, and released them on the beach.

Archie taught for years at the University of Florida in Gainesville. When a dinner honoring him on his seventy-fifth birthday was announced, the organizers had to rent a tent to accommodate the several hundred colleagues, former students, and friends who came from near and far.

Cooter

Congress has approved plans for the Archie Carr National Wildlife Refuge in Brevard County to preserve one of Florida's chief turtle beaches. The county government's hasty response was to issue building permits on beachfronts not yet acquired for the Refuge. Florida's Division of Beaches and Shores heedlessly adopted a policy that would permit sea walls and other beach "armoring" that would prevent turtle nesting. New rules now protect the planned Refuge from that fate.

Thousands of sea turtles have died in shrimp trawler nets. When the U.S. Secretary of Commerce initially backed away from rules requiring turtle excluder devices (TEDs) in the nets, Florida's Marine Fisheries Commission quickly moved to require them in Florida waters. By 1991 the federal law was in effect and the Coast Guard was apprehending violators. The TEDs aren't perfect and some fishermen use them carelessly, but it's progress.

Early one morning on Delray Beach, dead turtle hatchlings were found on and beside the oceanfront road. They had mistaken street lights for moonlight and headed away from the sea. Other beachfront communities shield or suppress their lights, as do many local residents. Delray Beach had been warned and was threatened with a $50,000 fine.

In 1992 several beachfront communities agreed to discontinue mechanical beach raking during the nesting season.

Today, before each turtle nesting season, volunteers sign up for nighttime beach patrols. Working quietly, without distracting lights, they watch the turtles laying eggs and mark the nests for protection after the female has covered them.

Gopher Tortoise

The gopher tortoise, a once-abundant relative of the Galapagos tortoises, grows to more than 14 inches long, digs conspicuous burrows, and prefers well-drained sandy habitats--the same habitats preferred by developers. As its population declined alarmingly, it became a protected species.

The problem for the Game and Fresh Water Fish Commission and environmentalists is the fast-dwindling acreage of prime sites. If well-drained sandy habitats were protected as strictly as wetlands are supposed to be, opportunities for developers would be much reduced. State and county governments, unwilling to halt development, have looked for a compromise.

Just as "mitigation" has become the excuse for loss of wetlands, "relocation" is the developers' strategy for usurping tortoise habitat. The Game and Fresh Water Fish Commission receives many applications for permits to relocate gopher tortoises from prospective building sites.

Relocate them where? A good tortoise habitat is likely to have an established tortoise population. Relocation has the dual risk of over-crowding and of spreading a disease that now affects some tortoises.

Mosquitoes

We could hardly blame Frank. Environmentalists fight to preserve every wetland in our county. We want wetlands included in phosphate mine reclamation plans. Before he retired, Frank Wilson's job in our county's government included mosquito control. Mosquitoes breed in wetlands. When citizens were bitten by mosquitoes, Frank heard about it. For him, wetlands were anathema.

Most histories of Florida attribute the slow development of the peninsula to the difficulties of travel over swamps and marshes. The hordes of mosquitoes were no less deterring. Some of the highest densities of mosquitoes ever recorded were here. One brave soul stood still while a scientist counted the mosquitoes that landed on him. The score: 500 landings per minute! The largest number we've encountered has been in the Everglades.

Small wonder DDT was applied heavily in Florida. Within a few years DDT-resistant strains of mosquitoes appeared, and the frightful effects of DDT on birds and other wildlife became apparent. DDT was outlawed in the United States, although it is still made here for export.

Draining or impounding marshes, where mosquitoes breed, was a popular strategy. That strategy, too, had serious drawbacks, and some coastal marshes have since been restored. Present controls are somewhat more sophisticated.

We spend more time outdoors than most people, hiking, canoeing, and camping, often in or near wetlands. We carry repellent, sometimes use it, and have no complaints.

Blind Mosquitoes

Some time between April and November, near a lake or stream, you may find yourself in a cloud of mosquito-like insects. They swarm, pelting you lightly. Two or three times a year we walk through swarms near our lake shore, and thousands cover our pool screening. They don't sting or bite, but they may fly into your ears, nose, or open mouth. They're aquatic midges, not mosquitoes. Most of their life cycle is in water. Adults emerge only to mate and die. Are they really blind? Our reference books don't say, but they're attracted to lights at night. Piles of dead midges a foot or more deep have been found in front of lighted store windows. They can stain painted surfaces. They've been known to blanket car headlights, make roads slippery, spoil food in restaurant kitchens, and stick in fresh paint. We've never witnessed these horrors.

No-see-ums

Cruising in a small boat rigged for camping, we anchored for the night in a salt marsh creek. The sky was clear, stars bright, so we left the top down and went to sleep. We were awakened by a mass attack of furiously biting insects. Frantic, we struggled to rig the top, one hand for the boat, one to slap at face, arms, and legs. We were bitten hundreds of times as we snapped the screens into place. The assault slackened then, but the tiny insects can pass through screening. Spraying the screens put a stop to that, and the itching quickly stopped.

The insects were no-see-ums. Called "sand flies" elsewhere, they're midges that breed in and around water. They seldom bite if there's any breeze. The Florida Cooperative Extension Service says, "Persons performing hard labor out-of-doors frequently are severely annoyed by these insects." We've met them only in marshes, never while performing hard labor in our lakeside garden.

The Monarch

As mentioned earlier, we began our butterfly garden only two years ago and have much to learn. Monarch and queen butterflies come to the milkweed we planted, feed, and lay eggs. Soon their caterpillars are munching voraciously on the milkweed leaves. We cut a few stems bearing caterpillars and put them in a vase on our breakfast table. As the caterpillars grow, they require more and more leaves. After a time, each spends a few hours motionless on a twig. Then it secretes a drop of white fluid with which it attaches its tail to the twig, and hangs motionless for a few days.

One morning we observed the next stage. A caterpillar began rippling contractions. One by one the segments of its outer body were compacted and shed, leaving a green chrysalis twitching energetically.

At first the chrysalis had bands of green and yellow approximating the caterpillar's segments. It gradually became a smooth, green, acorn-shaped shell with a band of golden dots.

A few days later the chrysalis turned transparent, disclosing the dark colors of butterfly wings. We put the vase outdoors. Shortly the shell split, and a new butterfly slowly unfurled and dried its wings, then flew away.

We had read about the long-distance migration of the monarch butterfly to Mexico. Once we saw the migration on a barrier island in New Jersey, hundreds of monarchs flitting about in what seemed an aimless way, but trending south. At the southern tip of the island, several trees were covered with butterflies awaiting a north wind to carry them on.

We had not known that monarchs don't make the entire journey. Our garden, like others, is a way station where one generation reproduces and the next continues onward. How do butterflies transmit their route maps from one generation to another? And how did the monarchs and queens find our newly planted milkweed? Scientists seek the answers.

Wildlife Corridors

One of the most promising developments of recent years is a proposal to establish wildlife corridors throughout Florida. In nature undisturbed, mammal populations can migrate and disperse in response to environmental changes. That's how they populated Florida when the sea subsided.

Towns, roads, farms, and other developments hamper this natural travel now. Habitats and populations are fragmented. If a species is eliminated from an isolated fragment by disease, hunting, or disaster, it may not be replaced by natural dispersal from another.

The proposed corridors would link the principal remaining wildlife habitats of Florida. These corridors would not be narrow pathways but extensions of habitats, with food and shelter. Animals would disperse into and through them.

On first hearing, the proposal sounds wildly impractical. When the plan is laid out on paper, it's breathtaking. The principal habitats and proposed corridors have been mapped. In Florida today it can still be done!

Land must be purchased, but not urban or suburban land. Some of the proposed corridors are river valleys and floodplains where development has been limited. Some landowners will sell easements.

The State is buying environmentally important land. The federal government, counties, The Nature Conservancy, and local land trusts are all potential buyers. It's a magnificent goal for the future of Florida's wildlife and natural areas.[16] It can be achieved.

As a consequence of savings and loan association failures, many properties, including some fine natural areas, were transferred to the Resolution Trust Corporation for sale. One such property, on the Wekiva River, has been acquired with Preservation 2000 funds. The Nature Conservancy and Seminole County have cooperated with the State in piecing together the Wekiva River Buffers project, adjoining Wekiva River State Park. This river corridor is home for several endangered species of plants and animals.

More Wildlife

This is already the longest chapter of our book, but our momentum is unchecked. We are alarmed by the stacks of unprocessed files and stories not yet told. We've said nothing about the bobcat or the Florida

[16]Inspired by the Florida scheme, a group of scientists contributed to a special issue of *Wild Earth*. (Special Issue. Canton, NY: Cenozoic Society, 1992.) *The Wildlands Project* audaciously proposes a huge, connected system of reserves throughout North America.

"You hold in your hands, I sincerely believe, one of the most important documents in conservation history," executive editor Dave Foreman wrote in a preface, with commendable modesty. After studying the articles and maps, we agreed. The Wildlands Project is not a goal for tomorrow but a magnificent design to guide conservation efforts for generations to come.

beach mouse, for example. Florida has 668 species of vertebrates. Populations of almost 300 of these are declining, many alarmingly. We could write chapters about fish threatened by overfishing, damage to seagrass beds and mangroves, and water pollution. (And there was the time a fish slammed into our canoe . . . .)

We have bought guides to help us identify the dragonflies and damselflies we see outside our office. Yesterday we saw twenty anthills built in the form of glacial cirques; now that's an ant we need to know more about. Conchs and sponges are endangered. (Conch chowder has long been a specialty of restaurants on the Keys. Conch fishing was outlawed in 1985, but poaching is not uncommon.) And how can we not discourse on frigate birds, roseate spoonbills gliding in at sunset, armadillos, spiders, tree snails, lobsters, starfish, walkingsticks, and other members of Florida's animal kingdom? Or the fascinating species of the plankton we have seen and photographed through our microscope?

Gary Player, the South African golfer, said it for us in one sentence. Apartheid was in full flower, Nelson Mandela still in jail. A headline-hungry reporter accosted Player as he left the eighteenth green. What did he think about race relations in his homeland? Player smiled. "Black, white, green, purple--I love them all!"

Chapter 23
Florida's Public Lands

W ho owns Florida? The *Florida Statistical Abstract* has 723 pages of small-print statistical information, but no data on State and county land ownership!

Land ownership by Europeans began in a tangle, although there were soon no Indians left. The Spanish crown made lavish land grants without benefit of surveys. Then came the British and their different system of land titles. When Florida was admitted to the Union, some grants had been abandoned. Private land titles were respected, but metes and bounds were fuzzy. Without so much as a map, the United States gave Florida all "swamp and overflowed lands." Thereafter the State made many poorly defined conditional grants. Often the conditions were not fulfilled, but records of State repossession are frequently unclear. To make matters more confusing, until 1836 the United States had no standards of measurement. As late as the early 1900s, land titles were based on several different foot measures.

Now the brass benchmarks of the U.S. Geological Survey have been planted statewide. Modern electronic surveying instruments are precise, but Florida doesn't stay put. Beaches erode; peninsulas accrete; rivers change course. After a tropical storm, several residents of Sanibel Island found they no longer lived on the waterfront. Sand swept from Captiva Island had extended the beach outward several hundred feet. The local government claimed the new land.

When the United States acquired Florida, the federal government became owner of untitled land. After selling or giving most of it away, only about 200,000 acres of the original public domain remained. The federal government has since bought back more than 4 million acres and is buying more.

The Bureau of State Lands gave us these estimates:

	Acres
State-owned land	1,756,203
Water Management Districts	1,539,589
Total	3,295,792

The State also owns 2.4 million acres of Aquatic Preserves and over 5 million acres of "sovereign submerged lands" — the bottoms of lakes and streams.

The combined federal, State, and county landholdings are almost one-quarter of Florida's land area.

State Acquisitions

In 1992 we camped on the 8,500-acre Walker Ranch. It was a working ranch with large areas of pine flatwoods, swamp forest, wet prairie, oak scrub, and wetlands. Developers were eager to buy and subdivide it. The owner wanted to sell and hoped the State would buy and preserve it.[17]

Many such private properties are scattered throughout the state: woodlands, islands, swamps, ranches, citrus groves--properties not yet subdivided and developed and that have desirable natural qualities. Included are planned subdivisions that failed as long ago as the 1920s, now forgotten and overgrown. One county of 68,000 residents has 208,000 platted lots! Because of present land use regulations, many of these old subdivisions couldn't be developed today.

Florida's Natural Areas Inventory identifies and studies environmentally significant lands. Some are the last pieces of prized ecosystems such as scrub. Some harbor endangered species of fauna and flora. Some are

[17]The Nature Conservancy guided negotiations leading to State ownership. The Disney organization bought the ranch and is restoring its ecosystems, chiefly wetlands. Title is being transferred to the State in increments. It is now named the Disney Wilderness Preserve.

vital to protection of watersheds. Such factors are weighed, and desirable sites are put on the Conservation and Recreation Lands (CARL) acquisition wish list.

The State's land purchases are financed by severance taxes on phosphate mining and oil and gas production, documentary stamp taxes, revenue bonds, and other funding sources. The annual CARL list is always much longer than available purchase money can cover, so projects compete. The competition includes public hearings, and it's not unusual for a hundred or more citizens to argue passionately for one or another project.

Florida's CARL, Save Our Rivers, and Save Our Coast programs were envied in other states. Then, in 1990, the legislature adopted the Preservation 2000 program, by far the most ambitious ever conceived in any state: $300 million for sensitive land purchases, every year for the next ten years, a total of $3 billion!

It's not guaranteed. The State's taxes are among the nation's lowest, and the needs of its growing population are great. Florida's constitution requires balanced budgets, and adoption of a budget is an annual crisis. Every year the fate of Preservation 2000 is in doubt. Thus far the program has been maintained.

FEDERAL LANDS WITH NATURAL AREAS

National Park Service

The National Park Service administers a number of National Monuments, Memorials, and Preserves. NPS sites with natural areas are:

	Acres
Big Cypress National Preserve	534,639
Biscayne National Park	96,483
Canaveral National Seashore	57,627
Everglades National Park	1,398,653
Gulf Islands National Seashore	28,976
(partly in Mississippi)	
Total	2,116,378

National Forests

Three National Forests are administered from a central headquarters in Tallahassee:

	Acres
Ocala National Forest	383,049
Osceola National Forest	179,732
Apalachicola National Forest	563,668
Total	1,126,449

The Osceola and Apalachicola forests had been heavily logged and virtually abandoned when the federal government acquired them. Both have been replanted. The Ocala and Apalachicola have numerous recreation sites.

National Wildlife Refuges

Florida has twenty-six National Wildlife Refuges, with a total area of 518,848 acres. Those of special interest to visitors are:

	Acres
Arthur R. Marshall Loxahatchee	145,666
Chassahowitzka	30,436
Florida Keys	23,851
Hobe Sound	977
J. N. "Ding" Darling	4,976
Lake Woodruff	18,506
Lower Suwannee	39,020
Merritt Island	139,153
St. Marks	65,248

Air Force

Eglin Air Force Base, 464,000 acres, and Avon Park Air Force Range, 106,110 acres, both maintain extensive natural areas that are open to visitors, with some restrictions.

State Lands

Florida's arrangements for managing State-owned land are often confusing to visitors and sometimes to State employees. When land is acquired, title is usually vested in the board of trustees of the Internal Improvement Trust Fund. (The trustees are the governor and the six elected cabinet members.) They decide how the land is to be used. In some cases it is leased to a State, regional, or local agency. The three principal State land-managing agencies are:

Division of Recreation and Parks, in the Department of Environmental Protection

Division of Forestry, in the Department of Agriculture and Consumer Affairs

Game and Fresh Water Fish Commission

Management responsibility is often divided. For example, when land on Lake Arbuckle was purchased, the Division of Forestry was designated as the "lead agency" and the site was named Arbuckle State Forest. However, the Florida Game and Fresh Water Fish Commission manages wildlife, and a portion of the site may some day become a State Park.

Dual management by the Division of Forestry and the Game and Fresh Water Fish Commission is common. Their objectives sometimes conflict.

Division of Recreation and Parks

The Division of Recreation and Parks manages 113 State Parks, State Recreation Areas, State Preserves, State Reserves, and historic sites, a total of about 420,000 acres. Florida State Parks have this admirable mandate:

> State park lands are managed to appear as they did when the first Europeans arrived.

Few of the Parks were pristine when the State acquired them. Each now has a plan to restore the original ecosystems. Visitor facilities are usually limited to a modest portion of each site. State Recreation Areas usually provide more space for recreation facilities than do State Parks, but preservation and restoration of natural areas is also an objective.

Hunting is prohibited in State Parks and Recreation Areas. Hunting is permitted in State Reserves, and is managed by the Game and Fresh Water Fish Commission.

Division of Forestry

Florida's eighteen State Forests, managed by the Division of Forestry, encompass 350,000 acres. Two large units, Blackwater River and Withlacoochee State Forests, comprise 87 percent of that total. Hunting is managed by the Game and Fresh Water Fish Commission.

The Forests are managed for commercial timber production, but they include many prairies, swamps, lakes, and other natural areas. Increasing emphasis is being placed on protecting and restoring native species. The forests are open to public recreation.

Game and Fresh Water Fish Commission

The Game and Fresh Water Fish Commission manages wildlife in sixty-four Wildlife Management Areas totaling over 4 million acres. However, only 135,000 of these acres are owned by the Commission. On 900,000 acres of privately owned land the Commission has lease agreements that permit public hunting and fishing. More than 3 million acres are State Forests, State Preserves, and lands owned by Water Management Districts, on which the Commission manages wildlife. The Commission also manages wildlife in National Forests.

Water Management Districts

Five regional Water Management Districts were established by the Florida legislature to protect and manage the state's wetlands, lakes, bays, rivers, and groundwater. To protect watersheds and other water resources, the five WMDs have purchased over 1.5 million acres of land and are buying more.

When we asked officials of the Division of State Lands if this 1.5 million acres is State owned, the first answer was "no." We had seen the land listed as "Not State-owned" in some official documents. But the WMDs were created by the legislature and land purchase money comes from State programs, so we pressed for a better answer and got it: the land is State-owned, but title is with the WMDs, not with the Board of Trustees.

The WMDs want to make much of their land available for public recreation. Hiking, horse riding, fishing, and boating are permitted on some sites. Others are kept closed for lack of budgets for supervision.

Several counties have parks on WMD land. Hillsborough County has developed outstanding parks by agreement with the Southwest Florida Water Management District.

County lands

Most Florida county parks are planned for swimming, ball playing, picnicking, and other intensive uses. Several counties, notably Hillsborough, have outstanding natural area parks with excellent interpretive centers and trails. Several are acting to identify and acquire significant natural areas and coastal beaches before they are developed. Some are providing matching funds for operation and maintenance of lands bought with Preservation 2000 funds.

Enjoying the Public Lands

Parks and other public recreation areas are scattered throughout the state. Away from the often-crowded beaches, picnic sites, and playgrounds are countless quiet places of rare beauty. Maps and guidebooks are useful, within their limits.

The maps included in State Park leaflets usually show only the developed portions, not the larger natural areas. National Forest maps show trails and unpaved roads but are sometimes out of date. State Forest maps show less detail.

To enjoy the quiet places, explore! Florida has thousands of miles of well-maintained dirt roads where one can drive at leisure. Leave the roads and walk. Florida has hundreds of miles of marked trails and hundreds more unmarked tracks that await your discovery. Rent a canoe or power boat and float into wetlands that have changed little since the first Europeans came.

Bringing a Dog?

We add this note because so many visitors discover to their dismay that the State of Florida prohibits dogs where other states do not. On our first visit, we were turned away from the State Park where we had planned to camp. Most Florida State Forest campgrounds also exclude dogs.

This is the published policy of the Division of Recreation and Parks:

> Pets are restricted from certain areas of the parks for sanitary reasons and to ensure a more relaxing retreat for millions of visitors each year. Pets are NOT ALLOWED in the camping areas, on bathing beaches, in concession facilities and may be restricted in other designated areas of the park.
>
> This rule was adopted after very careful consideration for the safety of visitors and pets, to reduce disturbances caused by pets, and to comply with public health and safety guidelines. Also, pets have a disturbing effect on wildlife and detract from the natural environment of the parks.

What nonsense! Pets are welcome in all National Park and National Forest campgrounds, including those in Florida. Florida's commercial campgrounds surely don't want their guests disturbed or injured, but almost all commercial campgrounds in Florida accept pets. We have camped with dogs in the state parks of forty-six other states. No other owners' dogs have ever imperiled our health or safety, kept us awake, or otherwise annoyed us. Almost all owners walk their dogs in designated areas.

As for hiking with a dog, we have hiked with a leashed dog in the parks, forests, and wildlife management areas of most other states.[18] The rules in Florida are inconsistent and confusing even to State employees. A State Wildlife Officer who ordered us to remove our dog from a Wildlife Management Area was taken aback when we called attention to his own rulebook, which says dogs on leash are allowed.

If you travel with a dog, it's best to avoid State-owned sites.

Privately-owned preserves

The Florida Chapter of The Nature Conservancy finds, studies, and acquires outstanding examples of ecosystems. It often buys land for subsequent transfer to a federal or State agency or assists in negotiations with owners. It owns and manages several fine preserves.

The Rookery Bay ecosystem was preserved from development by the pioneering efforts of a local land trust. Recently several other local land trusts have been formed.

Both the National Audubon Society and the Florida Audubon Society have sanctuaries around the state, open to visitors, several with interpretive trails and nature centers.

Barley Barber Swamp is a 400-acre freshwater cypress swamp preserve owned by the Florida Power Company. It is open to visitors by appointment.

[18]Dogs are usually excluded from trails where bears are common. They should be.

Chapter 24

What's Left?

Forty years ago we ended a magazine article with these words: "Clearly, our daughters will not have some of the things we enjoy today, things which are slipping away from us year by year. Our fear is that they may not know what it is they are missing."

Delaware's ocean beach was then our favorite weekend campsite. We pitched our tent among the dunes and often had a mile of surf and sand to ourselves. A year later the Chesapeake Bay Bridge opened. Crowds came, and beach camping had to be forbidden.

Places where John hiked and camped as a boy became suburbs. We climbed what had been a lonesome mountain and found a Good Humor wagon at the top. Our former island campsite on Lake George in the Adirondacks must now be reserved months ahead by Ticketron.

We miss many natural areas we once enjoyed. It is less painful to contemplate the wonders that vanished before our time. We have read about the Florida known to Sidney Lanier and John Muir, but it is not within our experience. We are keenly aware of how the Everglades and Sanibel Island have changed since we first saw them. Our baseline is that reality, not what was a century before.

For today's newcomers and visitors, our Florida of the 1950s is no more real than the Florida of Lanier and Muir. But no matter if their baseline is today; Florida is still glorious, still full of natural wonders.

We hope to engage the resident and visitor, but not by describing Florida past. Let them see Florida as it is today, as we see it, always finding more quiet places to enjoy and cherish. Let them discover Florida's cypress swamps, lonesome beaches, salt marshes, pristine islands, maturing pine forests, quiet canoe trails, spectacular wildflowers, splendid birds.

How much natural area remains in Florida? How much more will there be if plans for preservation succeed? Could even more be made public and restored?

No published statistics provide answers, so we constructed the following rough estimates. They are not authoritative. Several categories overlap, so don't try adding them together.

Today's Protected Natural Areas:
3.5 million acres

These are the areas owned by federal, state, or local governments, or by nonprofit entities, and dedicated to preservation or restoration of natural ecosystems. If a site has multiple uses, we estimated the portion maintained in or being returned to natural condition.

Some of these areas are pristine: undeveloped islands, undisturbed beaches and dunes, mangrove shores, salt marshes, remote wetlands. More have been altered by logging, drainage, tree farming, or other influences, but management practices or benign neglect are re-establishing natural ecosystems.

Natural Areas Awaiting Purchase and Protection:
2 million acres

Florida has led all other states in buying environmentally significant land to protect it from development. Adding to existing land purchase programs, the 1990 legislature enacted Preservation 2000, authorizing $300 million of land purchase money each year for the decade. It's a fantastic plan, although appropriation of the annual $300 million isn't assured.

These 2 million acres have been selected for future purchase. Many harbor endangered species of fauna and flora. Some are in excellent natural condition. Others can be restored.

Land purchase is not always necessary. Some other states have made excellent use of conservation easements. Mining companies have given some land to the State, and private landowners have made gifts or bequests. In 1992 the U.S. Department of the Interior obtained 108,000 acres of environmentally sensitive land in Florida from a developer. In exchange, the developer received 68 acres of federal land in downtown Phoenix, Arizona. The Florida land will be added to the Big Cypress National Preserve and several parks.

Lakes and Rivers:
2.9 million acres

The State asserts ownership of Florida's lake and river bottoms, up to the high-water mark. Well over half this area is seasonally exposed floodplain on which development is limited. It supports flora and fauna adapted to wet and dry periods. The principal commercial use is grazing.

Publicly Owned Managed Wetlands:
1,500,000 acres

The largest of these publicly owned wetlands are the three Water Conservation Areas in south Florida. Dikes and other control structures govern the control and release of water. Water management is their primary function, so they are not natural ecosystems. However, these areas support much wildlife and are protected from commercial development. One of the three is the Arthur R. Marshall Loxahatchee National Wildlife Refuge. Part of the Green Swamp is publicly owned.

The Merritt Island National Wildlife Refuge is a huge wetland managed for waterfowl. The original dikes were built for mosquito control.

Publicly Owned Areas That Could Be Naturalized:
1 million acres

Portions of State and National Forests now managed for commercial wood production. Clear-cutting, even-aged tree plantations, and suppression of understory growth have replaced original ecosystems.

Many people question use of taxpayers' money to grow wood for industry on public land, to the detriment of wildlife, water, soils, and recreation. A change of management policies could return 1 million acres to natural forest. Such restoration has begun in a few forests.

Because more than 90 percent of Florida's timber harvest comes from private land, the impact on wood supply would not be great.

Privately Owned Forests:
11.5 million acres

Timber companies have large holdings. Wood is also harvested on private woodlots. Although they are not managed for natural qualities, these forests support a variety of flora and fauna. Most of the large holdings include some wetlands. Some of the largest include or border on coastal salt marshes.

Large tracts are occasionally offered for sale. Some of this land could be returned to public ownership and restored. In any case, a forest left largely undisturbed between logging cycles is, in the naturalist's view, preferable to subdivisions.

Cropland / Pasture and Rangeland:
4 million acres / 6 million acres

These 10 million acres were once natural, and most large farms and ranches include some wetlands and forest tracts. They now support--not always to owners' liking--a variety of mammals, birds, and reptiles, including sandhill cranes, boars, caracaras, burrowing owls, and rodents.

Most future large-scale real estate developments will be on these 10 million acres. However, some owners love their land and don't want it subdivided. If they must sell, perhaps because of estate taxes, they'd rather sell to the State. It could then be restored.

The St. Johns River Water Management District, for example, has bought five central Florida muck farms for $20 million, intending to restore natural wetlands.

The District, The Nature Conservancy, the State, and them landowners have cooperated in piecing together 22,800 acres bordering Camp Blanding. Betsy Donley, land protection coordinator of the Conservancy, called it "one of the finest examples of intact sandhill and longleaf pine communities in the state. Pine and oak trees provide a canopy for 21 miles of Black Creek."

Other Wetlands:
(Acreage included in other categories)

Current and recent administrations, federal and Florida, have promised "no net loss of wetlands." Yet their policies and actions have permitted continued wetlands destruction. Various schemes give the illusion of "no net loss." A favorite in Florida is "mitigation." Developers may be allowed to destroy wetlands if they promise to create new ones. But artificial wetlands are short-lived; few of the promises are kept; and enforcement is lacking. The State's own studies demonstrate that the scheme is a sham.

A more recent scheme is mitigation banking. A builder buys "credits" in a land bank, and uses them to obtain permission to destroy a wetland. The money in the land bank buys other wetlands for protection. However, these other wetlands are also supposedly protected by law.

Advocates said mitigation banking gives builders a way to deal with small, isolated, damaged wetlands with little or no ecological value. Peter Belmont, a lawyer who has tried many environmental cases, called it "potentially a Pandora's box. . . . I have some doubt the agencies will say no when it's not appropriate." Eric Draper of The Nature Conservancy said it should be the last option. Yet the Florida legislature brushed warnings aside and ordered agencies to begin issuing permits.

One of the first cases was a wetland bank purchase of 345 acres in Broward County. Previously set aside as a preserve, the site had deteriorated because of neglect.

"The thought of setting something aside over and over again is a joke," declared Patti Webster of the county's Environmental Coalition.

Environmentalists blasted the Clinton administration's decision not to protect 53 million acres of farmland created by draining wetlands before regulation. Developers can now convert this farmland to other uses.

Mitigation would make sense if an applicant were required to buy, restore, and convey to the State a *former* wetland. In some cases, backfilling ditches would be enough to restore the former ecosystem. State agencies and Water Management Districts have many such sites on their wish lists, awaiting purchase money.

In 1992, Florida lost 3,824 acres of wetlands, all permitted by the Department of Environmental Regulation or Water Management Districts. Although "no net loss" has been an empty promise, at least the loss of wetlands has been slowed. Public opinion is quick to condemn threats to important wetlands.

Cities, Towns, Subdivisions, Roads, Industrial Parks, and Other Developed Land:
8 million acres

Except in their large parks, urban areas are unnatural, but a surprising assortment of wildlife inhabits them. Now that water shortages limit irrigation of lawns and gardens, many homeowners are turning to *xeriscaping*, landscaping with native species that need no extra water. Ground covers that require no irrigation, mowing, fertilizer, or pesticides are replacing some lawns. Water Management Districts offer advice. Many people are planning native shrubs and flowers that attract birds and butterflies.

Industrial Land with Natural Potential:
No acreage estimate

Mining companies, power companies, and some other industries own large areas that could become natural assets. Mined lands can be reclaimed in a variety of ways. Some formerly mined lands have become publicly owned parks.

Be Not Reassured, But Hopeful

These estimates demonstrate opportunity. Although only one-tenth of the state's land is now protected and managed as natural areas, almost one-fourth of Florida is publicly owned, and many more acres can be restored to natural condition.

Public ownership can be expanded to one-third of Florida's land area. Indeed, State biologists say 12 million acres, nearly one-third of the state, must be set aside if thirty-three underprotected species are to be preserved. They have prepared a habitat map showing where 5 million acres should be brought within the protected system, either by purchase or by arrangements such as conservation easements with landowners.

Biologists and conservationists are advocating broad wildlife corridors linking the state's principal natural areas. One such corridor is along the Peace River, where much of the land is owned by mining companies, and rules prohibit mining near the river. Another corridor will be the floodplain of the Kissimmee River, when its restoration is completed.

Some greenbelts and buffer zones have been established and more can be. Following deauthorization of the Cross-Florida Barge Canal, the land purchased for it has become a cross-state greenway.

Time is of the essence. The owners of many large landholdings are under pressure to sell, and developers are eager to buy. Should the legislature allow Preservation 2000 to lapse, many opportunities will be lost forever.

Chapter 25

Our Crystal Ball

L eaving Florida? Take a friend!" The Florida League Against Progress, FLAP to you, is at it again, publishing *Florida's Calamity Calendar* each year: 365 reasons why no one should even think about coming to Florida, 365 news items and cartoons culled from the daily press; for example:

- Man-of-war jellyfish zaps South Florida bathers.
- Polk County lifer applies for job as Secretary of Corrections.
- Bill would let teachers use stun guns on students.
- Boca Raton homeowner says 20 to 50 golf balls strike house daily.
- British tabloids label Florida "state of terror."
- Gulls tossed food by kids deluge Cocoa Beach sunbathers with droppings.
- Early red tide bans shellfish.
- Fire ants and termites spread to citrus groves.
- Save the Roach Foundation picks Florida roach.
- Biker calls Florida highways worst in U.S.
- Several government agencies classify sand as carcinogenic.
- Delray Beach swimmers plagued by biting sea lice.
- Santa Rosa County deputies go undercover to discourage nude beaches.

- Under Florida law, manslaughter is not a crime if an antique weapon is used.
- Unusually warm Florida winter benefits fleas.
- Florida ranks last in high school graduates, 45th in child care.
- Apopka family told their house's sinking was normal in Florida.
- HRS says 3000 classrooms have high radon.
- Sinkhole takes school.
- Allergists busy as pollen peaks.
- To beat heat, Floridians flock to malls.
- Beer-loving slugs invade Florida yards.
- Rooster awakens; attacks W. Palm Beach man.
- Camels loose in Venice hit car.
- SE Florida national leader for cancer-causing toxic air, water, waste.
- Freed Gibsonton giant snails could devastate crops.

The calendar, always good for headlines, has been published since 1981 by the Environmental Information Center of the Florida Conservation Foundation. They say, "FLAP is lobbying to triple the number of days in the year so that we can include more of the calamities we couldn't squeeze in."

Meanwhile, in Tallahassee, lobbyists and their dependable lawmakers are making their annual attempt to gut the Growth Management Act. The act was a modest attempt to bring order out of chaos. Developers want their chaos back.

It's election time, so candidates are appearing at Audubon and Sierra Club meetings, most of them not to be seen again until the next campaign.

Doctor, teacher, pizza salesman, or antique dealer--a citizen who speaks for nature in Florida is labeled "environmentalist" in the press. Like a polluter, he or she is considered a member of a special interest group. When a county commission appoints citizens to an advisory committee, one lonely "environmentalist" is often included among the developers, farmers, real estate brokers, builders, miners, and others concerned.

Legislators and commissioners do their nefarious work by day. The wage-earning environmentalist, who must cancel appointments or use vacation time to attend, is pitted against platoons of lawyers who are paid $200 an hour and call legislators "Tom" and "Nellie." Many evil deeds are committed in the heat of summer, when all good environmentalists are in Alaska or the Tetons.

Many an offense against land, water, and wildlife could be blocked if an able lawyer cited Section 432.b.12 or the decision in an 1899 case concerning groins. Few Florida lawyers will take environmental cases *pro bono*. Even for pay, few will endanger their practices by supplying pebbles for David's slingshot.

If the environmentalist has an employer or does business locally, he or she is at risk. Should his or her letter appear on the Op-Ed page, the boss or a valued customer may pass along a quiet warning. A few environmentalists have been fired. Some county employees have been warned not to attend Sierra Club meetings.

But candidates do come to Audubon and Sierra meetings, and a lawyer platoon is sometimes overwhelmed by a hundred or more citizens-called-environmentalists. Then the legislator or commissioner must choose: the money or the votes? A few hard cases have been replaced in recent elections.

At election time, the *Tampa Tribune* reported a poll it had taken, asking citizens what issues matter most to them:

> In Hillsborough County, it's declining water quality and school budget problems. In Citrus and Lake counties, it's protecting the fishing industry and improving recreation facilities.
>
> In Hernando County, it's controlling the development pressures.
>
> And everywhere it's crime.
>
> Every county, every neighborhood in West Central Florida has its own palette of concerns, its own grab bag of pressing issues.
>
> But for many residents in the region, their countywide concerns can be collected under a single category: protecting the environment.

The *Ledger* of Lakeland agreed:

> Among hot button issues in Florida, they don't get any hotter than the environment. Tuesday's presidential primary could shape up as a referendum on the state's most pressing environmental needs, from saving the wetlands to rescuing endangered species.

"There's hardly any ecology left," a taxi driver said sadly.

"We don't care how you do it up north," says a bumper sticker, next to another that announces "Native." Some good ol' boys still sneer at the tree-huggers and dickey-bird-watchers who bought the land the good ol' boys sold. The boys call the Growth Management Act a communistic import.

Their "Solid South" is no longer solid. Many natives don't like what's happening to their quiet countryside, and they support growth limitation. Many a native rancher or citrus grower would prefer to continue ranching or growing, but the tax assessor shares the developers' vision of Mobile Home Acres. The State can buy environmentally significant land only from willing sellers, but many are willing. Like the owners of the Walker Ranch, they have loved their land and, given a choice, would prefer to have it preserved.

There's a strange alliance now between developers and retired immigrants, the latter now outnumbering natives at many voting booths. Florida's climate is lovely, but for many of these immigrants its low taxes are lovelier. Dependent on Social Security, they threaten any politician who votes for tax increases. Retired couples don't have children in school, so they vote down bond issues. Florida's schools are among the nation's worst. Parks and libraries would be nice, but not if they cost money. Developers, too, are antitax.

Sooner or later, all who live in Florida must pay for the roads, schools, prisons, sewage plants, and other requirements of the growth that is eroding our quality of life. The Growth Management Act shifts part of the cost to the newcomers. It raises--slightly--the cost of new houses. Builders are horrified. They are even more horrified by "concurrency," the Act's requirement that a major development cannot proceed until the roads, utilities, and schools it will require are in place.

This was an editorial in the *Tampa Tribune*, a conservative newspaper:

> Remember, the state's growth-management process gives local governments plenty of latitude to decide their future. But the law does require that local plans be economically and environmentally responsible. Is that asking too much?
>
> It may be if you are a land speculator who doesn't want to worry about wetlands or a developer who doesn't care how much your project overloads surrounding streets. . . .
>
> Many North Florida politicians are anxious to turn loose any and all construction. Santa Rosa County, for instance, is unwilling even to curtail the use of septic tanks that pollute bays and rivers. Or consider the way Monroe County commissioners paved over much of the Keys during the '80s. Or how Hillsborough County's commissioners' development decisions in the '70s created the clutter-and-gridlock mess that the county is still trying to straighten out.

Pessimists believe developers and speculators and their politicians will always prevail. They believe growth can't be stopped. Thus far, few environmentalists have dared to say, "No more!" They say they want to manage growth, not stop it. But managed or not, growth cannot be sustained much longer. The infrastructure crumbles: roads, bridges, jails, schools. Faucets may run dry.

How Much Growth?

A University of Florida professor predicts that Florida's population, now 13 million, will increase to 37 million by the year 2050. We don't believe it. The state's resources can't support such an increase.

Water shortages alone will put a cap on growth. Water rationing is a temporary expedient at best. Salt water is invading more and more wells on which coastal cities depend. Some experts fear pollutants pumped underground are inexorably contaminating other well fields.

Many other species have inherent ways of limiting their populations. When a habitat becomes too crowded, reproduction declines. Matings occur at a later age or less frequently. Twins are produced less often. Ova are resorbed. When traditional breeding grounds are full, surplus seabirds alight on other islands but don't reproduce. Diseases are transmitted more readily in crowds. Cyclical droughts and unseasonable freezes are a natural control for many plant species as well as animals.

When a new organism is introduced to a habitat, it may multiply explosively, but growth has inescapable limits. A species that multiplies beyond the carrying capacity of its habitat destroys its life-support resources and crashes. After the crash the species may stabilize at a lower level the habitat can support.

We Believe

We are optimists. We believe nature and history are on our side.

Florida's population increased by 79 percent in the 1950s, only 33 percent in the 1980s. The number of people leaving Florida is increasing, not dramatically but significantly. Coastal towns that were attractive are now intolerably crowded. Housing costs have risen beyond the means of many would-be immigrants.

However they squirm and posture, legislators know taxes must be increased. The silence has been broken; a state income tax is openly discussed. Florida will lose its appeal as a tax haven.

Rural counties may wangle some exemptions from growth management regulations. Citizens of more populous counties won't tolerate retreat. If State controls are weakened, urban counties may impose even stricter controls on themselves, perhaps even the zero-growth rules adopted and tested in several communities elsewhere in the nation.

We are cautiously optimistic about the future of nature in Florida, for these reasons:

- Almost one-fourth of the state's land is publicly-owned now. That can be increased to one-third.[19]
- Although some public land is used for commercial timber production, that regime can be changed. Tens of thousands of clear-cut acres are reverting to their natural conditions. Even now State and federal land-managing agencies are restoring natural ecosystems on some of their lands.
- River pollution has been checked.
- Phosphate companies are required to restore the land they mine.
- Some wetlands have been restored, and more will be.
- The Kissimmee River will be restored. That's one wildlife corridor.
- The Cross-Florida Barge Canal project has at last been killed. The land acquired for it now becomes the Cross-Florida Greenway. That's a corridor. Lake Ocklawaha, backed up by Rodman Dam, is deteriorating so rapidly the dam will surely be removed, restoring lost habitat.
- Land along the Peace River can be acquired. Some has been. Another corridor.
- Completed and pending land acquisitions along the Wekiva River will create a corridor linking State lands at both ends of the river. Also pending is a link to the Ocala National Forest.
- The Upper St. Johns River marshes are being restored.
- The coastal marshes of the Big Bend, now largely owned by timber companies, can be preserved.
- The impact of Hurricane Andrew may bring about more sensible restrictions on future seaside building.

[19]In 1992, authorities raided a house near Cedar Key. Drugs were found; the real estate was confiscated, and the U.S. Marshal prepared to sell it. Harry Mitchell, manager of the Cedar Key Scrub State Reserve, heard this and made telephone calls. The Marshall agreed to delay the sale until the State could act. Result: 126 acres of prime scrub jay habitat were added to the Reserve.

There's more than one way to save a natural area!

- Marco Island will be the last large invasion of the mangrove coast south of Naples.
- The Everglades will never again have a natural water system, but the Park can regain a natural hydroperiod, and pollution by fertilizers, mercury, and pesticides can be reduced.
- Underground injection of hazardous wastes will be stopped. All underground disposal of wastes will be more strictly monitored and regulated.
- More storm water will be kept from entering lakes and streams.
- People will realize exotic plants are a menace and will support programs for their suppression.
- Enforcement of environmental laws will improve. Judges who once dismissed cases or imposed trivial fines are now getting serious.
- Leaking underground gasoline and oil tanks are being phased out.
- Solid waste landfills are being retrofitted with plastic liners. That may be a temporary solution, but the problem is recognized.
- Waste incinerators, once unregulated, must now meet strict emission standards. No more hazardous waste incinerators will be allowed.
- Counties are under mandate to reduce their volume of solid waste, to adopt recycling programs, and to provide special collection and handling for hazardous materials.

We are optimists because of what people are doing to save Florida:

- A State-funded environmental education program is reaching into every school. Imaginative projects have been funded. Children will lead the way.
- Students are learning how to test water quality in lakes. Environment is now the theme of many science fair projects.
- We have followed groups of children and young people visiting interpretive centers on their own. They're with it.
- The Nature Conservancy has raised millions of dollars for land purchases.
- There are more than 80 statewide and local environmental organizations totaling over a million members. They maintain a respected cadre of lobbyists at Tallahassee.
- Citizens turn out by the hundreds to support land purchases and good legislation. Often they travel a hundred miles and more to attend.

- Every weekend thousands of people, young and old, participate in canoe outings, trail hikes, visits to wildlife refuges, and wildflower excursions.
- Organized volunteers, young and old, gather trash from roadsides and stream banks, plant trees, take bird censuses, build and maintain hiking trails, patrol turtle beaches, act as docents at nature centers, care for injured wildlife, publish newsletters--whatever needs to be done. Soon after Hurricane Andrew, almost 17,000 volunteers took part in a massive coastal cleanup.
- "Ecotourism" flourishes, residents and visitors enjoying guided visits to see spring wildflowers, wetlands, reefs, wild rivers, and other natural areas.

Recognition is growing that artifact Florida cannot survive without natural Florida. If we first enjoy, then understand, and thus come to cherish what remains of natural Florida, it will be saved. Some of the lost will be regained.

APPENDIX A

Pathfinding in Florida

Less than half of Florida's roads are shown on ordinary road maps. To explore the parks, forests, wildlife areas, lakes, rivers, swamps, and marshes, one needs maps showing greater detail. Guidebooks are listed in Appendix B.

Road Maps and Tourist Information
Available at welcome stations and from:
Florida Tourism Industry Marketing Corporation
P.O. Box 1100
Tallahassee, FL 32302
Telephone requests: (850) 487-1462

Florida Atlas & Gazetteer
Freeport, ME: DeLorme Mapping, 1989.
Scale: 1 inch = 2.3 miles.
This Atlas is indispensable to Florida travelers. Its 103 color maps, each 9" x 14 1/2", show back roads, land uses, and features such as forests, parks, refuges, springs, lakes, hiking and canoe trails, and boat ramps.
The **Gazetteer** portion lists and locates hundreds of attractions: beaches, botanical gardens, campgrounds, museums, theme parks, zoos, aquariums, and much more. The *Atlas & Gazetteer* is available at bookstores, outfitters, and some newsstands.

National Forest Maps
Each of the 3 National Forests in Florida (Apalachicola, Osceola, and Ocala) has its own road system and map. Maps can be obtained from:
> National Forests in Florida
> 325 John Knox Road
> Building F, Suite F100
> Tallahassee, FL 32311
> $2.00 each

Wildlife Management Areas Maps
> Florida Game and Fresh Water Fish Commission
> 620 South Meridian Street
> Tallahassee, FL 32399

An outline map, available on request, shows the locations of sixty-three WMAs. Maps of many of these are available on request.

Hiking Trail Maps

    Florida Trail Association
    P.O. Box 13708
    Gainesville, FL 32604
    1-800-343-1882

Volunteers of the Florida Trail Association have developed and maintain over 1,000 miles of hiking trail. Sections of the Florida Trail on public land are open to all hikers. The Association has negotiated many trail easements on private land, and those sections are open to members only.

Hiking Guide to the Florida Trail, a looseleaf guide with maps, describes the terrain, flora, fauna, and facilities of each portion of the Trail. It is sold only to members. The *Public Trail Guide* ($11.95) has maps and information about Trail sections on public land.

Canoe Trails

Canoe Trails, a leaflet, provides brief descriptions of thirty-six canoe trails and a locator map. Leaflets with detail maps and more complete information on each canoe trail are available from

    Division of Recreation and Parks
    Marjory Stoneman Douglas Building
    3900 Commonwealth Blvd.
    Tallahassee, FL 32399

APPENDIX B

Further Reading and Reference

We won't list all books we read or scanned in the course of this project; Florida literature is extensive and diverse. Our Library of Congress computer search began with 3,724 titles. Too often we were enticed down pathways far from the scope of our work. Browsing in a good Florida library is delightful. Many of the fascinating books found there are long out of print.

Today Florida has many independent publishers, and we see new titles every time we visit a bookstore.

Here is a selection of books and pamphlets of general and special interest that amplify our text.

Guides

Perry, John and Jane Greverus. *The Sierra Club Guide to the Natural Areas of Florida.* San Francisco: Sierra Club Books, 1972.

The entries for two hundred parks, forests, wildlife refuges, and other natural areas describe each site's location, physical features, flora and fauna, interpretive programs, publications, and facilities.

LaFreniere, Barbara Brumm and Edward N. *The Complete Guide to Life in Florida.* Sarasota: Pineapple Press, 1993.

de Hart, Allen. *Adventuring in Florida.* San Francisco: Sierra Club Books, 1991.

Climate

Climate of Florida. Climatography of the United States No. 60. Asheville, NC: National Climatic Center, National Oceanic and Atmospheric Administration.

Hurricane Guide. South Florida Water Management District, PO Box 24680, West Palm Beach, FL 33416. (Leaflet with tracking map.)

Ecosystems

Myers, Ronald L., and John J. Ewel, eds. *Ecosystems of Florida.* Orlando: University of Central Florida Press, 1990.

Its 765 pages aren't light reading; parts of it are too technical for lay readers; but it stands alone as a basic reference.

Lord, Linda A., principal author, and Marcia Ramsdell, project director. *Guide to Florida Environmental Issues and Information*. Winter Park: Florida Conservation Foundation, 1993.

Dasmann, Raymond F. *No Further Retreat*. New York: Macmillan, 1971.

History
Tebeau, Charlton W.. *A History of Florida*. Coral Gables: University of Miami Press, 1971.

Blake, Nelson Manfred. *Land Into Water--Water Into Land*. Tallahassee: University Presses of Florida, 1980.

Carter, Luther J. *The Florida Experience*. Baltimore: Johns Hopkins University Press, 1974.

Derr, Mark. *Some Kind of Paradise*. New York: William Morrow, 1989.

Burnett, Gene M. *Florida's Past, Vols. I and II*. Sarasota: Pineapple Press, 1986, 1988.

Hoffmeister, John Edward. *Land from the Sea*. Coral Gables: University of Miami Press, 1974.

Fossils
Brown, Robin C. *Florida's Fossils*. Sarasota: Pineapple Press, 1988.

Parks
Florida State Parks Guide, a 48-page booklet, is available from the Division of Recreation and Parks. Each park has its own leaflet, with map and information. These leaflets can be obtained at park gates or by sending self-addressed stamped envelopes to the parks. The supply at Tallahassee is sometimes incomplete.

Camping
National Forests in Florida; Recreation Area Directory. Available on request from National Forests in Florida.

Grow, Gerald. *Florida Parks. A Guide to Camping in Nature*. Tallahassee: Longleaf Publications, 1993 (Fifth Edition.)

Woodall's and other national campground directories provide detailed information on public and commercial campgrounds in Florida.

The State Division of Recreation and Parks publishes leaflets describing State Park campgrounds and reservation procedures.

Hiking, Backpacking
Anderson, Robert. *Hiking and Backpacking Florida.* 3 vols. Altamonte Springs, FL: Winner Enterprises, 1991.

Canoeing
Anderson, Robert. *Canoeing Florida.* 3 vols. Altamonte Springs, FL: Winner Enterprises, 1990.

Glaros, Lou, and Doug Sphar. *A Canoeing and Kayaking Guide to the Streams of Florida. Vol. II, Central and South Peninsula.* Birmingham, AL: Menasha Ridge, 1987.

A list of outfitters and the rivers they serve can be obtained from: Florida Association of Canoe Liveries and Outfitters, PO Box 1764, Arcadia, FL 33821.

Rivers
Jue, Dean K., principal investigator. *Florida Rivers Assessment.* Tallahassee: Florida: Department of Natural Resources, 1989.

Marth, Del and Marty. *The Rivers of Florida.* Sarasota: Pineapple Press, 1990.

Flora
Bell, C. Ritchie, and Bryan J. Taylor. *Florida Wild Flowers and Roadside Plants.* Chapel Hill, NC: Laurel Hill Press, 1982.

Tarver, David P., John A. Rodgers, Michael J. Mahler, and Robert L. Lazor. *Aquatic and Wetland Plants of Florida.* Tallahassee: Bureau of Aquatic Plant Research and Control, Department of Natural Resources, 1986.

Coastal
Aquatic Preserves. (Leaflet with map.) Bureau of Land and Aquatic Resource Management, Department of Natural Resources, 3900 Commonwealth Blvd., Tallahassee, FL 32399.

Everglades

Douglas, Marjory Stoneman. *The Everglades: River of Grass*. Sarasota: Pineapple Press, revised edition 1988.

Douglas, Marjory Stoneman. *Voice of the River*. Sarasota, Pineapple Press, 1990.

Coral Reefs

Voss, Gilbert L. *Coral Reefs of Florida*. Sarasota: Pineapple Press, 1988.

Stafford-Deitsch, Jeremy. *Reefs. A Safari Through the Coral World*. San Francisco: Sierra Club Books, 1991.

Wildlife

Kale, Herbert W., II, and David S. Maehr. *Florida's Birds*. Sarasota: Pineapple Press, 1990.

Lane, James A. *A Birder's Guide to Florida*. Revised by Harold R. Holt. Colorado Springs, CO.: ABA Sales, 1989.

Dunkle, Sidney W. *Damselflies of Florida, Bermuda and the Bahamas*. Gainesville: Scientific Publishers, 1990.

Dunkle, Sidney W. *Dragonflies of the Florida Peninsula, Bermuda and the Bahamas*. Gainesville: Scientific Publishers, 1989.

Voice for the Silent Sirenian: Guardian of the Florida Manatee. Tallahassee: Department of Natural Resources. Pamphlet with illustrations, maps.

Van Meter, Victoria Brook. *Florida's Alligators and Crocodiles*. Miami: Florida Power & Light Company, 1987.

Van Meter, Victoria Brook. *Florida's Sea Turtles*. Miami: Florida Power & Light Company, 1987.

Lantz, Peggy, and Wendy Hale. *Lizards*. Casselberry, FL: Florida Audubon Society, 1988. (Reprint from *Young Naturalists*.)

Carr, Archie. *So Excellent a Fishe*. New York: Scribners, 1984.

Gerberg, Eugene J., and Ross H. Arnett, Jr. *Florida Butterflies.* Gainesville: Sandhill Crane Press, 1989.

Stiling, Peter D. *Florida's Butterflies and Other Insects.* Sarasota: Pineapple Press, 1989.

Gopher Tortoise: A Species in Decline. Gainesville: Florida Museum of Natural History. (leaflet)

Pamphlets and leaflets available from the Florida Game and Fresh Water Fish Commission, Tallahassee, include:

Planting a Refuge for Wildlife; How to Create a Backyard Habitat for Florida's Birds and Beasts
The Coyote in Florida
A Checklist of Florida's Mammals
A Checklist of Florida's Birds
A Checklist of Florida's Amphibians and Reptiles
Florida's Nonvenomous Snakes
Florida's Venomous Snakes
Nuisance Wildlife
Florida Panther
Florida's Burrowing Owl
Return of the Southern Bald Eagle
The Florida Scrub Jay
Florida's Wood Storks

Florida Government Agencies
A User's Guide. Tallahassee: Florida Department of Natural Resources.
This pamphlet explains the functions of DNR's Divisions. (The Department of Natural Resources has been merged into the Department of Environmental Protection.)

INDEX

ecosystem, 120; Indian River, 120; Tampa Bay, 119, 121; where to see, 125-126
Europeans, 31-32
Everglades, 18, 19-20, 165-171 (*see also* Everglades National Park): drainage, 166; Water Conservation Areas, 166-167; water supply, 83
Everglades National Park, 166-167: damage to, 166-169; efforts to save, 168-169; exotic plants threaten, 45; visiting, 170-171; water supply of, 167; wildlife of, 165
Exotic species, 44-51
Fire ants, 50
Fires, forest, 94
Fishes, saltwater, 120
Flagler, Henry Morrison,37-38
Flatwoods (*see* Pines)
Florida, geography of, 10-11: Central, 16-18; North, 13-16; Panhandle, 11-13; South, 18-20
Florida: rises from sea, 23; statehood, 32
Florida Bay, 20: pollution of, 169-170
Florida League Against Progress, 219
Florida Trail, 91, 97-98
Floridan Plateau, 23, 26, 43
Fossils, 22-29
Frogs, disappearance of, 192-193
Green Swamp, 17, 40, 131-133
Growth management, 39, 222-223
Gulf coast, 13, 14, 18, 119, 121
Gulf of Mexico, 180-181
Hammocks (*see* Hardwood forests)
Hardwood forests, 106-107: live oaks, 12-13, 107
Hog, wild, 186-187
Humans, first in Florida, 30
Hurricanes (*see* Climate)
Hydrologic cycle, 72-73, 81
Hydroperiod, 129-130
Indians, 30-31: Seminole, 35
Islands and keys, 20-21
Keys, reefs, and islands, 20-21, 37-38, 172-179
Kissimmee River, 17, 34, 36-37: restoration of, 147-150
Lakes, 136-141: ecosystems of, 138-139; meandered, 139; number and sizes of, 136; ownership of bottoms, 139; pollution of, 83, 137-138; restoration of, 140-141; water levels of, 136-137
Lakes: Okeechobee, 19
Land boom, 38-39
Land bridge, 27
Land sales and grants, 36-37
Lands, publicly owned, 205-212: county, 210-211; federal, 207-208; State, 33, 206, 208-210; State acquisitions of, 206-207